OTHER TRAVELERS' TALES BOOKS

COUNTRY AND REGIONAL GUIDES
*America, Australia, Brazil, France, India, Ireland, Italy, Japan,
Mexico, Nepal, Spain, Thailand; Grand Canyon, Hawai'i,
Hong Kong, Paris, and San Francisco*

WOMEN'S TRAVEL
*A Woman's World, A Woman's Passion for Travel,
A Woman's Path, Women in the Wild, A Mother's World, Safety and
Security for Women Who Travel, Gutsy Women, Gutsy Mamas*

BODY & SOUL
*The Road Within, The Ultimate Journey, Love & Romance, Food,
The Adventure of Food, The Fearless Diner, The Gift of Travel*

SPECIAL INTEREST
*There's No Toilet Paper…On the Road Less Traveled, Danger!,
Testosterone Planet, The Penny Pincher's Passport to Luxury Travel,
Shitting Pretty, The Fearless Shopper, The Gift of Birds,
The Gift of Rivers, A Dog's World, Family Travel*

FOOTSTEPS
Kite Strings of the Southern Cross, The Sword of Heaven

FOOTSTEPS: THE SOUL OF TRAVEL
*An imprint of Travelers' Tales, Footsteps showcases
talented voices in travel literature—one voice at a time.
Each Footsteps book will increase your wanderlust, enliven
your imagination, and nourish your soul.*

storm

storm

A

Motorcycle

Journey of Love,

Endurance, and

Transformation

ALLEN NOREN

TRAVELERS' TALES
San Francisco

Travelers' Tales and Travelers' Tales Guides are trademarks of
Travelers' Tales, Inc., 330 Townsend Street, Suite 208,
San Francisco, California 94107. www.travelerstales.com

Jacket Design: Stefan Gutermuth
Interior Design: Melanie Haage
Cover Photographs: North Sea photograph © Ernest Haas/Tony Stone Images.
Inset photograph © Bob Winsett/Index Stock Imagery, Inc.
Map: Keith Granger
Page Layout: Melanie Haage, using the fonts Fairfield and Disturbance.

Distributed by: Publishers Group West, 1700 Fourth Street Berkeley, CA 94710.

Library of Congress Cataloging-in-Publication Data
Noren Allen.
        Storm : a motorcycle journey around the Baltic Sea / Allen Noren.
            p. cm.
        ISBN 1-885211-45-7 (alk. paper)
          1. Motorcycling—Baltic Sea Region. 2. Motorcyclists—United States—Biography.
I. Title.
        GV1059.53.B27 N67 2000
        914.04'559'092--dc21
        [B]   00-023418

Printed in the United States of America
10 9 8 7 6 5 4 3 2 1

To everyone who helped along the way.

Here is the mother hooded seal on an ice floe with her cub. Thirty-mile-an-hour winds, thirty degrees below zero. Look into her eyes, silted, yellow, fierce, crazed, sad and hopeless. End line of a doomed planet. She can't lie to herself, she can't pull any pathetic rags of verbal self-glorification about her. There she is, on this ice floe with her cub. She shifts her five-hundred-pound bulk to make a dug available. There's a cub with its shoulder ripped open by one of the adult males. Probably won't make it. They all have to swim to Denmark, fifteen hundred miles away. Why? The seals don't know why. They have to get to Denmark. They all have to get to Denmark.
—WILLIAM S. BURROUGHS, *The Cat Inside*

Life to you is a dashing and bold adventure.
—CHINESE FORTUNE COOKIE

The Baltic Sea

N
W   E
S

●●●● Author's Route

100 k.
0   100 m.

Norwegian
Sea

North
Sea

Narvik
Alta
Kirkenes
Kiruna
Mo
Arctic Circle
Rovaniemi
Kemi
Luleå
Oulu
SWEDEN
Umeå
Kokkola
Ostersund
Vaasa
FINLAND
Trondheim
Gulf
of
Bothnia
Tampere
Helsinki
Gulf of
Finland
NORWAY
Bergen
Oslo
Falun
St. Petersburg
(Leningrad)
Stockholm
Åland
Harö
Saaremaa
Tallinn
ESTONIA
Parnu
RUSSIA
Visby
Kuressaarev
Gulf of
Riga
Goteborg
Gotland
Riga
LATVIA
Åseda
Oland
Baltic
Sea
LITHUANIA
DENMARK
Århus
Lund
Kaunas
BYELARUS
Malmo
Bornholm
(RUSSIA)
Copenhagen
Slupsk
Vilnius
Roskilde
Rugen
Gdansk
Minsk
Hamburg
Kolobrzeg
Mazurian
Lake District
NETH.
Szczecin
Bremen
POLAND
GERMANY
Warsaw
UKRAINE
CZECH.
Kiev

ONE

"It's raining," I said to Suzanne, my face framed by my hands as I looked through the window of the train. The sky was almost dark as we moved north toward Bremen, Germany. The bright lights inside the train reflected off the glass, projecting ghostly images of the passengers around us. "Suzanne," I said again. "It's raining."

"Hmm?" she asked, and I watched her reflection in the window as she lowered the book she was reading. She made a mark with a pencil so she wouldn't lose her place and turned her face toward the back of my head. "What did you say?"

"It's raining."

"Let's see," she said, and leaned across me. As she moved, the air around my face filled with the perfumy oils of her scalp, and I leaned toward the crown of her head to breathe them in. A middle-aged woman across the aisle lowered her newspaper and stared at us.

"A spring shower," Suzanne said. "Everything is being washed down and freshened up just for us." She sat up, kissed me, and went back to her book.

Her breath left a cloud on the glass, and I watched the dark world beyond reemerge as the shadow of moisture evaporated. The air around the glass was cool against my forehead and nose. It smelled of rain and metal. Silver rounds of water had pooled on the earth and shone like moons.

As the train entered Bremen, Suzanne and I gathered our things and moved sideways down the narrow aisle toward the door as our helmets, bags, and tent scraped and caught against the seats. We stopped next to the door and watched the city's lights streak past like tracer fire.

"I'd like to stay in a hotel tonight," Suzanne said. The driver applied the brakes and she leaned into me. "I'd like it to be a nice one."

"We should save it for later on, when we really need it," I said, thinking of all that was before us. "We should save our money for the Arctic Circle, Russia, or some place in Estonia or Poland."

"Oh, come on," she said and nuzzled my chin with her nose. "Let's celebrate the beginning of this trip."

The train braked harder and I grabbed hold of a handrail to keep us from falling. Outside, the lights of Bremen slid like illuminated drops of rain across the glass.

Why not? I thought. *What better way to begin a motorcycle trip around the Baltic Sea?*

~~~

Suzanne and I were sitting on the floor of our apartment one evening, flipping through the pages of our atlas, when the idea for this trip came to us. We'd just finished a late dinner, and a candle dimly lit the pages. It was spring and the front door was open, letting in the scent of the sweet peas and jasmine blooming outside. A year had passed since the end of our last trip, and our savings, though still low, were showing signs of recovery. For several weeks we had allowed ourselves to begin dreaming of our next destination. Our atlas lay open and the two of us were leaning over it, admiring the possibilities as though it were a catalog. We had just flipped past Mongolia and China when Suzanne stopped.

"Here," she said suddenly. "What do you think of this?"

I watched as her finger described a clockwise rotation around the Baltic Sea. It began in Denmark, rolled across the flatlands of southern Sweden, up Sweden's east coast, through Stockholm, and continued north to the Arctic Circle. She then drew a ragged line southeast across the interminable forests of Finland before sweeping through the mysterious landscapes of Russia and the Baltic States. Her finger continued across the north coasts of Poland and Germany and came to a stop again at the Danish border.

I was transfixed. But Russia was still closed to independent travelers in 1990, and the Baltic States—Estonia, Latvia, and Lithuania—were still controlled by Moscow and only vaguely recalled on the pages of our atlas by pale lines demarcating disputed borders we strained to see with a magnifying glass. We spent a week making inquiries but were informed that such a trip by independent travelers was an impossibility. We continued the delightful task of roaming through our atlas and dreaming as we saved our money.

For two years the idea of traveling around the Baltic Sea remained in the back of our minds. There was something appealing about traveling in a great circle, circumnavigating an entire region from beginning to beginning with thousands of miles in between.

Suzanne and I kept talking about it, and the world began to change in our favor. Then, in the spring of 1992, the idea surfaced for real. The Iron Curtain had come down, and the world was under the spell of Gorbachev. Russia was opening, and, one by one, the Baltic States declared their independence. Suzanne and I decided to try again and found we could get visas. Night after night we opened our atlas to page sixty-eight and hovered there as we plotted a route and talked about how we would make the trip. Suzanne suggested we buy a used car in Europe, some kind of van we could live in as we traveled. She described how we could fill it with food, clothes, camping gear—everything we needed—and when the trip was through we could sell it. We had done that once before in Australia. We had bought an old van and lived in it for four months as we drove through the Outback.

I suggested we try another means of transportation and convinced her a sea kayak was the way to go. I reasoned that the history of the nations bordering the Baltic had been largely established on the sea, and to approach each of them from the water would be fitting. We checked out navigation books from the library and pored over nautical maps. We imagined the solitude that would envelope us as we paddled together on the open sea, exploring the hundreds of islands, coves, and beaches the maps promised. We imagined the wildlife we'd discover and what it would be like to paddle into the great cities of Copenhagen, Stockholm, Helsinki, St. Petersburg, and Gdansk knowing we'd arrived at each of them one paddle stroke at a time. We spent months researching kayak brands, shipping costs to Europe, navigational aids, coastal patterns, and restricted zones. We took an ocean kayaking class. We plotted the miles, over and over again, and realized the short northern European summer and long distance would force us to spend the winter months somewhere along the way. It sounded like a wonderful idea until we counted our money. Even on our usually Spartan budget, we calculated we'd have to save for one more year.

One afternoon I was driving home from San Francisco, stuck in the afternoon traffic, and was passed by a motorcycle laden with packs and duffels. Two people in worn black leather suits were riding it, and I watched them weave in and out of traffic and speed ahead onto the Golden Gate Bridge. The two people looked so together, so naturally complete riding as if they were one. They moved through the cars and trucks as if they were trifling obstacles, and were gone. As I sat in my car I imagined Suzanne and myself riding like that and immediately got excited.

Because they were travelers I bet they would pull off the freeway at the vista point, a pullout at the north end of the bridge that allows for one of the most astonishing views of San Francisco, the islands in the bay, and of the bridge itself. I went there, too, and found the bike parked like a sliver amid ponderous tourist buses, minivans, and RVs.

The bike was a well-worn Moto-Guzzi with a German license plate. It was dented and spattered with mud. The vinyl on the seat was cracked and worn through to the foam padding below. Aluminum boxes filled with gear were bolted to the back of the bike and were covered with stickers from national parks in Canada, the United States, and Mexico. My mind filled with images of all that the two riders had seen and done along their route. Though I searched through the milling crowd I could not find them. I waited. They were probably walking across the bridge. I walked partway across looking for them but then I had to leave. I thought about the motorcycle all the way home.

"But you've never really ridden," Suzanne said, "and it's such a long way."

There were good reasons why a motorcycle would be preposterous: our lack of experience, the possibility of getting hit, theft, fuel shortages and bad roads, especially in Russia and the Baltic States. But the more I thought about it, the tighter the idea held me. We could learn to ride. Poor roads would slow us down. Finding fuel would be an adventure. A motorcycle would be the ideal means of transportation because we *weren't* experienced. We'd see the world in a new way, and we'd meet people we wouldn't have met otherwise.

There were also many other advantages, and Suzanne and I listed them on a piece of paper. The bike would be a self-contained unit much smaller than a lumbering car, one that would be spare, stealthy, and agile. It would be as good in cities as on the open road, and fuel-efficient in a part of the world where gasoline sold for four to six dollars a gallon. Riding a bike would be like flying through the landscape. We'd become intimate with the briny smell of the sea, the perfume of spring meadows, the tang of pine and birch forests, with summer fields ripe with grain, the clean Nordic air. We liked the idea of having everything we needed—tools, clothing, food, cooking, and sleeping gear—on two wheels. I welcomed the new perspective of the world we would gain from a motorcycle, just as I had gained something crucial the first time I flew in an airplane or paddled along the California coast in a kayak.

We both started to get excited about the idea of a motorcycle, and we lay in bed at night and imagined the first tentative miles of the trip as we departed from a foreign land. We talked about riding down the main streets of Copenhagen, Stockholm, and St. Petersburg, and crossing over the Arctic Circle with the midnight sun low on the horizon. We envisioned the endless coastline and the uninterrupted months together.

Suzanne and I visited several motorcycle shops. We went to see bikes listed for sale in the newspaper. We talked to mechanics and people who had toured on motorcycles. Then one weekend I stopped by a local motorcycle shop and along one wall spotted a used BMW that kept tugging at me. I knew a little about them. They are excellent long-distance machines and the engines are long-lived and relatively easy to work on. The owner of the shop agreed that such a bike would be the perfect machine for our trip. He pointed out how comfortable this particular one would be for two people. It had just been serviced, and he said that parts, if we needed them, would be readily available throughout Europe. It was outfitted with luggage cases and had room to tie on the rest of our gear. The paint was a subtle bronze that wouldn't attract attention, and the bike had an ample fairing—a shield and windscreen around the front—that would protect us from any weather we encountered. It was also on consignment and priced for a quick sale.

Suzanne and I test rode the bike on a clear, fall morning, and we wanted to just keep going. I made calls to embassies and shippers and discovered that shipping a motorcycle was relatively easy and cheap. We realized we could complete the trip in one summer and fall. We bought the bike.

~~~

Our train stopped beneath the steel and glass cavern of the Bremen train station. A shrill whistle blew, the door opened, and Suzanne and I slipped into the congested flow of people as they left and entered trains for the city, the suburbs, and beyond.

We worked our way through the press of travelers and commuters, past men and women in suits carrying briefcases as they smoked and paced and waited, past old people on benches, groups of gum-chomping kids on school trips.

We entered the heart of the station. It was framed in iron with a ceiling so high it could contain its own weather. On the periphery were small shops selling flowers, liquor, newspapers, and magazines. There was a currency exchange office, a restaurant with a blue-and-orange neon sign, and to the right was a small kiosk with mounds of green apples and cans of beer, bottled water, and rectangles of neatly wrapped chocolate. Inside a woman dressed in a white smock and hat stared at a rotating grill of tumbling sausages, waiting for one to go awry.

A harshly beautiful prostitute, dressed in a white leather bolero that exposed a bloated stomach, walked in strung-out circles around the interior of the station, trolling. She wore a white skirt with what looked like greasy handprints on her rear and a pair of scuffed white cowgirl boots she dragged across the cement floor. There was a bank of public phones, and around those was a collection of drunks checking for change each time someone completed a call.

When we were outside I thought, *Here we are. This trip has really begun.*

Until then I had been afraid it wouldn't begin. In the back of my mind there was always a voice that suggested this trip was outrageous, that something would happen to keep us from getting this far. I worried that one of us would break an arm or leg while learning to ride, that our motorcycle would be destroyed in shipment from our home in California, that we'd have to call the trip off. I felt hot with excitement.

"What's the matter?" Suzanne asked.

"It's going to happen," I said.

"What's going to happen?" she asked, concerned.

"The trip," I said. "It's really going to happen."

"Of course it's going to happen," she said with a smile. Then she turned and walked between lines of waiting taxis and buses, toward a gold neon sign that shone "Hotel."

two

Suzanne and I had met at work seven years earlier. I had recently returned from a trip through Eastern Europe and was planning another. I got work in a factory building wooden shipping crates around the heavy equipment manufactured there. Each morning I went into the front office to collect the appropriate forms for the machines shipping that day. Suzanne was working as a receptionist, and each morning I passed her desk. Her smile caught my attention.

She always smiled. Not just at me but at everyone. It was her nature. For months we only exchanged greetings, and then she learned that I was saving my money to go away again. We arranged to meet in the parking lot for lunch one day and sat on the tailgate of my truck as we ate. She had never traveled but had studied French during high school in preparation for the day she would. She was putting herself through school, attending the local junior college at night before transferring to a university. We promised to meet again, but I left shortly thereafter on my trip.

I was gone six months and was arranging to take a job driving new Mercedes transport trucks from Germany to the Ivory Coast via the Sahara when I received news that my father had cancer. My mother asked that I come home, and after his operation I resumed my job crating machines while he healed.

I discovered Suzanne had been promoted to the copy room where she assembled parts manuals and sales catalogs. My job also required that I make copies of shipping labels for each machine that left the factory. Suzanne usually had a big copy job running, so I often had to wait a few minutes to use the machine. We'd fill those minutes with talk. One morning I realized I was anticipating our daily visits, and not long after, Suzanne reminded me that I'd promised to meet with her again.

Our dating began tentatively. I'd been in relationships that had ended because of my travels, and I warned Suzanne that I'd be leaving again. I explained that I had always traveled alone, and I had acquired a routine of visiting odd places and finding myself in dangerous situations. I explained that I couldn't compromise my spontaneity—the joy I felt to move when and how I chose. It was something I had to do—a compulsion for which I sacrificed bank accounts, jobs, and relationships. I warned her that I craved the encounters that unfolded as I moved through the world alone.

And then I realized I was in love.

Ten months later I moved out of my small, one-bedroom apartment and into a smaller one-bedroom cottage with Suzanne. It was set at the back of a narrow lot, behind a house, and beneath a towering cork tree that served as a second roof. The cottage was very old. An elderly neighbor told me he remembered it was once a chicken coop. It was crooked and riddled with termites. The whitewashed shingles on the exterior walls were peeling, but it was cheap, and the owner had repaired the place enough to make it cozy for Suzanne and me. Its size required an intimacy that suited our love. There was just enough room for our books and maps.

As we passed through our first year of living together, I considered us very lucky. We suited each other in so many ways. Suzanne even embraced the austerity that was required to travel on paychecks like ours. We scrimped and saved all that first year, and soon we were able to begin planning a trip together.

Our first trip was to Europe. We gambled on the weather and planned it for the late fall to take advantage of cheap airfares. A false winter preceded our arrival, but it was only a bluff. Mild, clear days followed us through Czechoslovakia, where we witnessed the first demonstrations that would result in the Velvet Revolution of 1989. Suzanne liked how I traveled without a guidebook, going to each place without opinion. Our immersion into the life of each village, town, and city to find even the most basic things erased any shyness she may have had. We met Austrian bakers and Italian postmen, French butchers and German road crews, who told us about trails, lakes, beaches, places to stay, and events we would never have discovered within the cover of a book.

We ended our trip in the Bavarian Alps, where it began to snow. The cold crept down from the mountain peaks and froze the little stream by our room. During our time there we discovered that our plans for the future had merged, and everywhere we looked we saw each other. I discovered that the richness of the life Suzanne and I had together was portable and extended as far into the world as we wanted to take it. By the time we left Europe, we knew we would spend the rest of our lives together.

On the plane home, Suzanne and I began planning our next trip. After work we devoted our evenings to reading about the places we wanted to visit. Our list grew impossibly long as one year passed and then another. We pinned a map of the world to our bedroom wall and marked the places we wanted to see. At night we'd lay together and try to connect one place to another and make a route. I found a company that specialized in discounted round-the-world airfares. We counted our money and measured it against the great distances on the map. We edited our list, sold possessions, and measured again.

Finally, we were ready. We gave notice on our place and bought a wad of airplane tickets to Hawaii, New Zealand, Australia, Indonesia, Hong Kong, Malaysia, Singapore, Mauritius, South Africa, Kenya, Egypt, and Greece. It felt as though we were holding a million dollars in our hands.

We were gone the better part of a year. Rather than satisfying our curiosity, we realized we'd only scratched the surface. Contrary to the popular saying, the world wasn't getting any smaller. It was as big as ever. Our list of places to visit was twice as long as when we'd left. We found a place to live, and new jobs. Our world map went back up on our bedroom wall and we began planning again.

~~~

I was too excited to sleep that first night in Bremen, and when I finally did sleep, I dreamed of getting on the bike and riding badly. In my dream the bike was out of balance, as if the engine turned an eccentric cam that made the frame twist wildly out of control. Suzanne was screaming in my ear as I tried to make the bike right itself and run smoothly. And after my dreams had exhausted me, I lay awake on the bed staring into the darkness of the room trying to figure out what could have gone wrong.

I could hear the sound of vehicles thumping over the cobbled street outside our hotel room. Suzanne slept soundly beside me, her breath regular and warm against my shoulder. Her calm soothed me, and I began to make a mental list of all we had to do before getting on the road. We had to find the office of the company that had handled the shipping of the motorcycle from California, clear customs, and carefully check the bike over after having spent twenty-eight days at sea. We'd have to get it started, and then, if anything was wrong, find a shop and buy parts.

I was thankful for our experience in the logistics of getting a trip under way, and in our thoroughness. I recounted the surprises and challenges of each trip and how we'd made it through them all, despite engine troubles, floods, political turmoil, and illness. I imagined everything that could happen on this trip and reasoned with myself why I shouldn't worry: crashing—we were careful; bad weather—it was summer and we had the right gear; mechanical troubles—I'd been over the bike and learned how to fix all but catastrophic problems. Most importantly, we had each other.

The hours passed and the city of Bremen gradually moved toward another day. Our room passed through steadily lighter shades of gray until I heard the sounds of morning traffic in the street below and I could lay there no more. Suzanne stirred as I turned to look at the clock beside the bed. It read five-thirty. I got up and walked to the window, pulled back the light gauze curtain, and opened it. A rush of cold air spilled into the room carrying the sounds of engines and brakes, the rush of a commuter train as it left the station, a blaring horn. The day had begun and I felt as if we were running late.

Our alarm went off at six. "I have minutes," Suzanne said. "I have five minutes."

"We've got to get going," I said, and recited all the things we had to do.

"Just a few more minutes," she said again, and fell back asleep.

I leafed through a phone book and wrote down addresses and numbers for motorcycle shops on a piece of hotel stationery. I found a bus schedule and plotted our route to the shipping company. I started to pack our gear. Twenty minutes passed and I turned on the radio beside the bed. The even voice of a woman filled the room as she read the news in German, followed by a pause, and then the first happy notes of a polka.

"Okay, okay," Suzanne said. "I'm awake."

She rolled over and pushed herself upright onto the edge of the bed. She yawned, ran her hand through her paint-black hair, and let it fall.

I wanted her to hurry, to feel the same urgency I did to dress, gather our things, find the bike, and get on the road. We had planned to ride through the flat, industrial north of Germany that first day, to ride the two hundred miles to Denmark. Over the border our map revealed many inlets and coves along the Baltic coast. We knew we'd find a beach there, and on it we'd make our first camp. I wanted us to have plenty of time to select one with fine sand, enough shade to protect us from the afternoon sun, where we could swim if we liked, and make a fire to cook our dinner on and fall asleep as we searched the sky for falling stars.

~~~

Two buses and a long walk brought us to the office of the shipping company. As we walked toward the entrance we looked for our motorcycle along the side of the building, but there were only cars and transport trucks. A woman greeted us from behind an immaculate desk. She placed a call and then announced that "Eddie" would be with us in a moment to settle our account. She offered us coffee or tea and showed us into a conference room.

Eddie entered the room, shook our hands, and sat down with a stack of papers he quickly sorted into three piles. He was short and slight with close-cropped blond hair. Eddie assured us the bike was fine. He said it was in the company's warehouse a few kilometers away and that he'd drive us there when we were finished with the paperwork.

After looking at our passports, he smiled with a twitch and said he'd been to California twice. "To El-Ay," he said, and pronounced the name as though he knew something intimate about the place. Eddie had thin, pale fingers with inflamed tips. A layer of skin was peeled from around the nail of each, leaving a seared shade of red. As he consulted each document he absently picked at the skin and peeled it off. I wanted to reach across the table with my own hand, lay it on top of his, and tell him to stop. He asked for all our papers, our insurance documents, registration, passports, driver's license, and then disappeared.

While Eddie was gone, Suzanne and I looked around the room. Along one wall was a large window. It looked onto a parking lot and a tall, brick factory building. The rest of the window framed a perfect blue sky. The sun streamed through at an angle. I took Suzanne's hand and we stepped into its warmth.

"Hmmm," she said, and turned her face to collect it.

"I'm so happy we did this," I said as we put our arms around each other. "This is going to be a wonderful trip."

A single cloud floated around the edge of the factory building and drifted into the open sky. It was slate blue and shaped like a cauliflower, its lobes separated by deep, purple valleys. Around it was an armada of sculpted white clouds as fine as those in a German romantic landscape painting.

The door opened and Eddie resumed his place at the table. He picked up a telephone and called customs. "A friend," he assured us with a wink. Because it was Eddie, the customs officer listened to his description of us, asked a few questions that Eddie answered after flipping through our documents. Eddie laughed, gave us a thumbs up, and hung up the phone. The customs official had waived our inspection.

~~~

The bike was wedged between crates of machinery and palettes stacked with hundred-pound bags of fertilizer and sunflower seeds. A long screw auger used for moving grain blocked the way out and Eddie had one of the workers move it with a lift truck. The bike was covered with a layer of fine dust that made it look old. My first thought was to clean it off as I would clean the dust off a friend. I went over to it and was thankful that it didn't appear to have been dropped or scratched or broken in any way. When the auger was moved I took the handlebars in my hands and pushed. The wheels turned easily, and I maneuvered the bike between several pieces of machinery and an antique Cadillac sedan. Then I sat on the seat and rolled down a ramp into the loading yard.

Suzanne was standing beside an empty shipping container. She smiled as I rode the bike beside her.

"Not a scratch," she said after walking around it.

Eddie pulled beside us in his car and helped us unload our bags from the trunk. He wished us well, shook our hands, and left.

Suzanne and I checked the bike's oil levels, the brakes, and the air pressure in the tires. We connected the battery. I turned the key but the lights on the instrument cluster were dead. I wondered if we had let Eddie leave too quickly. Our only way into town for parts now would be an expensive taxi ride. I felt in my pocket for the list of motorcycle shops and then began a methodical check of all the wiring. I found a wiring harness that was loose. I removed it, cleaned the terminals, and put it back together. Before turning the key, I remembered a Russian custom where travelers sit a moment before departing on a long journey. I threw my leg over the bike and sat down. I closed my eyes and gave a silent prayer for the engine to start. I felt for the key and turned it. I heard a familiar click as electricity pulsed through the bike and brought it to life. I opened my eyes and the instrument lights were on.

"I've got my fingers crossed," Suzanne said.

I touched the starter button with my thumb. The engine turned over but didn't start. I waited a moment for the fuel to work its way toward the spark plugs. I touched the starter again. The engine caught, then revved.

We attached the two side bags to the bike. I strapped the tank bag to the top of the gas tank. I slid our map of northern Germany and Denmark into the clear plastic envelope that attached to the top of it and pushed our compass into one corner. We arranged our stove, fuel bottles, pots and pans, rope, plates and bowls, lantern, spare parts, and extra tools in a trunk box behind the seat. Then we tied the tent across the back and wound our lock around the fuel tank.

I rode up and down the street alone several times, testing the brakes, the steering, and the balance of our load. Other than an annoying flat spot on the front tire from being tied down on the ship, everything seemed fine. I felt so good riding the bike again. I had missed it for the past month. As I rode up and down that street the familiarity of the handlebars and seat, of the engine's vibration, of the bike's smell and weight, made me feel something close to kinship. I'm not a fool when it comes to machines. I didn't give the bike human traits like trust and friendship. I knew that a machine like ours would just as surely carry us around a sweeping bend as it would carry us straight into an oncoming car. But as I leaned into each turn and thought of all that was before us, the bike meant everything. It was our vehicle to a new world.

I rode over to where Suzanne waited for me on the side of the empty road. I looked into her eyes, took her hand in mine, and I cleared a place in my mind for all the things we'd see, for the people we'd meet, for every glorious morning, day, and evening in the months ahead.

"I love you," I said.

"And I love you."

"You ready?"

She nodded and climbed on behind me.

tHRee

We merged into traffic on the Bremen/Hamburg autobahn toward Denmark at seventy-five miles an hour and then accelerated to eighty-five to match the flow of traffic. It felt extreme. It was not extreme on account of the speed. On a solid bike like ours, on an open road, one can achieve those speeds almost accidentally. It was extreme because of our combined weight and the weight of our things. It was extreme because I was still not sure of the bike, whether the front tire with its slight depression, which I could feel like a frantic pulse, was damaged more than I knew. It was extreme because to our left, in the fast lane just five feet away, cars blew past at an easy one hundred miles an hour and created shock waves that buffeted us. And it was extreme because it was our starting pace and the speed at which traffic in the middle lane moved and merged with a randomness that suggested we could, with the slightest flinch, end up a stain on the seamless concrete road.

Cars and trucks jockeyed for advantage around us. They brushed past us in a way that reminded me of how a precision flying team is always on the verge of complete destruction. Suzanne was stiff behind me. Her hands were dedicated to holding my hips. Her knees and thighs were like pincers. A blue Mercedes sedan changed lanes and sped around us as though we were a slalom pole on a ski slope. The driver never offered hints of his intentions through his blinkers. The smooth curve of his bumper barely missed our front tire as he pulled before us. Suzanne gripped my pelvis with her knees and shook my shoulders. I looked in the rearview mirror at a grill and headlight. I turned my head to look back at the intent stare of a woman who wanted to pass. She flicked her lights so the high beams filled our mirrors and my eyes with a flash I could not see through.

At eighty-five miles an hour there was nowhere to go but forward. The Mercedes was still in front of us. A transport truck barred our right side as solidly as a cement wall. My ears were overwhelmed with the sound of racing engines, the whine of tires over the roadbed, the adrenal pumping of my heart. A white car rapidly occupied the fast lane to our left. The woman behind us swerved in front of it anyway. I scanned the road for an escape but there was none. I braced myself for a crash and I wondered if I'd feel anything when it happened. The white car slowed rapidly and settled what appeared to be only inches behind the woman with the urgent need to pass, and then they both sped out of sight.

I felt the inward collision that accompanies an expected disaster many times in those first miles, though almost immediately I began to perceive the competence of the drivers. Watching them, looking at their faces as they passed, I saw that they weren't concerned or excited. Quite the contrary, they looked relaxed and poised at eighty to one hundred miles an hour. They moved with a machinelike precision. I wondered if we weren't on one of those futuristic roadways where cars are controlled by a computer that sends them speeding precisely along on autopilot. Though I was not ready to match their perilous all-out weaving and tailgating, I realized it was not anarchy, and I began to relax.

The autobahn had only infrequent exits, but every twenty or thirty miles there were large rest areas with gas stations, emergency repair shops, and fast-food restaurants. We pulled off at the first one. The bike needed fuel. I wanted to see about the tires, the load, and to check in with Suzanne.

I pulled beside a gas pump and felt Suzanne climb off behind me. I got off after her and pulled the bike onto its center stand. I watched as she shed her gloves and began pulling at the chin strap of her helmet with both hands. She did it with an urgency I didn't recognize, as if her lungs were short of air. Then she pushed it from her head and breathed deeply. Strands of black hair fell across her face. She wiped them back and I could read the stress and exhilaration of the first few miles in her eyes.

"God, what a beginning!" she said with a look that was both excited and appalled.

"I think I understand the rhythm now," I said. "It's not as dangerous as it seems."

"I was expecting something a little gentler," she said, eyeing the flow of traffic on the autobahn suspiciously.

She walked back and forth beside the bike, stretching her arms, shoulders, and back and working them back into her familiar ease.

"We'll be in Denmark in no time," I said as I finished filling the tank. "Our beach is calling us."

We settled into a middle lane of traffic at eighty miles an hour. Within just a few miles I began to feel easier with the speed and flow of traffic, and I began to appreciate the singular design of the autobahn. There were five lanes, all of them generously wide so even large trucks had plenty of room. The roadbed was seamless and as smooth as a racetrack. All the turns were gentle and well graded so traffic never slowed. Barrier walls on the outside edge of the lanes kept one from becoming distracted by the surrounding countryside. Traffic moved like water in a smooth channel. I felt Suzanne begin to relax behind me as we ate up miles. An old couple in a camping van slowed alongside us. They smiled and waved approvingly at us. We waved back and I heard Suzanne giggle happily. I moved one lane to the left and accelerated past one car, then another. The blip in the tire disappeared. The bike felt incredibly smooth. It felt as though I could have let go of the handlebars and it would have continued on its own.

∽∽∽

A gust of wind came from nowhere and shoved against our left side so the bike veered toward the edge of the lane. Suzanne grabbed my waist, wobbled, and pulled herself against my back. I immediately countered by leaning the collective weight of the bike against the wind and it righted itself. I quickly looked around to see that traffic hadn't been scrambled across the lanes like we had. Another gust blew us back across the lane and pinned us there.

"Be careful!" Suzanne yelled through my helmet.

Vehicles continued to whiz past us. I leaned hard against the wind until it subsided, and then we were stable again. I looked for a way to move to the slower lanes and had to speed up to get around traffic to do so. Another blast of wind hit and this time it carried a chill. I moved over a lane and felt the turbulence created by the large transport trucks that made an almost continuous wall in the slowest lane.

My hands began to ache from gripping the handlebars, but within a few miles I had learned how to lean into the wind and keep the bike in our lane. I noticed a bank of clouds as dark as smoke begin to appear over the barrier wall of the autobahn. Within minutes they had consumed the sky. I pulled off at the next rest area so we could put on our rain suits.

Somehow I knew the weather would be better in Denmark. Looking north we saw an expanse of blue sky, and I convinced Suzanne our beach lay beneath it. The storm was probably a local one, something we could out-run or out-maneuver if we just kept moving north.

Back on the autobahn the wind seemed to taunt us. Each invisible gust blew across the roadway as if meant only for us. The rest of the traffic was four-wheeled and stable. I noticed the way trailers tilted and shimmied, the way a car leaned, but that was all.

I envied their stability as the wind treated us like a sail, blowing the bike to the far side of our lane, so close to other vehicles that drivers looked at us with concern as the bike neared them and I wrestled for control. One time a middle-aged man driving a yellow car swerved and then braked as we neared him. He was smoking a pipe and had filled the interior of his car with a plume of calm smoke. His abrupt maneuvering caused the smoke to slosh like water in a tank. It collided against the windows on one side, contracted, and then expanded throughout the car again.

Traffic became congested just south of Hamburg, but it didn't slow. It pressed closer, as if everyone was trying to outrun the coming storm. In that closeness movements became more precise. I tried to move back from the vehicles in front of us to give us extra room, but each time we fell more than a car's length behind, another vehicle filled the void we had created.

As we rounded the edge of Hamburg the wind changed. It had been gusting from the left but came now in violent swirls that shook the bike as if a tire was loose or the forks were coming uncoupled. I gripped the handlebars tighter and pinched the gas tank with my knees. Suzanne's hands reached around my stomach and her helmet pressed against mine. The first drops of rain ticked against my helmet and the windscreen of the bike, where they quickly accumulated to obscure my view of the road.

It was the way the rain fell, combined with the wind and the speed and movement of the traffic, that made the rest of our ride such a difficult one. The rain came down with a force that made me think something was fundamentally wrong with the weather— perhaps we were in the midst of an anomaly that would claim the lives of hundreds of people and would be featured in the world news. It fell so hard that I felt the bike's tires cut through a layer of water on the roadbed. The windscreen and my face shield were like melting glass. The noise of the rain, the noise of the cars and trucks around us, the noise of the bike, the sound of my own heart, were so loud that I waited for something to shatter.

Still the traffic did not slow. It moved dead-on, crazily. It moved with the assurance of a very fast assembly line. But this flow of vehicles was no machine. It was thousands of individual cars and trucks being driven by people lost in their own thoughts, who just wanted to get somewhere—quickly.

The wind increased. Water was lifted from the road and thrown up by the tires of the vehicles around us until I was almost driving blind. To my left I saw a vague hand through a wet window. I felt the first cold drops of rain squeeze between the visor of my helmet and fall onto my face. I felt them as they began a slow slide down my neck. The hand moved again, a rapid movement up and down. A car slipped in front of us. A heavy spray of water washed over my visor, and I envied each car for its wiper blades. The hand moved once again. A flash of brake lights illuminated our windscreen. The hand moved more rapidly and I looked over at it. It moved intently, up and down, up and down, and I realized someone was waving, urging us on.

We were east of Hamburg when I saw what looked like a black granite wall moving across the lanes of traffic. I wanted to apply the brakes, to slow down and approach with caution, but we were caught in the rushing current of traffic. The dark rectangle became the hull of a ship. A white flying-bridge sat atop one end, and the whole of it moved in a steady glide directly across the autobahn. I anticipated a sudden flare of brake lights as vehicles slid to a halt to avoid being crushed, or perhaps a quick turn in the roadway that would lead us safely around the ship. Instead the traffic moved steadily forward. My head ached as all my senses resisted rushing blindly on. Then the roadway began a gentle dip and I saw the open mouth of a tunnel. I stole glimpses of the ship as we slipped beneath it, and I tried to understand the physics of the forces at play.

The tunnel was still and warm. The sound of the wind and rain was replaced with the smooth droning of engines and tires as they turned over the hard, dry surface of the road. The droning was punctuated by the hiss of a truck's air brakes and the throaty rev of a diesel engine as the driver changed gears. The bike felt extraordinarily smooth and stable again, and for just a moment it seemed as if we were floating. I shifted my weight from side to side to see if anything felt loose or broken. The bike responded with a series of precise weaves and then righted itself. Suzanne's legs relaxed their hold on my pelvis. Her hands slid from around my stomach to my hips and rested there.

The road leveled and then began a slow rise toward the surface. Vehicles around us accelerated in unison and the air filled with exhaust. The air grew thick with gases, and I tried to breathe as little as possible. Light filled the end of the tunnel, and I felt like a moth as we rushed toward it.

I breathed deeply as we reentered the storm. I pulled the air into my lungs and cleared them of exhaust. A gust of wind shoved us toward the right edge of our lane and held us there. I leaned hard to the left and won back our position in the middle. Rain blurred my vision, and I focused on the tail lights of the car ahead. I welcomed the protection of Suzanne's arms around my waist and the pressure of her legs as she pulled herself against me.

The storm raged as we rode past Hamburg and Kiel. As we rode across the flat, exposed shank of Germany that merges with Denmark, I concentrated on the wind and how I could minimize its power over us and discover a way through it. I studied the way it lurched and rose and twisted, the way it harnessed the rain and dove in on us. I tried to read its progress—how it bent grass and trees on the side of the road, and pushed the rain up just before it hit. I tried to lean smoothly so we didn't wobble and oversteer. I learned to use the throttle like an imperfect rudder—a little less power helped us to lean against the wind, while extra power lifted us when the wind declined. I was thinking that with time I could master the weather, that I could learn it as some sailors learn the sea.

And then we began a long rise over a bridge spanning a canal. It rose in a high, fine arch that caught the bottom of some clouds, and as we began the climb to meet them, we entered different layers of the storm. The wind changed from violent gusts to blasts and swirls that pushed and pulled at the same time, so it felt as if the bike would suddenly change directions or begin spinning out of control. The winds raced over us, then relaxed for an instant, like a tide before it rushes back. It swirled and pitched and pulled

against the windscreen and wheels, against our bags and our bodies, as if trying to tear something away. It reached down the neck
of my rain suit like a cold hand and blew under the base of my
helmet, filling it with wet air. The chin strap tightened against my
throat as the wind tried to pull the helmet off my head. My face
shield popped open and wind rushed across my face and out the
opening like a frantic bird.

My hands, arms, and knees ached as I held onto the bike. The
wind shoved us toward the guardrail, then sucked us back toward
cars that never seemed to slow or even notice us. We rode over the
apex of the bridge and then down the other side. A yellow van
wedged itself into the small space between us and the car ahead. A
mess of seagulls whipped past. I braked carefully to create a buffer
between the van and ducked to avoid the worst of the spray from
its tires. An extended gust blew us from our lane. I leaned against
the wind and felt the bike inching back, and as I leaned and coaxed
the handlebars and throttle, Suzanne began to pinch me with her
legs. I glanced in the left mirror and could see only a headlight. It
remained just a few feet from the rear of the bike. Even if I could
have moved, there was nowhere to go, and all of my strength and
concentration was focused on the middle of our lane and on getting the bike there. Then Suzanne began to laugh. I felt it through
my back—a series of high notes that I heard over everything else.
She laughed hysterically, madly, to the bottom of the bridge.

We left the autobahn at the next exit and stopped under the
wide metal roof of a fuel station. While the storm continued
around us we climbed off the bike, removed our gloves and helmets, and I asked Suzanne why she was laughing.

"Because," she said, her voice strange to me, "I thought we
were going to die. It wasn't a matter of *if*, Allen, but only *when*. And
didn't you see that car, the one so close to us? The people inside
were kissing. They were two feet from us and the couple was kissing. We've got to stop, Allen. This is getting crazy."

~~~

On a narrow road that encouraged low speeds, we rode east toward the Baltic Sea. We rode past farms with straight fences and neat yards, through villages buttoned up as tight as a coat, past cows huddled together, their backs humped against the weather. We rode beside planted fields of grain the wind had pressed against the earth like slicked hair, through small wooded areas that filtered the storm momentarily. There was only an occasional car on the road, which made our experience on the autobahn seem otherworldly and remote.

Near the village of Wacherballig we found a campground beside the sea. It was at the end of a lane that followed the subtle curve of the beach. I stopped the bike and for the first time looked across a portion of the Baltic. The sea lay gray and agitated before us, and in the distance it merged seamlessly with the clouds in the sky. The wind blew unimpeded off the sea and against us like a firm hand trying to push us away.

A narrow pier led into the water and at the end were dozens of sailboats. Their thin masts scratched at the belly of the sky, and through them I made out the stormy coast of Denmark. Somewhere in between a fishing boat pushed through the water. Its bow rose on the crest of a wave and then plunged, creating a flash of white foam. Over its stern a constellation of seagulls wheeled in a chaotic orbit. The wind gusted and pushed the weight of the bike onto my right leg. Suzanne shivered behind me. I'd lost the feeling in the ends of my fingers long ago.

~~~

A small outbuilding marked the entrance to the campground, and through its roof a chimney exhausted a stream of smoke the wind swept away. Faded brochures and notices were taped against a window, and between them and the glass was a collage of dead insects. Three children interrupted a game of cards long enough to take our money and tell us we could set up our tent anywhere we wanted.

Most of the camp was either too wet or wind-swept to pitch our tent on, and we spent a long time searching for a site that lay just a few inches higher than the surrounding ground. We found a place behind a hedge and positioned the bike as an added barrier against the wind and rain. It took both of us to set up the tent: to hold the ground tarp down, stake the corners, erect the poles, and fix the rain cover in place. Suzanne went inside first, and I handed her our bags through the tent door. I knelt in the opening and felt the cold of the earth seep into my knees.

Three bags held all our things, and as Suzanne arranged them at one end of the tent, it struck me how inadequate their contents seemed. She opened our two hard cases that fit on either side of the bike and removed our sleeping bags. At the bottom of her bag I noticed the blue plastic that protected the dress and sandals she'd brought in case we were invited somewhere. Suzanne unrolled the bags and smoothed them out with her hands like sheets on a mattress. She lay down on them, looked at the ceiling, and breathed a heavy sigh. I took her hand and kissed it.

"I'm sorry about this beginning," I said.

"So am I. Quite a day. But we made it this far," she said with a smile.

"Yes. We made it this far."

The wind shoved hard against the tent and lifted one corner, pulling a stake with it.

"This won't go on," she said. "It will be over soon."

After dinner Suzanne lay down for a rest that became sleep, and I walked through camp toward the sea. Three children wrapped in yellow rain suits and red boots kicked a soccer ball through the wet. Across from where they played was a large blue tent with a car parked to the side. A family of four sat in the car, staring at a small television set on the dashboard. I passed a cluster of enviably large trailers, each equipped with a tented extension that created an extra room big enough for a table and chairs and for people to stand and walk around in. A plastic picture window I could see through fronted each, and inside one was a family sitting around a table. They watched me as I walked past. I smiled and waved, but no one waved back.

A group of older men huddled in the lee of the camp toilets. They were talking animatedly, laughing, and smoking. I wanted to be invited into their conversation. I wanted to tell them about our day, have them ask where we were from and where we were going. I wanted to be offered a cigarette, to have one of them invite Suzanne and me back to his trailer for a drink, where the weight of our day could be softened with some laughter and conversation. I slowed my pace and said *"Guten abend"* and watched them close in on themselves as if I'd said something offensive.

I walked to the pier, then onto it and out over the sea toward Denmark. The boards were slick from rain, and the pier heaved and fell in the surf. I walked stiff-legged, with my hands out to keep from falling. The wind was icy and the rain fell in numbing drops against my skin. The boats pulled at their ropes. Their bellies slurped and slapped as they were lifted and then dropped in the water. One boat had a bell that sounded in time with the swells: clang-clang, clang-clang; clang-clang.

I walked to the end of the pier and balanced against the wind and the roll of the waves. Straight ahead was the coast of Denmark, a line of green that looked like a low hedge across an open field. The wind filled my ears, and to hear the bell I had to cock my head. I pulled the sleeves of my rain suit over my hands and squinted my eyes against the wind. My lips became numb and I thought to myself that it shouldn't be like this.

Our first day should have been free of storms. It should have been an easy ride to Denmark. We should have been sitting on a beach, our jackets off, our feet covered with sand, and we should have been deliciously drunk with thoughts of all that lay before us. The weather should have been as it was the year before when Scandinavia had what many called a "California" summer.

I watched as a sleeper wave at least two feet higher than the others formed in the distance. It rolled darkly toward me and I waited for it to break and flatten into a harmless froth. The wave grew higher. It seemed to stand on hind legs and gain speed. It didn't break, and I realized it was going to hit the pier. I spread my legs and tried to grip the planks with the soles of my boots, and when the wave hit, I thought of people we read about in the news—people who get caught in flash floods, or pulled into the surf and swept away, because they don't believe anything can happen to them. The pier bucked and knocked me forward. I landed on my hands, and my arms and feet were covered by water. My left foot slipped out from under me and over the edge of the pier. I heard ropes straining, the hulls of boats lifting and slapping the water, the bell ringing wildly: clangclangclangclang; clang, clang-clangclang, clang, clang.

four

The storm breathed down on us throughout the night. It came in furious exhalations and coughs, in pants and wheezes that carried torrents of rain, bits of trees, and spume from the sea. I thought the hedge behind us would tear and break, that trees would fall. The side of the tent pressed against my thigh throughout the night as I tried to sleep. I listened to the storm fold in on itself and build until it seemed uncontainable. I listened as it crested and crashed down on us again and again and again. And as I listened I thought how terrifying travel can be, especially beginnings; how travel can feel like the first awkward stage of flight when the plane is neither high enough to glide to safety should anything happen nor high enough to turn back. It's a feeling that I have done something irrevocably wrong, a feeling of utter failure.

I envied Suzanne for her ability to shut it out and retreat into sleep. As I watched her, I thought about the day's ride and what I could have done better. Though I had ridden in all kinds of weather since we'd bought the bike, I'd never encountered rain or winds like these. In the dark of night, under the storm, I practiced riding. I leaned the bike each time the wind rolled against the tent, and I brought it upright when it subsided. But inevitably, out of nowhere, the wind blew us so hard that I lost control of the bike, and of my imagination, and we fell. I watched the whole thing unfold in slow motion: the bike, with us holding on, slid beneath a car, and we were rolled and smashed beneath the wheels and undercarriage. Our bodies were thrown aside, and the bike disintegrated. Our sleeping bags and stove, our clothes and tent and notepads and dreams, tumbled over the surface of the road.

I listened to the storm and willed it to end.

With the first light of morning the storm began to recede. At first the change was so subtle I had to mark the sound and force of the wind, the heaviness of the rain, as I would the movement of a ship across the horizon. The pressure of the tent against my thigh decreased. The roar of the wind through the hedge and trees became a moan. The rain became a steady shower.

Suzanne woke. Her eyes opened and the skin around them gathered as she smiled at me, and as she smiled the weight of the night fell away.

I felt small and grateful.

I suggested we return to the autobahn. The break in the storm was our opportunity to get to Denmark quickly and, quite possibly, beyond the weather. As we rode I felt an urgency to move on, as if escaping a building just before it collapsed. Within sight of the autobahn the sun momentarily broke through and illuminated the wet surface of the road like a phosphorus fire. I could feel the sun's warmth through the damp leather of my gloves, on my nose and cheeks, as though a warm hand was laid there. And then the space in the clouds closed again.

We merged again with traffic. I settled the bike in the middle lane and positioned it so we were out of the blind spots of the vehicles on either side. I thought how easy it was without the wind and rain, how pleasurable riding was. I thought that all we needed was a patch of blue on the horizon, an end to the clouds we could fix on, and we could go like this forever. Then the sky began to darken like a false night. The wind began to blow with a wail. The rain began to fall like tears. It filled the air and covered the road. It worked its way through my helmet and began running down my neck. Suzanne pulled herself against me. The tires of all the vehicles around us picked up the rain again and spun it into the air like fountains.

Traffic began to slow near the border. I shifted down through the gears and we came to a stop with the rest of the traffic. It started again, slowly, and we became part of a halting mass of vehicles that moved a car length at a time.

"This is still pretty crazy, Allen," Suzanne said. "Don't you think so?"

"There's got to be an end to it," I said. "Let's go a little further and see what happens."

Most cars were packed with people and luggage for a vacation or weekend away. I saw bicycles, small boats, toys for the water, and took these as confirmation of better weather ahead. They're locals, I reasoned. They know what's going on.

The wind and rain lost a degree of their gloomy influence. I focused beyond the inconvenience of the elements and thought of how it would be when we hit our stride, when the weather had passed and the trip acquired a life of its own. Our trips always did. In a single moment they rose like a wave that Suzanne and I caught together and rode. And, as with all the others, we would be brought inextricably together by the challenges and wonders of the road. We just had to be patient now, and it would happen.

~~~

The first thing I noticed about Denmark was how the road differed. The precision of the autobahn was replaced by a highway constructed from much softer materials. Each lane had two troughs running down it that had been formed by the weight of millions of tires, and a ridge that welled up in the center. The troughs were filled with water, like rain gutters on the side of city streets. I tried to ride along the crown of the center ridge, but the wind kept pushing us down the sides and into the troughs. The bike slowed abruptly as the tires cut through the water and sent up a cascade on either side of us. Then we surged ahead again as I maneuvered us out.

I found myself making deals with God to appease the weather. I offered to accept the rain so long as the wind ceased, even a little. I offered to accept the wind so long as it blew at a dependable speed I could lean into. Instead, it continued to blow cruelly in blasts and swirls, in eddies that careened off trucks and cars and threatened to sweep us away.

I found myself anticipating gusts and reacting to my anticipations. I usually guessed wrong. I reacted to feigned punches, and by reacting, I left us open to the actual blows. I began to take the weather personally, to feel as if it was out to get us, and I tried to think of ways to strike back. A transport truck crossed through our lane in front of us, creating a shower that blinded me. I felt the tilt of vertigo and resisted the temptation to turn or brake sharply away. Instead, I relaxed my grip on the handlebars and let the drape and pull of my legs down each side of the bike orient the rest of me. And when I could see again we exited at a sign that promised the town of Sonderborg, just twenty kilometers east toward the sea.

~~~

"Taller du Engliska?" I asked across a paper-strewn desk.

"Of course," the man said without looking up. His big hand gripped a pen he guided quickly through a form, writing short notes and making slashes through boxes. He was a big man with red hair and a thick beard. He looked like a fisherman, not a youth hostel warden.

I waited for him to reach the bottom of the page before I asked about a room for the night, but when he arrived there he pushed the page aside and continued to another. I listened to the rolling of his pen as it slid across the paper and to the dripping of water as it fell from my clothes to the floor around my feet. Behind him was a large window that looked onto a small yard of shrubs and trees, and from my position I watched as the storm assaulted it.

As he neared the bottom of the next page I turned and looked at Suzanne across the lobby, where she sat with our bags. She was already out of her rain suit and was rubbing her face with both hands, as if to align the parts again.

"So," the man said, and paused to sign his name in a tight scribble at the bottom of the page. "You want a bed?"

"For two people."

"*Two* people?" he asked, as though it could be a problem.

"Yes. For two people."

"Two people," he repeated, and then looked at me for the first time. "You are early."

"Yes. I saw the sign. We're on a motorcycle and we wanted to get out of the weather."

"Motorcycle?"

His eyes left mine and he peeked around the corner to where Suzanne sat. "Hmmm," he said, and opened a ledger on his desk. The thick pages crinkled as he turned them. "You do not mind children?" he asked. "We have a school group this night. They can make some big noises."

I looked through the window into the storm and said the children would not be a problem. The man handed me a key.

He must have felt sorry for us. Suzanne and I expected a dormitory filled with double bunk beds as in most hostels, a room filled with hyperactive children away from home for the first time. Instead, we had a room to ourselves. Two beds were pushed against opposite walls, and between them was a wooden table and two chairs. Above the table was a window that looked onto a yard. The floor was carpeted, and attached to our room was a bathroom and shower.

"This isn't a hostel," Suzanne said while stretching her body across one of the beds. "It's a hotel."

"Try ordering room service," I kidded.

"Mmmmmm. What would I order...let me see. How about some hot soup to begin?"

"How about some wine?" I asked.

"White or red?"

"White. No, red," I said, and lay down beside her. She moved against the wall, making room for me, and then pressed her face into my neck.

"And then a big roasted chicken with potatoes," she said.

"We're in Denmark," I said. "Land of fish. How about salmon?"

"Yeah," she said, and kissed me. "With roasted garlic, and lemon. A big salad on the side."

"Do you think they'd bring candles?" I asked, and ran my fingers slowly through her hair to work the knots free.

"I'd insist. Any dessert?"

"A big, juicy orange would be perfect."

"I'd have some kind of pastry," she said. "I think I deserve it after everything."

I turned my head and looked back through the window at the sky. The wind carried clouds like a river at flood stage carries debris.

"Yes," I agreed. "After everything, you deserve it."

~~~

In the afternoon the storm waned enough for us to walk into town. Compared to riding through the storm, it seemed benign now. Like the ocean from shore, I thought. From shore, the ocean is like a wild animal viewed from afar. It is something to contemplate, a thing to wonder at, a backdrop to hang a day on. But when on the ocean, one must be aware of its raw power and its fickle ability to disrupt and spoil a life. Even the experienced can disappear in a moment of fatigue or laziness, or while gazing up to gauge the weather and lingering for too long on the sweep of a gull overhead.

We walked through a neighborhood of yellow brick homes. Each yard was precisely trimmed, like the hair of a man who has it cut weekly. The homes had narrow planting beds along the foundations where small flowers were in bloom. Windows were polished like fine lenses, magnifying the order within: a windowsill draped with a tatted runner; a clear glass vase of blue flowers placed squarely in the middle of a table made up for dinner; a woman stirring a simmering pot as she stretched and rubbed the small of her back.

Sonderborg begins on the edge of the sea and radiates inland like a bloom of lichen on a rock. It begins with a castle on the water, its massive stone walls and battlements still poised against Germany. Suzanne and I walked along the breakwater and watched two boys with a butterfly net try to catch a crab hiding in the algae. Around them thousands of saucer-sized jellyfish pulsed rhythmically against the slow current.

"Mens of war," one of the boys explained.

"Jellyfish," Suzanne said, and the boys laughed.

"Jolly-fish," they repeated, "Jollyfish. *Jollyfish.*"

The water teemed with them. Further out I noticed how their thin white and pink mantles pierced the surface. A fishing boat left port for the Baltic and caused a wake that pushed hundreds against the stone jetty. The jellies sloshed back and forth against the pier, continually pulsing like an unhurried heart. Their aimless travel fascinated me. It was as if movement, and not the direction, was all that mattered. Watching them made me think of movement as an ideal, and how, a few times, I had arrived at a point during a trip when the direction became just as meaningless. At those times the only important thing, the only logical thing, was to keep moving—to find the place farthest on the map, to strike off and keep adjusting the endpoint farther and farther away. A friend explained it perfectly to me: He had been traveling for many months and was hitching in Spain, on his way to Barcelona, but no one would stop for him. He stood on the side of the road for hours waiting for a ride. Half a day passed. He grew weary of waiting, and finally, it occurred to him it didn't matter where he went. So he picked up his bag, walked to the other side of the road, put his thumb out, and got a ride in the opposite direction.

Farther along the breakwater Suzanne and I passed a granary that stood between the waterfront and the edge of town. Pigeons perched fatly in every recess sheltered from the weather, staring as we passed. Around the corner was a children's clothing store, and beside that an identical store with "Porno Shop" written in large black letters along the front. In the window was a faded mannequin in cheap lingerie, her skin blotched and dusty. She wore a white G-string decorated with lace and white stockings held in place by a garter belt. A spider's web spanned the area between her legs and several flies were stuck there like dried currants. Beside the mannequin was an inflated dildo as high as her hips, and around that was an array of smaller dildoes that rose like mushrooms after a rain. An old woman wearing a brown raincoat and matching wool hat walked in front of the shop and stopped for a look. She stood in front of the window as if looking at shoes, checking to see if anything had been rearranged or added to the collection. Perhaps a sale item would have drawn her in.

Suzanne and I kept walking and met a man sitting on a bench near the center of town. He stopped us with a slurred command issued through his long mustache. His skin was stained with dirt, his clothes worn. A bottle swaddled in brown paper rested between his legs. He wore a floppy fedora that was black from the rain. I used my few words of Danish to say that I didn't speak the language. A look of bewilderment crossed his face, followed by a flash of anger that suggested he didn't like me making fun of him. He said something to himself and began to giggle.

"*Deutsch!*" he accused.

"*Naj.* American," I said.

He seemed confused. He looked away and pushed back the brim of his hat to scratch his brow. The bottle tipped and he reached to catch it.

"Mo-ment," he said, and thought very hard about something. Suzanne and I waited longer than a moment. We watched his mouth work and waited for his thought to come.

A very fat man sat poised on the edge of the next bench as if he'd forgotten to sit down completely. His bald head was swollen. His face was a deep blue.

"Moment!" the drunk said urgently, his thought ripening.

The fat man held a cigarette at the opening of his mouth and pulled on it with each breath like a respirator. His eyes were wide, as if they'd been fixed there after some astonishing fact had been revealed to him years ago.

"Eew iss frahm Amerika?" the man with the hat finally asked.

"Yes," Suzanne said.

"Frahm Amerika? Eww," he pointed between the two of us, "iss frahm Amerika?"

"Yeah," I said.

"*Naj!* I loves Amerika. Cowboys!" he said, and crudely mimed how a man might position himself on a galloping horse. His eyes shone briefly. A smile split his lips and for a moment he was riding a very fast horse across the American West.

"What would you do in America?" I asked.

"Texas! I sahmday goes to Texas," and the faraway look in his eyes grew acute. He continued to ride, and Suzanne and I began to edge away.

"Nooooo! Chee-cago! Gangster!" he blurted, and then he stood and gripped an imaginary machine gun. He scanned both ends of the road for a rival. A woman and a child walked quickly by and the drunk let them pass unharmed. The fat man sucked on his cigarette unaware of us, his eyes wide and unblinking, the astonishing blue of his face so rich I thought it could be beautiful on a wall.

"Chee-ca-go, Chee-ca-go!" the drunk sang and danced a stiff-legged jig. He danced jerkily, enthusiastically, and then gripped his head as if he was in great pain. His body lurched backward and collapsed on the bench. He looked dazed, his eyes wide, his chest heaving. "Amerika," he said through quick breaths. "I loves to see Amerika."

Suzanne took a dollar bill from her wallet and held it in front of his face. He took it and stared at the image of George Washington on the front. "For your trip to America," she said, and we continued on.

That night I dreamed that Suzanne and I were riding the bike along a beach. It was wide and smooth, bordered by steep dunes and the sea. The sun was so bright I had to ride with sunglasses on and my jacket unzipped. Suzanne was humming behind me and occasionally pointed to things that interested her: the curl of a wave, a group of sea lions resting at the base of some dunes. We rode for a long time in a straight, relaxed line with nothing in our way but coils of kelp and mounds of white shells, and gulls, which lifted themselves on heavy wings through heat vapors. From nowhere a wave began flooding the beach. I turned the bike toward the dunes but the water became deeper. It washed through the spokes and began to carry us with it like a piece of driftwood. The water rose higher still. Suzanne reached around my waist for something to hold. We went under and were twirling in a powerful eddie. I lost the bike. My helmet filled with water and sand. Suzanne's hands tore at my hips and then slipped from around me. I could hear her screams through the water.

~~~

The children woke us at seven. A group of them ran up and down the hall knocking on doors, squealing with delight. They began singing Danish folk songs, but sometimes their voices disappeared beneath the sounds of the storm. Suzanne and I retreated into the shower together and took turns lathering each other's skin until it felt like grease. The water was hot, and the small space quickly filled with steam. I worked on the knots in her neck and she murmured what sounded like a prayer. I worked on her shoulders, on the corded muscles down the length of her back to where they tied into her hips. I worked the muscles down her arms, past her elbows and wrists, to the wooden segments of her fingers. Her breasts filled my hands, and my fingers traced the span between each rib until they fell across her stomach and thighs.

"Allen? I'd rather not go out there today" she said. "Not yet anyway."

"We can stay another day," I said.

When we were done, we held each other in the steam and listened to the dripping of the faucet against the tile floor.

"A few of our trips began like this," I said, and wrapped my arms around her waist.

"How so?"

"With rain. Remember Australia? New Zealand? Even that time in Hawaii."

It had rained for a month in Australia when we were there. They were record rains that submerged portions of the arid Outback and stranded travelers on temporary islands. In New Zealand it rained for two weeks straight until most of the major rivers on the north island were swollen past flood stage. One night we were stranded on a road between two landslides. That night I took a long walk on a black-sand beach at the height of the storm. The waves were stained a coffee brown with soil washed from the mountains. On the tidal boundary, an unusual assortment of flotsam had accumulated: large sections of a house, entire trees, beds of seaweed, and the bodies of fish and bloated sheep. I found a doll's head upside down in an open clam shell. The doll's glassy eyes were opened wide. Where the neck had been connected to the head was a hole, and the inside was filled with water. A small fish swam in circles in search of a way out.

In Hawaii a storm raged for eight days. On one of them we decided to visit the Mauna Loa lava fields during an eruption. We got to within feet of an oozing wound in the earth. We could feel the heat as the lava spilled over the land toward the sea. We could smell the raw earth and hear it hissing as the rain fell on it. But we couldn't see a thing through all the steam.

"I remember," she said. "But we weren't on a motorcycle then."

"But everything worked out," I said. "The rains passed and everything was fine."

~~~

We used that day to rest and watch the fury of the storm expend itself through the window of our room. After a number of hours we noticed a change in the sound of the rain. Some birds came out of hiding and flitted across the sky as if a cease-fire had been declared. We decided to go back through town for a walk along the sea.

On the way Suzanne found the dismembered remains of a crab along the breakwater. It was the same place where the two boys had been working their net. The pieces were spread like broken glass over the stones. Suzanne looked at the mess and nudged the pieces over the edge with the toe of her boot. They made little splashes and then tumbled and twirled between jellyfish to the bottom.

We walked along an old waterfront promenade. Fine old homes with big yards looked onto the sea. At the base of the breakwater was a narrow beach strewn with washed-up algae and bits of broken shells, and we climbed down onto it. The waves tossed stones onto the shore where they clattered and rolled before being pulled back. The wind blew off the water and we pulled the zippers of our jackets to our chins. A gray veil of clouds hung down to the water like a curtain. I knew they must end somewhere. I imagined how, just a mile out, perhaps ten, the weather was warm and sunny. At any time the gray could lift and part and reveal the weather we had hoped for. When that happened I knew we'd forget the discomforts of these first days, just as we had on previous trips. I said to Suzanne that in just a few days the weather could be warm and dry, and that she and I could be complaining about how hot we were in our jackets, gloves, and helmets. We'd probably get to the point where we welcomed a little rain and cool air. I said that in a few days we'd look back on the beginning of this trip as something extraordinary, and we'd be glad for the experiences and the stories.

"I'm sure you're right," she said. "It's just that everything feels so harsh. I know it's because of the weather and because we're so exposed on the bike, but I feel as though my skin is being eroded."

"Be patient," I said. "This is going to be a great trip."

"I hope so," she said.

The muted clatter of the stones in the waves appealed to me, and I imagined how we'd hear variations of that sound along the thousands of miles of shoreline in the months ahead. I suddenly wanted to hear them all at once.

~~~

Suzanne and I returned to the hostel as the storm gathered itself again. From a rise on the edge of town we watched as the sky darkened and closed around us. We walked the last block as the rain pelted our backs and the wind twisted around our legs. Suzanne pulled her jacket around herself and lowered her head. She moved closer to me. "I'm being patient," I heard her say under her breath. "I'm being patient."

When we arrived back at our room she lay on the bed and turned her face toward the wall. I sat beside her.

"If things don't improve," she began, "we should think of going somewhere else. We could go south. France. Spain. I don't know."

I was shocked. How could she, after all it took to bring this trip to life, say such a thing? We had never turned back before. We took our time and figured a way through difficulties.

The thought of going somewhere else terrified me. My heart and soul were already on the road north. I'd studied and prepared. To change our plans now would be like telling someone who'd prepared to live in Europe that they were going to the middle of a desert.

"Give it time," I urged. "You didn't give yourself time to prepare."

"What do you mean by that? There was no way to prepare for *this*."

Until just three days before leaving California, Suzanne had been focused on school and work. She'd had a busy semester at college because she'd squeezed in an extra class that wouldn't be offered again. She was also working thirty hours a week, so most of the planning and preparation had been left to me. She hadn't had time to research with me the places we'd visit or to help me choose our route and select the gear we'd take. I, on the other hand, had steeped myself in Nordic mythology and stories about the peoples of the far north, on histories of early development and the spread of Christianity and the Hanseatic League. I pored over accounts of colonialism and invasions. I studied current events and a multitude of maps. The places became a part of me. I had done my best to convey all that I learned to her, but I knew it wasn't the same as preparing together. She assured me repeatedly that she trusted my judgment, that she'd catch up once we were on the road. Through no one's fault, the trip had become too much my own. Even the motorcycle became my responsibility.

Our original idea was that we'd both drive, and Suzanne carved out time to take a motorcycle safety course over a weekend in the early fall. The instructors were a father-and-son team, ex-military, and adept at barking orders with an intimidating authority. The class was held in a parking lot and the students were a mix of men and women of all ages. There was a paunchy middle-aged banker who planned to buy a Harley-Davidson, a teenage boy who dreamed of racing Japanese sport bikes, and two middle-aged women who'd never ridden before but who had just ordered matching Harleys. Suzanne told me how several people had not returned to class after the break, how others had continued to disappear throughout the weekend, and how the remaining students were increasingly on edge. She told me of the point in class when one of the women with the Harley on order had suddenly lost control of her bike during a simple maneuver and panicked. Instead of braking, she applied full throttle and sped across the parking lot. The students and instructors could only watch in disbelief as she raced straight toward the trailer of a gravel truck parked in a far corner. She came to a stop against a cyclone fence after passing untouched beneath the trailer. Though she was unhurt except for a few scrapes, she left the class with her friend.

Suzanne stayed. She learned to ride and to negotiate all the obstacles smoothly and was awarded her certificate. But when it came to riding our motorcycle, she hesitated. With its size, our combined weight and gear, she decided it was more than she could handle. She relegated herself to the position of passenger. "It just means I'll be able to sit back and enjoy the ride," she said good-naturedly, and dove back into her studies and work.

I did have time to prepare. I rode all fall, winter, and spring. I took the bike out in winter storms as they battered the California coast. I practiced on muddy, rocky roads not meant for a street bike. I rode at night when there was frost on the ground. I loaded the bike with fishing weights and sandbags and rode through snow whenever storms blanketed the surrounding hills. At least once a month I rode along the busy freeways around Oakland and San Francisco. Over time I came to think of the bike as the vehicle we had logically evolved to after having moved through the world in planes, trains, buses, and cars. I came to think of it as the perfect vehicle.

To ride a bike is to be part of the machine. You're essentially sitting on top of an engine and a raw steering mechanism, and your arms and legs are the linkages that make it all work. To ride well every part of my body had to work together in minute ways. With the fingers of my right hand I controlled the starter, the front brakes, right turn signal, and throttle. The fingers of my left hand controlled the horn, the left turn signal, and the clutch. My right foot controlled the rear brake, and with my left I moved up and down through the gears. My whole body was involved in steering the bike. By shifting my arms, hips, legs, or even my head, the bike moved in subtle ways. Every aspect of riding required preparation, thought, and coordination.

To negotiate a turn I had to think about where I was in the lane, when to begin leaning and how far, how fast I was going, whether there were obstacles like gravel or oil I had to avoid. If I had to stop, I could not just stomp on the brakes as I would in a car. I had to set the bike up before applying them so the bike wouldn't begin sliding. I applied the front brakes a little harder than the rear. At the same time, I carefully worked the clutch and shifted down through the gears, steered and balanced, and kept an eye on the traffic in front of me and behind.

To drive a car is to remove yourself from the surrounding environment with sheets of steel and glass, with soundproofing and loungelike seats, with heating and cooling and audio, and with so many springs and cushioned parts that you may as well be sitting in a movie theater.

To ride was to place myself in the environments I rode through. I felt every bump and dimple in the road through my hands and arms. I was aware of subtle temperature changes and smells. I tracked cars like an air traffic controller tracks planes. It was as if my mind expanded and I was super-aware of all that was around me. At times it seemed as if I could see without really seeing, as if my mind could peer around turns and over hills. Best of all, my view of the world was only limited by how far I could turn my head.

"Were you prepared for this?" Suzanne asked, her hand pointing out the window.

"No, but since when did that stop us? We've stumbled upon the unexpected, and incredible things can happen if we work through it."

Suzanne looked at me as if I'd just spoken in tongues.

"We can get through this," I said more reasonably. "It will pass."

I looked from Suzanne to the window. A gull whipped past out of control. The trees bowed under the force of the wind. A dove called from somewhere nearby, perhaps under the eaves where it was hiding. Three children ran outside and back again, as if on a dare.

five

It rained all night.

My mantra willing it to fall—willing it all to come down because it can only rain so much in a year—became a mantra willing it to just go away, to leave us alone. And in the morning I woke to a calm that was filled only with the sound of birds and the dull beat of water dripping from the eaves to the ground. The sky was blue and clear. A strong wind blew from the west, carrying nothing.

I woke Suzanne and together we wondered if our break had come, if the storms had finally passed. We showered, ate quickly, packed our things, and pointed the bike north.

I felt extraordinary as we left Sonderborg, as though we had passed a test and were now free. I allowed myself to imagine a perfect Baltic Sea day, one where Suzanne and I were lying in the sun on the edge of the sea. As we stretched out, we'd safely recall the despair of the previous days, then laugh. Afterwards we'd swim in the cool water of the sea and lie back down on the rock until our skin was dried by the sun.

On our way out we passed an old couple on bicycles, their heads wrapped in wool scarves, their long jackets flapping like flags as they pedaled heavily into the wind. They appeared like har-bingers of summer, like some migrating species of bird the growing season could be set by. I only had to twist the throttle and we moved smoothly around them. We continued on, past a field of grain smeared with patches of blood-red poppies. A forest enclosed us and we crested a small rise. Suzanne leaned forward and yelled something to me.

"What?" I called back to her, and at that moment, through the branches of the trees, I saw clouds.

"It's going to start raining!" Suzanne yelled into my neck. "I can smell it!"

Remnants, I told myself about the clouds. Just stragglers.

I opened the visor of my helmet and breathed in. Suzanne was right. The scent of rain was as heavy as fog. I tried again to will it away, to make the storm turn south toward Germany and to make the road bend in a way that would take us around it. We crested another rise and a familiar mass of clouds was waiting for us. The wind began to blow harder, and while we were still under blue skies, drops of rain began ticking against my helmet.

I leaned against the gusts that now rolled over us. The rain began to fall in sheets, and both Suzanne and I assumed a defensive curl that was now all too familiar. The wind whirled harder than it had before. It pulled the chin strap of my helmet into the skin of my throat. It pulled my helmet back and shook it from side to side. The wind took my glasses and pulled them off my face.

All I could think of was how to remain upright until there was somewhere I could pull over. Then Suzanne began to laugh behind me. Her laugh was high and full, as if the weather was really just a joke she'd finally gotten. I began laughing too, hysterically, holding the handlebars so tight my hands ached. As each gust shoved us across lanes, I yelled and laughed and heaved the bike back into place. I yelled and laughed as water ran down my face and neck and chest. I laughed as Suzanne's hands pulled at my waist, as trucks and cars streamed past us, until everything around us be-came liquid, and it seemed as though the rain would never stop.

And then it did. Just as it had started. The wind eased. The clouds rolled over us and left behind an unblemished blue sky. The bike settled onto the road. I didn't have to lean and shove to keep in on track. The cars and trucks around us moved with what seemed like politeness. They gave us room. A woman in a blue car waved, and I waved back.

~~~

We arrived in the city of Århus in the late afternoon, just as the shopkeepers were taking in their sidewalk displays and locking doors for the night. People leaving work crowded intersections and crosswalks. Lines of cars formed at each streetlight, and drivers raced to make it across before lights changed. I followed signs to the center of town, navigating cracked and pitted streets through a warren of bunker-gray buildings.

A strong wind blew through the streets like water rushing through a gorge. People moved quickly, as if strolling or lingering in front of shop windows was something they did elsewhere. Many buildings were boarded up. Windows were uncharacteristically dirty for a Danish town. It reminded me of Eastern Europe during the eighties when maintenance was something that was performed only in cases of extreme need.

We rode past a park where people waited for their dogs to relieve themselves on the grass, and I remembered that Århus had been the seat of the occupying Nazi government during World War II. The gray aspect and neglect took on a new meaning then, like the broken face of a violated woman.

We found a hostel north of town, an old octagonal dance hall in the middle of a wooded park. The main room was barnlike with tall ceilings and open beams. In the far corner was the registration, a small closet with curtains around it. Notices written in blood-red ink were posted to the side: "ABSOLUTELY NO ENTRY BEFORE 17:00!" "YOU MUST VACATE YOUR ROOM BY 10:00!" "YOU MUST CLEAN ROOM BEFORE LEAVING!" and "BE QUIET!"

I checked the time, rang a small bell on the desk, and waited. A woman with severe acne and short red hair came through a door, consulted her watch, and huffed. It was thirty minutes past five, and she acted as if it was our fault. She impatiently tapped a pen on the counter as I filled in the registration form, and Suzanne asked her if she knew what the weather report was.

"Look on the outside," she told her.

The hostel was surrounded by tall beech trees. The wind was blowing in long, wavelike rushes through their canopies. We removed our bags and gear from the bike. I threaded the lock through both tires and the frame, covered it, and we moved inside. Suzanne put her things down and sat on the edge of the bed. She looked tired and sullen.

"So," I began. "What would you like from room service tonight?"

I expected to see her smile, to hear her repeat our game and suggest something extravagant: lobster, champagne, boiled potatoes, a nice salad. Instead she rubbed her face, leaned back on the bed, and stared at the ceiling.

"How about some soup to begin?" I suggested, and began to feel foolish. "Or something to drink?"

"I just want to sleep. I'm tired, Allen."

I continued to talk as I unpacked our sleeping bags and clothes. I suggested we take a walk. The sea wasn't far away, and a walk along it would be good for both of us. I arranged our bags and helmets and unrolled our sleeping bags on the beds. I asked Suzanne if she wanted to go but she gave no answer. I bent down to kiss her. She was asleep.

~~~

As we ate the last of a packet of bread for breakfast, finished the last few slices from a square of cheese and ate two apples, Suzanne and I watched the storm rage through the window of our room. We ate silently, like seasoned soldiers watching a battle rage. We heard a sharp crack and watched a branch bend and fall to the ground with a percussive thud. A moment passed. The wind paused, and then rushed again. Suzanne swallowed, and then looked at me.

"We need to get out of here," she said.

"Checkout time isn't until ten," I said, and handed her another slice of bread.

"That's not what I mean."

"You mean out of Århus. Out of this weather."

She nodded.

We were out of our room at ten, just as the sign at the desk warned. The red-headed woman who had checked us in was making her rounds as we left. Our bags and helmets, the tent, and tank bag weighed us down and caused us to move awkwardly toward the bike. She gave us a suspicious look, as if our gear might contain furniture from the room.

Suzanne and I decided to take the noon ferry east to Denmark's main island of Zeeland. We'd head toward Copenhagen, and from there Sweden would be within sight across the Øresund, the narrow body of water that separates the two countries.

After loading the bike we settled on a bench under the eaves of the hostel porch to wait. I watched the storm and wrote in my notebook about how the angle of the rain changed preceding each gust of wind. I was timing them and thinking of ways to use it as a warning, as a gauge of when to brace and lean. But it wasn't working. Each gust was a little different than the last. I became distracted by the clatter of leaves as the wind rolled them over the gravel drive. Suzanne nudged me and said, "Take a look at this."

She was reading a tourist brochure about Denmark. It was filled with pictures of smiling families and people lying on sun-bleached beaches, riding bicycles along country lanes, canoeing on calm lakes, and hiking through woods and meadows. In each picture the people were wearing shorts, short-sleeved shirts, and swimsuits. Everyone was tanned and smiling. Suzanne laughed and said the pictures were probably taken in Greece.

A door closed with a slam. A deep voice muttered something on the verge of a yell. Heavy footsteps and grunts preceded our first view of the body that owned them.

"Bitch! Ga' dam bitch. Write a letter. Get 'er fired."

Suzanne looked up from the pictures of tanned bodies enjoying themselves under the Danish sun and said, "American."

We watched as a huge black man moved across the parking area with an armload of stuff: a stack of videocassettes, a bundle of clothes, a coffee pot, boxes of food, and plastic containers holding things that rattled as he moved. The man walked as far as a faded sedan and dumped his load onto the wet hood. Cassettes, boxes of food, and plastic containers slid to the ground. Clothes and papers blew across the lot, and I ran to catch them.

"Shit! Look a 'dis!" the man yelled toward the hostel. "Look what ya done! Ragged no good bitch!"

As he yelled, the remaining items on the hood of the car began sliding to the ground.

He ran back and blocked their fall with his open arms and chest. When everything was corralled, he unfolded a sweatshirt, made a kind of barrier, and then stepped slowly back.

"Can I help?" I asked, and handed him the things I'd collected.

The man glanced briefly at me, and then back at the hood of the car. His eyes were wide, alert, and he was poised to jump. "Na'ta thang," he said, and cautiously stepped back from the car. "Everthing is under con-*trol*."

Just then a blast of wind rolled down through the trees, across the parking lot, and caused the stack of videocassettes to begin sliding.

"Bas'ards!" he said, and caught them.

"What a pile of stuff," I said.

"Yeah. Ol' redhead in there didn' even le'me pack. Ain' no way to treat a man," he said. "Ain' no way." Then he laughed, as though he'd discovered the humor in his situation. "Hey. You from the States?"

"California," I said. "I'm Allen. And over there," I said pointing, "is Suzanne."

"Aw right!" he said, and offered his hand. "King. Jesse King."

"Like Bond. James Bond," I said.

"Ya got it! No one ever gets it, an' ya got it. Cool!" and he repeated his name slowly to savor the sound of it. "King. *Jesse King*."

A box of crackers wavered and I reached to catch them.

"Thanks, man. Wha'cha all doin' here?"

I told him about our trip up from Germany and pointed to the motorcycle. He looked puzzled. "Tha's it?"

"What's 'it'?"

"Tha's all ya got? Tha's all yer stuff? There on yer scooter? Shit, man. You travel *light*. Take a look in my car."

I followed Jesse around to the passenger's side and he opened the door. A box of fruit, a pillow, a box of music cassettes, and more clothes fell to the ground. The car was stuffed with a vast assortment of things. An electronic keyboard was pressed against the inside of the car. Beside it was an amplifier. There were more boxes and bags of food, piles of clothing, an unrolled sleeping bag, plastic containers, coffee cans. Plastic water bottles, piles of paper, silver and copper coins littered the floor. The dash was jammed with maps, receipts, bird feathers, shells.

"So Jesse. What do you do?"

"Can' ya tell? I play music, man. I play the *blews*," and when he said "blues" he closed his eyes and pursed his lips as if offering a kiss.

Jesse told me he'd been traveling the music circuit in Europe solo for the past fifteen years, ever since a band he was in toured the continent. They did pretty well and then broke up before they made it. "I decided to stay right here," he said, and shoved the box of fruit back into the car. "Ge' mo' 'preciation here than home."

Jesse said he was following the example of a long line of black performers who'd settled in Europe, including Josephine Baker and Paul Robeson. "But," he said, "those days is gone. Now, I got 'nother plan. Know what it 'tis?"

"No."

"The *lotto!*" he said with a whisper, as if revealing a guarded secret. "Ya see, all these countries here," he said, and described a semicircle beyond the forest. "They got the lotto, and I plan on winnin' *big*, ya know? Big, man. Lotsa money, and then I'm gonna help my family out."

"Where's your family?"

"Philadelphia. Got a boy there, too. When I win the lotto, I be livin' eight months in Philly, and the rest here, playing ma music. Yessir. That'a be fine."

The rain began to fall harder and I helped Jesse gather his things from the hood of the car. He plunged his hand into the mass of items inside the car, felt around for something, and then removed a yellow rag that he used to wipe the rain from the things I handed him.

I asked Jesse where he had come from, and where he was going.

"Been ta Oslo, in Norway," he said. "I was suppose ta play a gig up there. Been doin' the same one five years, but things went bad, know what I mean? They canceled on me, man, and I gone all that way. No way ta treat a man. Ain' like the old days. No sir."

I handed him the videocassettes and the plastic boxes of food. He wiped each against his shirt and then shoved them into the car. I helped him with a piece of plastic he wanted to fold, and I helped him with the amp, which he turned and then shoved with his foot deeper into the car to make more room.

"Don' know where I'm goin'," he said. "I'm waitin' for a phone call, but tha' red-headed bitch in there run me out. I told her I was havin' a cash-flow problem. Jus' temporary. I says to her, 'I'll have the money in a coupla days,' but she run me out!"

I helped Jesse fill the back of the car and the passenger's seat, and then watched him try to close the door. He shoved it hard, but the latch only caught partway. He slammed it, but still it wouldn't close. "Gimme a hand," he said, and counted to three. We both shoved and the door closed, sending a cascade of gear onto the driver's seat.

"Now fer the trunk," he said. Inside the trunk was a boom box, boxes of vinyl records, more cassettes, pairs of worn shoes, all of which he began to move from side to side and push into recesses.

"What was better about the old days?" I asked.

"Ah, man! Like I say—'preciation," he said. "Back then we used ta jam with everone—Beatles, Aretha, Stones, Dionne Warwick. Hey, you know Paul? Paul McCartney?"

"No. Never met him."

"Well, ya ever see him," he said, and pointed at my chest, "ask 'im 'bout Jesse King. He 'member me. We jammed lot'sa times. Ol'

Paul. *Those* were tha days. Not now." And after a moment's reflection he added, "Don' forget. Ya ask him. Ol' Paul 'member."

"I don't think it will close," I said when Jesse was finished loading the trunk.

"Sure it will," and he pressed the trunk down on his things lightly, as though playing *pianissimo*.

"We can move that box there," I offered.

"Watch," he said, and hefted his bulk up and onto the lip of the trunk, snapping it shut. "Hah! See that? I told you. Jesse King don' travel light!"

~~~

I steered the bike into line behind a long queue of cars and trucks that curved along the outer bounds of the pier. We stopped beside a white camper van with an older couple in the front seats. They were bent over their laps, so the crumbs from the sandwiches they were eating would fall on the papers they had spread across their knees. I waved at them and they stared like two startled birds.

We dismounted, and Suzanne looked toward the horizon. "It looks like there could be some clearing," she said, and I followed her hand out over the sea toward Zeeland.

The couple in the car beside us looked, too, and then returned to their meal. There was a glimmer of blue at the edge of the horizon that shone like a precious stone.

"It's difficult to tell from here," I said. It was something to hope for, and as we waited for the ferry, both Suzanne and I watched for any change one way or another. The ferry ride would take three hours, and I tried to guess whether the horizon and the strip of blue was over three hours away. I tried to guess the speed of the ship. I dimly remembered something about the curvature of the earth and the distance one could see before the horizon bent away.

"Of course," Suzanne said. "Zeeland must be on the other side of those clouds because we'd see the land from here if it wasn't, right?"

"I'm not sure," I said, but I liked Suzanne's hypothesis anyway.

A woman in a white car pulled behind us. A smile spread across her face as she looked at the bike and us. She waved urgently before getting out as if we were old friends.

"Where on earth are you from?" she asked us.

As Suzanne told her the story of our trip the woman kept shaking her head and saying, "No! Don't tell me!" But her disbelief was not out of incredulity. It was because she thought our trip was such a fantastic one.

"You've come all that way? How wonderful!" she said. "How very smart. Yes, this is a pleasure to meet you."

She held out her hand to both of us, introduced herself as Hanne, and made a point of explaining that she loved to travel, too.

The old couple in the car beside us seemed annoyed with our conversation. The woman looked as though she was about to say something, and then twisted her face as though she'd smelled something foul. Her husband reached across her lap and rolled up her window.

Hanne told us she was returning home from a visit with her parents for the past week. "They're old," she said. "And I try to see them often. But before that I was in Greece. Such a wonderful land. The people there are so open and warm. Not like us Danes. They're...like the sun."

A whistle blew. Hanne said it was time to load the ferry. "I'll see you on the ship," she said, and got into her car.

The bike was considered unstable cargo. A man in an orange safety suit directed us to ride it onto the lower deck along with the large transport trucks where we'd be close to the waterline and any movement caused by a swelling sea would be minimized. We were first in and rode the length of a football field through the cavernous belly of the ship to the front. Several trucks pulled tightly around us and filled the space with the hissing of their brakes, the heat and clatter of their engines, and acrid exhaust.

I tried to pull the bike onto its center stand but it slipped on the slick metal deck. It was covered with a film of oily diesel fuel. I tried again and my feet began to slide beneath me. Suzanne took a grip opposite me. We pulled together and the bike settled onto the center stand.

Suzanne gathered up her bag from the bike, her gloves and helmet, and stood waiting for me.

"I want to tie the bike down," I said, "so it doesn't slip and fall over."

"They'll take care of it. Let's go. It stinks down here."

"No. I want to look after it."

"Don't be ridiculous, Allen. It'll be okay."

"It's our responsibility. If the bike goes over, we'll be the ones to lose."

"It won't be my loss," she muttered.

I felt my face go wan. A wave of hurt moved through my chest.

"Oh, come on, Allen. This is ridiculous!" Suzanne yelled above the noise and hiss of the trucks.

"What's ridiculous?"

"This!" she said with a sweep of her hand, as if it was everything in the ship. "*This* is ridiculous. The bike. The weather. We should be in a car, Allen. Everything would be so much easier."

Her words came from nowhere, like the rolling jabs of the wind. I stared at her, and after a moment her eyes and face began to soften. I saw that she was relieved. She'd needed to say it for a while. I realized, too, that I should have seen it coming, that the signs were there.

"What do you want me to do?" I asked. She could have said almost anything: that she wanted to quit the trip, she wanted to go on, that she was just tired.

"I'll help you," she said finally, and together we found a length of rope among some tackle and tied the bike against the side of the ship.

~~~

"Wonderful!" Hanne said when we met her again on the ship. "Follow me. I know a perfect place outside away from the weather. I always sit there."

Hanne led the way to the back of the ship, and as she pushed a door open, she said she'd spoken with the navigation officer. He'd told her that most of our passage would be sunny and calm.

We wiped rainwater from three deck chairs and set them beneath an overhang out of the wind. The rain had stopped, and Hanne assured us that in no time we'd be in the sun. "It's often like that," she said with an amused laugh. "Sun on the sea, rain on the land. Sometimes I think summer occurs only on the water."

Århus slipped behind us and faded into the clouds that hung over the land. The clouds above the ferry fractured like ice during spring thaw on a lake. Hanne suggested we move our chairs closer to the stern.

I watched as the ship's wake fanned out from the back of the ship. To our right a small fishing boat rocked easily on the water, then lurched and fell and rolled as the wake slipped beneath it.

"So," Hanne said as she settled into her chair. "Tell me more about your trip."

I waited for Suzanne to respond, but her gaze was fixed over the water, and I knew she was leaving it to me. So I told Hanne how we had shipped the bike from California and how we had begun in Bremen. I told her about all the rain and wind, about our first night in the tent, about the hostel in Sonderborg. I gave her my impressions of the people we'd met, including Jesse. I told her how good it was to be moving through the world again.

Hanne reflected on what I'd said, and as she did, I looked at Suzanne. Beneath the bottom edge of her sunglasses I saw a tear work its way down her cheek.

"Has anyone told you about the summer in Scandinavia that occurred on a Saturday? Don't worry," she said, noticing the look on my face. "It's just a joke. But you know about jokes, how they contain something of the truth. You will have to be careful on your journey."

I waited for Suzanne to say something. I wanted her to talk of the storms, of riding on the autobahn, of camping, and how she felt about moving on. I hoped she would tell me something through Hanne, something she hadn't said before.

"Did you visit Ribe?" Hanne asked suddenly.

"Ribe?" I asked.

"Yes, Ribe. You must have gone right past it."

"We didn't go there."

"Too bad," she said. "Such a beautiful town. So old. You really missed something."

"Look. The sun," Suzanne said, and pointed over the water where burning shafts of light etched the surface of the sea.

"How about Esbjerg?" Hanne asked. "None of the islands either?"

A smile spread across Suzanne's face as she watched the sun illuminate the sea. She tilted her face so she could absorb as much of it as possible.

"There were many places we had planned to stop," I explained. "But the weather wasn't cooperating."

"You really should have seen Ribe, though. You can always visit on your way back."

"The world becomes so big when you're out in it," I said in defense of our route. "The more you know of a place, the more you try to discover, the more unknowable it becomes."

"How do you mean?"

"Take Ribe for example. The more you think you know about it, the less you really know. You may know some of the most interesting sites in Ribe, and some of the history, but that's only part of the story. It's like searching for the center of an onion. You keep peeling only to find more layers. We could spend the rest of our lives in Ribe and never know all of it."

"Interesting," Hanne said, and removed her jacket. "It's the same with people."

Hanne was quiet for a while. She and Suzanne were fixed on the same spot on the sea. I stared too and let the rhythm of the ship's engines and the warmth of the sun work through me. We passed a small island, and a flock of gulls flew from it like predators after a wounded animal. They hovered over the bow of the ship and dove into the churned-up water to snatch stunned herring.

"Yes," Hanne said. "I suppose you're right. As you were talking,

I couldn't help but think of my husband. I've never really known him."

A muscle along the edges of her mouth pulled the remains of a smile from her face. "He's from Iceland. He lives there now, with our son. My husband is an architect, a brilliant man, but he can't work here. When we were first married we lived in Denmark. We were so full of hope and love. Everything seemed so promising. For years it was like that. But then he got sick. A—how do you say? In the head...."

"A breakdown?" Suzanne offered.

"Yes. That was it. A breakdown. What a word: *break-down*. Anyway, I thought our love would take care of it. I thought that if we really loved each other, it would pass. But it didn't. He just got worse and worse. Finally, I sent him back to Iceland to recover. He never came back. So, like your towns, I tried to know him. I really tried."

I thought Hanne would begin to cry, but instead she forced a smile. She sat up in her chair and ran her fingers through her hair. She stretched and pushed her hands into the sky. "Oh!" she said. "How beautiful! The way the sun shines off the sea."

We all looked. The clouds had become sparse, and much of the sky was a deep blue that seemed almost foreign to us. It had only been a matter of days—less than a week—since we had good weather, but it felt much longer. For the first time the horizon wasn't black with the next storm, and even the wind had subsided. As the ferry neared the port of Kalundborg, the flock of gulls over the back of the ship thickened. They circled overhead, reeling in mosaic patterns of white on blue, etching the sky with what I hoped were greetings.

<center>~~~</center>

The docking alarm sounded and Hanne quickly gathered her things. "I'm sorry!" she said. "The road to Copenhagen is narrow, and I must be off before the trucks block it up. You're so brave," she said while hugging Suzanne. "Have a wonderful journey." She put her arms around me, then pulled back to look me in the eye. "And you be careful."

The bike was as we'd left it, upright and alone in a far corner of the ship. The rope was pulled taut as if it had tried to wander away. We pulled our helmets and gloves on as the ship's engines reversed their thrust and sent a prolonged shudder through its cavernous belly. We heard voices outside, the shouting of commands, and I could picture dock workers hurrying to secure lines and prepare for the opening of the ship. There was a loud banging of metal on metal as though a piece of stubborn machinery were being beaten. Around us truck drivers climbed into the cabs of their vehicles and anticipated the opening of the ship and the road ahead. Many of them bore license plates from Sweden, and as far away as Finland. Home was a long way off for them, and as they stared out their windows they looked hungry.

A hydraulic ram beside us began to whine as fluid was pumped through it to lift the huge nose of the ship skyward, flooding us with light. The short high-pitched whine of starter motors engaging the diesel engines, and then their heavy clatter, filled the space around us. Suzanne climbed on and I started the bike. I couldn't hear the engine or feel that it had started. A continuous rumble from all the motors and the movement of the ship overrode any sensation from the bike. The only way I could tell it had started was to rev the engine and watch the tachometer dial rise and fall.

Trucks inched toward the front of the ship and jockeyed for position to get off first. I moved the bike forward also, and squeezed around the bumper of the first truck. A man in fluorescent orange coveralls removed a chain that blocked the way out. Behind us I heard diesel engines rev, gears engage, and I felt their urgency to get moving. I revved the bike and released the clutch. The back tire spun on the oily metal deck and edged sideways before gaining traction. Then we were on asphalt and the bike moved smoothly forward. A sign pointed the way toward Roskilde and Copenhagen, and we followed it.

We found a room in a hostel on the edge of Roskilde. It was ten o'clock in the evening and the sky had just become dark. The young couple we shared the room with had obviously assumed they had gotten lucky and had it to themselves. The contents of their bags were spread across our beds. The small table in the middle of the room was covered with bread crumbs, three empty soup cans, and a bottle of water. I could see they were disappointed. I told them we were just the cleaning crew. They laughed, and we introduced ourselves.

Aaron and Deirdre were from Tel Aviv, Israel. Aaron had just completed his military service as a medical officer in the Gaza Strip, and Deirdre a degree in psychology. They were celebrating by taking their first trip abroad, a thirty-day excursion that took them from France to Denmark. They were both impressed with the size and beauty of Europe and spoke animatedly of all the places they'd been, a long list that mixed regions with cities and countries: Nice, Provence, Paris, Burgundy, Belgium, London, Wales, Scotland, Denmark, and finally, Roskilde, their farthest point north. Tomorrow they would catch a bus south, and in two days they would be leaving for home on a plane from Amsterdam.

"Thirty days seemed like a lifetime," Aaron said in the monotone of someone condemned to a long exile. "But now it's time to go and it feels terrible. We should have another month, or the rest of our lives."

"It's disappointing," said Deirdre, her hands moving softly as she talked. "It's been so good to be away from Israel. We haven't read a newspaper since we arrived here, and I can't tell you how wonderful that has been."

"I never knew how much stress we live with in Israel. Always this or that happening—the politics, the fighting. You can have it," Aaron said, and cupped and threw his hands as if the problems of Israel were a ball that he could toss my way.

"We've been so relaxed," Deirdre said as she began clearing their food from the table. "No worries, except we couldn't go through Germany."

"*She* could go to Germany," Aaron corrected. "But I couldn't."

"I wanted to meet some Germans," Deirdre added.

"She always wants to meet some Germans. A psychologist, you know?" he said. "She wants to talk with them about some things. What's to talk about? It's the same in Israel."

"Relax, Aaron," Deirdre said, as if to contain what was coming.

"It's true. For two years I was in the Gaza, and such terrible things, *terrible things*, happened there. I saw it all. Pathetic. All of us are wrong—Israelis and Arabs. I used to visit one man—a Palestinian. He looked sixty years old, but he was only thirty-five. His house, it was just a shack," Aaron said. "It was often bulldozed by the army, and each time it was bulldozed he'd build it back. Then, one day, he was smiling. He wanted to show me something, and I followed him to his house, the same collection of sticks and metal, just rearranged. 'What do you think?' he asked me. 'Think of what?' I asked him. 'The roof,' he said. 'It's new.' I told him I thought it was nice, but it wasn't. It was just new metal on a bad house. He told me he had saved for six years for that roof. Six years! Can you imagine? Six years for a few pieces of metal. In the meantime his family was in rags. They had just enough to eat, and I knew through our Intelligence the army was going to bulldoze the entire place in a few days again. And she," he said, motioning toward Deirdre, "wants to meet some Germans. I ask you, what are we going to say to one another?"

"But this trip has been worth it," Deirdre said as she wiped crumbs from the table with a cloth in spiraling swipes. "It's a beginning. It's given us hope."

SIX

A thin layer of moisture lay on the inside of the window the next morning. It looked as if someone had begun to wash it and was called away. Everything on the outside looked thick and blurred through the glass. A tree branch quivered in a breeze, and the red bud of a rose moved nervously back and forth like the brush of an indecisive painter. I tried to gauge the sky through the glass. It appeared as blue and unmarred as a cobalt bottle.

Roskilde looked like Shangri-la beneath the clean light of a post-storm sun. Suzanne said it looked unreal and that the atoms of every brick and stone and slate shingle were vibrating.

We parked in the heart of town. From there we walked through the streets with the ecstatic glow of the blessed. I smiled and said, *"Godmorgen,"* to everyone we passed. Suzanne walked with the ease of a dancer and kept pointing out tiny details of architecture and dress that caught her eye.

The central square was filled with tables and stalls for a market. A pile of radishes neatly tied into bundles, their red bodies like bright balloons, looked remarkable to me; fat raspberries, carefully laid in shallow blue paper trays, oozed promise. Weathered men and women did the selling. Their thick hands, cracked and dirty from their work, moved like aged machine parts as they measured and wrapped goods in paper cones and sacks. One woman sold nothing but fresh bouquets of wildflowers she'd probably picked early that morning while we slept. Each bouquet was held together by a piece of white string and set in a canning jar filled with water. Suzanne and I stood in front of her table and looked at her flowers for a long time. She smiled at us from beneath the dark blue scarf that covered her head, her mouth a wide crescent that seemed the whole of her.

We moved past the Roskilde Cathedral, a red brick building that still retains its sacred height above all other structures in town. Its massiveness cast a long shadow that held the cold from the previous night. The perimeter was paved with round stones the size of apples that were difficult to walk on. It was as if they had been placed there as a test of one's devotion to enter. An elderly couple walked arm in arm for support, the balls of their feet shifting as they carefully picked their way over each stone. As they opened the door of the cathedral, the bright tones of an organ escaped on the morning air.

We walked to the shore of the Roskilde Fjord on the edge of town. We got as far as the breakwater and then lay down beside each other, as flat as possible, and in direct line with the sun. The stones were warm and their warmth radiated through our clothes and skin like a salve. I felt myself unfold. I was made light by the sun, by the lapping of the water against the stones, and by Suzanne's closeness. It was one of those moments when I am so full and content that I could peacefully die.

"Look at the swans," I heard Suzanne say.

I sat up beside her and our legs dangled over the stones where spray from breaking wavelets collected on our boots. I looked to where she pointed in the middle of the fjord and saw flecks of brilliant white on the water.

"See them?" she asked, and there was delight in her voice as though she had discovered something very rare.

The swans' long, curved necks were like script against the agitated surface of the sea.

"Aren't they beautiful?" Suzanne said.

Their heads drooped like heavy flowers as they swam across to another shore. Around them were several gray goslings, barely visible against the cold, blue water.

"Yes. They're beautiful," I agreed.

I put my arm around Suzanne and pulled her close. Her head rested on my shoulder and I kissed her.

"Tell me what happened on the ship," I asked after a while.

She became still for a moment, and then turned her face toward mine. The dark brown pupils of her eyes were wide and looked into mine.

"It feels as though we're in over our heads this time, Allen," she began gently. "We're in too deep. But I don't think you see it. Or maybe you just don't agree."

Her words struck me hard. "Tell me what you mean."

The voices of excited children filled Suzanne's pause. A group of girls and boys quickly rode their bicycles down a grassy slope to our right and ditched them near the water. They ran to the edge and began scanning the surface of the fjord.

"It's difficult to describe," she said. "Maybe you're right and I just wasn't prepared. But something makes me feel that it's more. The weather. The bike. It makes the world feel enormous. Dangerous. And sometimes when we're riding along, I get the feeling you're part of the danger. You should see yourself riding, the way you're hunched over the handlebars, your hand on the throttle, riding right into it."

For the first time in our years together I had the feeling that we were living separate lives.

One of the children shrieked and pointed into the water. The others reacted as though the shriek was an alarm and began to rush around and gather stones.

"It's the weather," I said. "And it's getting better. If the mistral in France can cause people to go crazy, I'm sure this much rain and wind can do the same. I'd say we're doing pretty good."

"I don't know that it's just the weather," she said. "Tell me, do you like this, how the trip is going?"

"I wish the weather was better, but, yes, I like it. We're doing just the right thing by being here," I said. "I think this will be an important trip for us. I love being out in the world again, and I'm really glad we're doing it on the bike."

The children let loose a volley of stones that tore at the water. A small girl squealed with joy. She thrust her arms toward the sky and performed an abbreviated dance.

"So you think things will get better?" she asked.

"Sure. We're already feeling better today," I said. "I think we just need a few good days. In the past we've had bigger challenges, and we worked through those. They brought us closer together. We'll do the same this time."

I heard another shriek, another volley of stones hitting the water, and a furious exchange of orders followed by a cheer.

Suzanne took a deep breath and looked again at the swans. "Just remember I'm trying my best," she said. "I really am."

"I know," I said. "I am, too."

After a while we moved arm in arm along the breakwater in the wake of the children. We wondered what they could be trying to hit. I thought it must be the small fish I'd watched scoot from stone to stone along the shore. Ahead of us the children scanned the water. One pointed. Directions were shouted and rocks were thrown.

"Jellyfish," Suzanne said. One lay inert and crumpled, almost fluid, as the waves pushed and pulled it among the rocks. Farther on were others, immobile and limp, half suspended in the water. Others were damaged, their mantles punctured and torn, causing them to flutter against the current in slow, graceless circles. The children were about fifty yards ahead of us. They began running relays for more stones as the others maintained a frenzied barrage. I thought of running up to them, telling them to stop because what they were doing was wrong. But then they were off again on their bikes, furiously pedaling along the water in search of more. Suzanne pulled my arm. We turned left.

～～～

We found a campground on the edge of Copenhagen. It was pressed between the main road into the city and a business park. A woman with pink and brown moles on her face checked us in. The moles supported long hairs like the fronds of an exotic plant, and as she talked or wrote she combed them with her fingers, pulling lightly at the ends so the moles rose like eruptions on the landscape of her face.

"You is good lucky," she said, and wound some hairs around a finger as some men caress their mustache. "This camp open yesterday," she said with a smile, "so you sleep anywhere, all over!"

"Thanks," I said. She smiled, let the hairs loose, and straightened them gently.

We pitched the tent on the softest piece of ground we could find. Over it was a thin layer of clipped grass. A row of spindly birch trees grew behind us and their leaves sounded like rain as they shook in the wind. While I knocked tent pegs into the ground, a man walked by. I waved, said "*Hej* (Hello)," and he returned a shy wave as he moved past. Then he noticed the bike and stopped abruptly. He wore the clothes of a biker: black leather boots, a ragged denim jacket without the sleeves, stained denim jeans, a red kerchief tied around his neck. His hair was scruffy, his eyes and cheeks were swollen, as if he'd ridden a long way with his face full-on into the wind.

"Where you from?" he asked. His eyes were on the bike, as if he'd directed the question to it.

"California," I said, and pulled the tent taut as Suzanne secured the opposite corner.

"Kalforna?" he asked, slurring the word as if he was drunk.

"Yes. California," Suzanne said, and knocked another stake into the ground.

"*Kalforna*. Hahahahahaha! I no believe!" he said, as if our joke was a lousy one.

Suzanne and I went back to staking the tent and I waited for the man to continue on. He didn't move.

"Kalforna?" he repeated a moment later.

I watched him walk to the back of the bike and study the license plate. His lips began to part and a smile spread across his face. "I no believe," he said slowly.

But his smile said he did believe, and that he was very pleased to have stumbled across us, as though we were something worthwhile left in the grass. He walked past the bike and edged closer to us.

"I'm Allen," I said, and held my hand out for his.

"Kary," he said. "Your woman?"

"Suzanne," Suzanne said quickly. "I'm Suzanne."

"I no believe," he said yet again. "From *Kalforna!*"

"Believe," Suzanne said.

"And you? Where are you from?" I asked.

"I? Gothenborg, Sweden. Not so far. I come for little vacation. My camp is there," he said, and pointed through the birches to a tent set on the far side of an empty field.

"Is that your motorcycle?" Suzanne asked him.

"Ja. *My* bike. My *wife!*" he said. "You must come for beer. My camp. We make some party. You come, ja?"

~~~

"What a strange guy," Suzanne said as we walked across the field to Kary's camp. "We should just send the bike over. That's all he's really interested in."

Between us we carried the last of our food to share with Kary—a half box of crackers, a wedge of cheese, a cheap bottle of wine, and three apples. We also carried our own cups because we guessed Kary wouldn't have extras.

"He's a character," I said.

Suzanne rolled her eyes. "You'll talk to anyone."

"He seems like a nice guy," I said.

"He barely even noticed me," she said. "He asked you what my name is."

"I think he's just shy. If we don't like him, we can leave."

"Meet my wife," Kary said as we walked into his camp. "My lovely Virago Nine-Hundred."

Kary held his arm out toward his bike, a dirty, gray thing with rusting chrome, and he made kissing sounds through his pursed lips. He sat cross-legged in the doorway of his tent and motioned for us to sit as well. He looked satisfied with himself, content and at home in his camp, the lord of his field. He had all he needed, and now company, too.

"My wife," he said yet again, pointing at the bike with a graciously upturned hand. "My house," and he twisted his torso and pointed to his tent. "You must see inside," he said, and opened the fabric door like a curtain that concealed a fine sitting room. Inside was a pile of empty beer, wine, and schnapps bottles. There was an open duffel bag stuffed with clothes, and a rumpled green sleeping bag stretched down the length of the tent.

"Drink beer," he said and handed each of us a dark green bottle. "Strong beer. Only in Denmark this beer."

I took a drink and told Kary it was good. Suzanne sipped hers and made a face.

"Hahahaha. Too strong for she!"

Suzanne and I cut the apples and cheese into slices and spread them on a plastic bag. We arranged some crackers along the edge, and Suzanne reached behind her and plucked a dandelion and set it in the middle.

"Have some," she urged Kary, and he put a slice of apple on each knee.

Kary removed a pipe from his jacket pocket and began packing it with tobacco from a worn leather pouch. Suzanne asked him about his work, and he explained his job at the Volvo Heavy Truck factory in Gothenburg assembling chassis. He said he would quit working soon for medical reasons.

"Mine belly," he grimaced, rubbing the portion that hung over his belt as if it was bruised.

Kary lit his pipe with a plastic lighter he had to shake before it would work. He cupped the bowl with both hands and hugged it to his chest as he would in a storm. He drew from it deeply. He inhaled and held the smoke in his lungs for a long time.

"All finish when I go home. They give me money—two-hundred thousand kroner. My pension. I lives on that," he said with a smile, and halfway hoisted his beer in salute before he drained it.

He opened our bottle of wine with his pocket knife by pushing the cork through the neck of the bottle with the blade. A little geyser of wine shot up over his hand and he licked it off. He poured some for Suzanne and me into the cups we'd brought, then tipped the bottle to his mouth and sucked so greedily that each swallow drew air through the corners of his lips.

A moment of silence passed between us. Suzanne and I made sandwiches from the apples, cheese, and crackers. We sipped our beer. Kary pulled again at his pipe and inhaled, then let the smoke loose from his lungs in a long exhalation.

"I am Sooomi-man," Kary said.

"Sooomiman?" I asked.

"*Sooomi*-man. You know?"

"You mean Finland?"

"Ja! I am Finn-man. From Loviisa. Near Russia. On the sea."

"Really?" Suzanne asked. "We're going that way."

"Nothing to see," Kary declared emphatically. "Willage on the sea. Nothing."

"When did you come to Sweden?" Suzanne asked.

"Ahhhh, was sixty-two. Many Sooomi goes to Sweden. Was so poor there," he said, and then explained how he had been swept up in one of the periodic Scandinavian migrations. Finland was poor after World War II. Sweden needed workers, and a lot of Finns went there.

"I am Sweden-man now. Sooomi not my home," Kary scowled. He reached for another beer and popped the metal cap with the butt of his lighter. He put the mouth of the bottle to his lips and drank half of it in two swallows as if to wash away a bad taste.

I asked Kary if I could take his picture. He smiled and sat up straight in the doorway of his tent as I focused the camera.

"Moment," he said. He smoothed his hair and bared his teeth. He held his beer bottle to the center of his chest, and I snapped the shot.

"On my wife?" he suggested, and leaned forward to get up. The two apple slices on his knees fell into the grass. He picked them up tipsily, wiped the face of each slice against his dirty jeans, and then carefully arranged them in the door of his tent.

Kary sat on his bike and I focused the camera.

"Moment," he said again. He pushed his right hand into the pocket of his jeans, removed a key, and started the bike. "Now you take," he said over the rumble of the engine, and as I focused he revved it.

Kary and I sat down and he put the apple slices back on his knees. Suzanne and I ate the rest of the cheese and crackers, and Kary turned our bottle of wine to his lips. He lifted it to the sun and squinted inside to see if it was really empty. With a shrug he flung it through the open door of his tent, where it landed with a clatter on the others. He reached inside for another. He leaned farther until he fell onto his back, grunted a little as his face reddened, and produced a bottle of schnapps. Suzanne rubbed her arms and looked at me to say we should be going.

"I had a girl," Kary said as he opened the bottle. "I had the *bess* girl."

"Another motorcycle?" I asked him.

"Motorbike? Nej. A wooman girl. I loves her so much. She be mine true love, this girl." Kary tipped the bottle to his lips and drank. "This girl," he began again. "You like to see picture?"

He reached into his back pocket for his wallet, a worn-out thing stuffed with old paper, and removed a dog-eared Polaroid he held against his chest.

"Don' be shocked! You not be shocked?"

I took the picture from him and held it between Suzanne and me. The girl was standing beside a white refrigerator, her face turned down as if she'd had just enough time to look away from the camera. She was naked except for a cigarette between the fingers of her right hand. She'd just exhaled and a halo of smoke was visible around her head.

"I loves her," Kary said again. "I says to her ever day, ever day, 'I loves you. I do anything for you.' But, she be only fifteen. Now she have another man, and a small boy. She say to me I be too old. Ah...she be a *good* girl. *Bess* girl."

I handed the picture back to Kary. He drank again from the bottle and then slipped the picture into his wallet.

"Now mine wife is she," he said, and pointed to his motorcycle.

I said we had to go and Kary nodded his head. We gathered our things off the ground and I said we'd see him around the next morning. Suzanne reminded him to eat his apples. Kary smiled, and we left.

~~~

The next morning I accelerated across two lanes of traffic and then worked the bike into the flow of Copenhagen's commute. The driver of an immaculate blue Mercedes with gold accents and smoked windows braked to let us in. I waved and a gloved hand fluttered above the steering wheel like a bird. The diesel engine of a bread truck ticked and smoked alongside us. Its driver, a young man with a wedge of brown hair along the length of his jaw, noticed the bike. He waved for us to go, then changed his mind and accelerated and cut in front of us to make it through a light. But he didn't make it, and I had to brake abruptly as the truck lurched to a halt before us. Suzanne grabbed me around the waist to brace herself and her hands felt good there. It was the first time she'd touched me that day.

We should have slept in that morning. We should have stayed in our sleeping bags and dozed, made love, and then dozed again. Afterward, we should have crawled through the door of the tent and lain in the sun as it warmed the earth. We should have blessed the sun, the absence of any wind, and devised some ritual to give thanks because it was the first cloud-free, sun-filled, windless day of the trip.

"The sun," I said to Suzanne when she stirred. "It's beautiful outside."

I wanted her to open her eyes, look outside, and smile. I wanted her to say, "Allen, everything has changed. I'm so glad we're here."

She was still again. "Hey, sleepyhead," I said softly.

"Let me be," she said. "I hardly slept all night."

"You feel okay?"

"Just let me sleep a while longer."

As I crawled out of the tent, she rolled over and absorbed the space I'd occupied. She sighed. Her face settled into her jacket and she was asleep again.

I leaned against the bike facing the sun and looked at it through squinted eyes until its fire burned its image onto my retinas. *"We're in over our heads this time, Allen,"* she had said. *"We're in too deep."*

Our trips had always taken on lives of their own, lives we had embraced almost blindly. We'd put our trust in them. The challenges along the way were never hurdles. They seemed instead like the most valuable lessons, ones that we experienced together and which bound us in the same way that marriage binds other couples. In fact, when people asked if we were married, we said yes. We were married many times over. Our ceremonies seemed all the more substantive because they happened on the road, at some crucial moment when everything was going to hell and we pledged ourselves to each other yet again.

At one time she hadn't been afraid. At one time the enormity of our trips had inspired her. She'd led the way plenty of times. As I sat against the bike and waited for her to come out of the tent, I thought of a time in South Africa. We'd rented a cheap, broken-down car that had to be push-started from a wrecking yard in Pretoria, and we were making our way south across the Great Karroo toward Cape Town. It was six months after Nelson Mandela's release from prison, and every day the country was on the cusp of euphoria and extreme violence. It was also the middle of winter, and one particular morning it was so cold that we could not sleep and decided to begin driving.

We had only gone a mile when a man stepped from the tall grass on the side of the road and stood in the lights of our car. I swerved around him and kept going. We'd heard and read plenty of stories about hijackings and murders on the road, so I was surprised when Suzanne told me to stop. I asked her if she was crazy, but she insisted and said it would be fine.

By that point in the trip I knew she was right. She'd become almost clairvoyant when it came to the people we met and the places we went there. I backed the car up and the man, a small black man dressed in rags and covered with weeds, timidly approached us and motioned to the empty seat.

Though we had no language in common, and though the man could not read a map, we discovered that he was trying to get home, which he pointed to vaguely across the empty plateau. And so we drove.

We drove for three hours on a combination of small roads and dirt tracks, guided only by his hand signals. In that time we assembled his story. He had been traveling for more than two weeks to attend the funeral of an aunt in the north. He could not afford a bus ticket and had walked most of the way at night and slept during the day in the bush. He said the roads were very dangerous, that they were patrolled by rival tribal and political mobs that killed many people. He said he'd been chased several times before we picked him up. At one point I asked him why he let us pick him up. It had been dark and he couldn't tell who we were. He smiled then and pointed to Suzanne, as if to suggest that he'd sensed her.

After three hours we drove to the end of a dirt track where a number of dumpster-sized brick houses stood on a cold, windswept plateau. Tufts of snow clung to the low-lying scrub like cotton. We pulled up in front of one of the houses and a young woman's face, and then a child's, filled the only window in the house. The man waved, and the look of relief and happiness on the woman's face was plain to see, and then her tears.

We all got out to say good-bye. As we were standing there, the man did what I thought was an extraordinary thing. He took Suzanne's hands in his, then he hugged her and kissed her cheek. They both cried and I felt as though I was intruding. They looked into each other's eyes for a long time, and only parted reluctantly.

A numb circle radiated from the middle of my back as I leaned against the bike. At its center was the ellipses of the motorcycle tire, and at the center of that was the feeling we may have made some terrible mistake. What was happening to us?

For the past few years Suzanne had been hinting there may be more to life than just our trips. After one discussion we'd had about long-range plans, she suggested the time could come when she would have seen enough of the world on a shoestring and that she'd have had enough scrimping and sacrificing. She said she was getting weary of quitting jobs and starting over. She suggested we establish a base. She spoke more and more about having a career, about wanting to buy a house, and taking "normal" vacations. Such talk scared me. I agreed that a house would be a good thing for us but said that we didn't have enough money for both. The standard two weeks of vacation a year wouldn't do. She asked me how else we were going to get money without paying our dues in the working world. I reminded her of my desire to make a living as a writer. She gently pointed out all the rejection notices I had taped against the bathroom walls like shingles. Why, I asked her, should we compromise the freedom we had worked so hard to attain? In the end we didn't have answers for each other, and the questions disappeared as the prospect of this trip became real and as Suzanne grew bored with her job and school. Our passions were ignited once again.

A breeze rattled the leaves of the birch trees behind me and then rustled the roof of the tent. I heard Suzanne putting on her clothes inside the tent. I heard the drag of the zipper as she opened the door. Her hands appeared, followed by her head and shoulders, like a diver in slow motion. She stood up and stretched. Her body floated on the perfect blue background of the sky.

~~~

I maneuvered the bike through abrupt stop lights, impatient cars, and swarms of bicyclists. We rode past apartment blocks decorated with drying laundry that flapped like flags, past sex shops that offered live entertainment, past corner markets with displays of exotic fruits on the sidewalk, and past newsstands that sold papers and magazines from half a world away. We were honked at and rushed. A city bus pulled in front of us and forced us to swerve into the next lane of traffic. I used the brakes often and had my thumb over the horn like a trigger.

I had been looking forward to exploring Copenhagen, to being on foot and walking with Suzanne through the gradations of architecture that define historical ages and neighborhoods. Now I wasn't so sure. I found myself wanting to start at the beginning again. Press a button and rewind back to Bremen—to erase it all and start over.

We parked the bike in a small square near the National Museum. Kary had warned me to use our lock, and we threaded it through the tires and frame, through our helmets, then around a lamppost. I checked my pockets for money and keys. I checked the lock again, and then Suzanne asked, "Which way first?"

I looked around. We were surrounded by museums, churches, parks, cafés, galleries, and exhibits, but they all seemed hollow and insignificant.

"Where to?" she asked again.

I was lost. Not lost in the sense of taking a wrong turn, but lost completely. The kind of lost that comes to mind when someone says they have lost their bearings. Rather than feeling elated by the opportunities of Copenhagen, I felt overwhelmed. While standing there looking at the traffic that streamed down Vestervolgade and trying to answer Suzanne, a wave of vertigo caused the buildings, Suzanne's face, the street, and the traffic on it to ebb suddenly. In that ebbing everything about the trip seemed meaningless.

"Which way, Allen?"

I tried to remember why we were doing this trip. I struggled to recollect the essential aspects of it and of all the other trips we'd taken. I thought instead how they were all part of the same ridiculous and vain dream. I leaned against the bike and said I just wanted to look at the map. I held it open in front of me and hid in the maze of streets and symbols. I could feel Suzanne's eyes on me.

I wanted to tell her what I was feeling but was afraid she'd agree. I was afraid she'd say that I'd come to my senses.

"Come on," I heard her say.

It was as though my neatly constructed framework for this trip, for my life, was slipping away like the point of a dream I was on the verge of forgetting.

Just begin walking, I told myself. *It will come back to you.*

I folded the map and Suzanne stood before me with her hand out. Her fingers stretched across my palm and pulled.

She pulled me across the street toward the center of town, and for a time we walked with an aimless abandon. For the most part we walked in silence except for brief exchanges where one of us pointed something out: the manicured green of the Tivoli Gardens and the way two gardeners moved quietly through a flower bed like foraging animals; the way every bench in the city's main square was occupied by people sunning themselves, their faces tilted and cocked just-so to catch the sun's rays; the ancient facades that lined the old town square; and the busyness of countless buses, pedestrians, and pigeons that assembled and left with a cosmopolitan regularity. There was the odd juxtaposition between a model of the world's tallest man seen through the door of the Ripley's Believe It Or Not Museum and the slender granite columns that supported the vaulted ceiling of Helligånds church just a block beyond. An occasional breeze funneled through the streets. If we were caught in the shade, it chilled us, so we kept moving.

We walked through the quiet, tree-shaded grounds of the university on paths dappled by shards of sunlight that broke through the canopy. Just beyond the university grounds we watched a young mother urge her toddler to drop a silver coin into the stained paper cup of a beggar outside a tram station. We kept walking, past the Workers' Museum and the Musical History Museum, where we thought of stopping, but to stop made me feel awkward.

It was awkward because each step was like a pulse, a biological rhythm that promised another would follow. Each footfall rose through my legs and knees, then rose again through my hips and into my chest, where it resonated with hope.

And when we were too tired to go any farther, we found a tourist boat that pushed through the antifreeze-green water of the city's canals, then out through the harbor and back. A young woman narrated in five languages as the boat wound its way through the waterways past significant sites. She recited a memorized paragraph in Danish, Swedish, French, German, and English about each of the cathedrals, castles, museums, forts, and palaces. She spoke so quickly the flow of her words sounded like a stream of noise, like stones in a river that are worn round and almost identical. Suzanne and I made a game of guessing when we thought she was switching tongues, which she did in the space of a comma as the boat moved on according to schedule.

"I'm surprised," Suzanne said.

Our guide had just explained how the statue of the Little Mermaid, one of the city's significant landmarks, had once been decapitated, but I knew Suzanne meant her surprise had been at me.

"Are you disappointed with me?" Suzanne asked. She took my hand in both of hers and caressed it.

"No. It's just that I feel lost at the thought of us not being together on this trip," I said. "We've been through too much for that to happen now."

"Hush," she said, and laid a finger across my lips. "Don't talk like that."

I welcomed her ability to silence me.

seven

"Touring is like that," David explained. "It's the most diffi-cult part of playing music. All the time away can do a lot of damage."

The ferry shuddered beneath our feet as it began the fifty-minute voyage across the sea to Malmö, Sweden. David leaned against the steel railing on the sun deck between Suzanne and me, and together we watched the land and sea revolve around us as the ferry turned in the harbor.

Suzanne had spotted David when we walked onto the deck. "I bet he's an American," she whispered to me

"How do you know?"

"The way he stands. His hair. And look at his glasses."

David looked like a model for a Levi's advertisement. He wore faded blue jeans that looked tailored, and his tousled brown hair was cut to look reckless. His comfortably worn leather jacket and polished boots made my own look cheap and rough. David heard us speaking and asked where we were from.

"Me, too," he said. "I live in L.A."

David was the drummer for the The Hooters, a rock band

that experienced top-of-the-chart fame in the mid-'80s. "We're touring through northern Europe to promote our new album," he said, and motioned to a table where the rest of the band sat in plastic deck chairs playing cards and talking. "That's Rob, Eric, John, Fran, and Mindy," he pointed. Each of them waved or nodded to us.

"How long have you been on the road?" Suzanne asked David.

"Too long. Two weeks," he said, as if it was a sentence. "I left a wife and baby boy at home, and this tour is just beginning."

A stiff breeze blew against us as the ferry moved from the harbor into the channel that separated the two countries.

"Where have you been?" Suzanne asked.

David turned to answer her and his voice became faint. I thought he said Bremen, or Berlin, perhaps both. David's voice became inaudible through the wind and the sound of the ship's props churning the sea.

As the ferry pushed farther from the coast, buildings and trees became flecks on a slim wafer of green wedged between the empty blue of the sky and the deeper blue of the sea. As I watched I thought of our progress to this point in the trip. I thought of the winds and rains, the discoveries that were unfolding between Suzanne and me, and I thought I began to see our place in the landscape of this journey. I thought that if I just kept looking I would realize something very important about what lay beyond.

I looked past the front of the ferry at Sweden. I saw dim shapes emerging from the dark wedge of land there: buildings, ships docked along the harbor, sparks of sunlight reflecting off car windows as they moved along the coast road. It looked so promising. I thought to myself, *We can begin again*.

~~~

I had already put on my helmet when David appeared beside us in the hold of the ferry. It had stopped moving, and outside it men shouted as they secured lines and prepared to open the front of the ship.

"You should come to Lund," David said. "We play there to-night. I can have passes for you at the door."

I looked at Suzanne to see if she was game. The front of the ferry began to open and around us drivers started the engines of their vehicles. "It's just thirty minutes from Malmö!" David yelled above the noise. "It won't cost you a thing!"

"Yes!" Suzanne said. David smiled and then disappeared between a maze of vehicles.

Southern Sweden was like a desert after Germany and Denmark. The sun was so bright my eyes teared from the glare, and as we moved north toward Lund we rode across a rocky landscape covered with a weave of ripening wheat and barley fields that radiated a Van Gogh gold against a cloudless sky. We'd stopped briefly in Malmö to change money and I noticed there how Suzanne seemed transformed. She was animated and a smile was fixed on her face.

Watching her now it was difficult for me to remember how it was that I'd felt so lost in Copenhagen just a few days before. I felt embarrassed at the memory of my indecision and confusion, of my sudden doubts about this trip. *We're hitting our stride,* I told myself. *I can feel it.*

Everything about the bike and us seemed synchronized as we moved effortlessly north. The road was smooth and banked around turns. There was no wind. The bike felt perfectly tuned and responsive to my slightest touch, and Suzanne's thighs and chest and arms felt as much a part of me as ever. *Even if we were to die along this route,* I realized, *we could not fail.*

A middle-aged woman at a gas station on the edge of Lund gave us directions to a campsite. Her smile was genuine and her manner so pleasant she could have worked for the Swedish tourist authority. She was meticulous with her directions and drew a map with pictures that made it unnecessary to communicate with a common language. From her drawing I imagined a campsite set in a meadow surrounded by trees. There was a clear lake and a sheer granite precipice that made me think of Yosemite. I said to Suzanne, "It must be beautiful here."

Instead, the forest was a thick hedge, the meadow a length of lawn. The clear lake was a municipal swimming pool filled with squealing kids, and the granite wall was a phalanx of high-rise apartments that would block the morning sun until at least ten or eleven each morning. The campground was empty except for two house trailers set beside each other in the parking lot. A rusted purple car was parked between them. The sound of a radio turned on too loud spilled through the open door. Two families sat sullenly in folding chairs on the asphalt and watched us.

Suzanne and I lay on the grass in the sun and let sweat simmer through our pores. We had closed our eyes and begun to doze in the sleepy doldrums of the afternoon when a car pulled up with the stereo blaring the music of the rock band AC/DC. *"I'm on a highway to hell! I'm on a highway to hell!"* The car stopped with a chirp of the tires beside the bike. Two young men wearing dark glasses and frowns began carrying gear from their car to a part of the grass just beyond us. I waved to one of them. He flipped his head in acknowledgment and continued awkwardly past carrying a heavy cooler and other supplies stacked on top of it.

I watched as the two of them assembled a large tent with a vestibule attached to the front where they could store things out of the weather. They inflated an air mattress as big as a raft, then spread their sleeping bags and pillows on top of it. They carried bags of beer, wine, and food from their car and set them in the shade of the hedge behind their tent. And when they were done, they sat on the grass and leaned back as if that portion of the earth were an old recliner in their home. In unison they reached into one of their bags, pulled out a bottle of beer each, and opened them with their teeth. They tipped the bottles together so Suzanne and I heard the clink of glass, and swallowed hard until the bottles were empty. When they were done they tossed the empties onto the ground in what was almost an elegant movement, and reached inside the bag for another.

Just then a van pulled beside the edge of the lawn and seven clean-cut boys climbed out. They were laughing, and looked as if they'd just arrived at camp. They too began removing bags, and a long bundle they unrolled on the other side of us. They were gawky and loud, and they giggled incessantly as they shabbily erected a blue-and-green tent the size of a shack, spread their sleeping bags inside it, and popped the tops off a few beers. One of the boys had a guitar and gently strummed some broken chords. He sang a few bars of the Beatles' "Let it Be," and the others joined in. "Let it be," they breathed. "Let it be, let it be-e, let it beeeee...." Behind us the opening chords of something very hard and metallic eclipsed the sing-along. The boys stopped their singing and looked beyond our tent to where our other neighbors stood hunched over a boom-box, madly strumming imaginary guitars. Their music was startling under the warm Swedish sky, like stumbling across graffiti on a rock in the forest.

"It won't last long," I assured the boys. "I think they've been drinking a lot of beer."

"Swedes," one of the boys said. "They can do that all day."

The boys were from Växjö, a small city two hours to the north. They explained how they'd pooled their money to rent the blue VW van for the trip to Lund. "Our first time," one of them said with a smile.

"First music fest," another clarified. "First time for a music fest."

I asked the boys about Växjö, what it was like to live there. I imagined its location carved from the thick Swedish woods, a town of cobbled streets and neat homes painted in pale pastels and rich reds. I imagined small shops and a weekly market in the town square.

"Boring," they agreed, as if to wash it from their skins, except for one boy who wore a pair of narrow rectangular sunglasses with fuchsia lenses. "Great fishing," he said, and then told me how the forest around Växjö is pocked with lakes. "Pike," he said, holding his hand against the middle of his chest. "Pike up to here."

Our neighbor's concert arrived at a crescendo of bobbing heads and thrusting guitars. Three staccato chords ripped across the lawn, followed by a flurry of drums. The boy from Växjö with the guitar played a quick riff as the music died and sang, "Now let *us* be."

In no time the boys from Växjö had accumulated a neat stack of empty beer cans on the grass. Two of them smoked cigarettes clumsily, and I couldn't help but stare as they drew smoke through their pursed lips and squinted eyes. They asked our names and were surprised at the distance suggested between them. "Noren," the boy with the guitar said, "is Swedish. Valenzuela...Spanish? And you are from America?"

Suzanne explained the dynamics of American immigration by giving them an abbreviated version of her family's five generations in the United States, and then told them how my grandfather had followed his brother to California from Åseda, a town smaller than Växjö and about an hour farther to the north. "We're going to visit the uncle there," she said. "He moved back after living in California for forty years."

They listened with great interest. They shook their heads at the distances involved, the odds of our coupling, of their having even met us. A boy with a gold hoop through his ear sucked on his beer, then raised his hand to ask a question. "*Åseda?*" he said. "But Åseda is a shit town."

We had thought The Hooters would play in a bar or hall, but while walking into Lund we found a handbill stapled to a tree. The Hooters, it said, were the opening act for a three-day outdoor festival. Farther along we became part of a stream of people moving in the same direction. In the distance we heard guitars and a bass being tuned. We felt the percussive shock of a drum beat.

A long line of people wound down a cobbled side street but Suzanne led me to another entrance. She spoke to a plump woman with shorn green hair who pointed us toward another woman holding a clipboard. The roar of the crowd made it necessary for Suzanne and the woman to lean into each other to talk. The opening chords of a song caused people around us to surge in the direction of the music as though summoned. The woman flipped papers over the top of her clipboard, noted something with a pen, and then attached purple bands with gold stars around our wrists with a plastic rivet.

I took Suzanne's hand and we penetrated the edge of the crowd, then wound between several thousand bodies until we reached the front of the stage. Lund is a university town and the crowd was mostly students. For the most part they were unusually wholesome and polite kids with a smattering of punks and others who did their best to look as though they lived on the fringe. But in Lund, as The Hooters played their upbeat opening tunes, it struck me as the safest kind of crowd. Even the fearsome ones smiled and moved their bodies in polite gyrations, careful not to bump anyone.

Suzanne and I came within thirty feet of the stage and a place materialized for us to dance comfortably with the rest of the crowd. The top of David's head bobbed above his drum kit and occasionally either Suzanne or I waved, but he didn't see us. The band was tight. They played with a practiced ease that allowed a seamless transition between songs. The lead singer, a lanky man with long black hair, sensed just how much the crowd knew of each song and periodically leaned the microphone over the lip of the stage and invited the crowd to fill in. At one point the boys from Växjö danced by us in a line. They were all smiling as though they knew the money for the van was a shrewd investment. In their eyes was the look of living, as if the buildup for the event carried a momentum of its own that would propel them all into adulthood.

The Hooters played long and hard. They navigated their show to a frenzied crescendo and through two encores. Somewhere near the end they succeeded in sustaining the energy of the crowd like a single note. The audience moved more quickly and surged forward. Their cheers became wails and screams. Occasionally people began flailing and spinning out of control, like dervishes, until they caught themselves.

And then the music stopped. Each member of the band put his or her instrument down. They assembled at the lip of the stage, bowed, and disappeared.

Behind the stage was a bar for the press that our wrist bands allowed us admittance to, and behind that was a cyclone fence. There was a gate that a security guard filled, and on the other side of that we could see several of The Hooters on a second-floor balcony. The lead singer was sitting on a patio chair with his feet up, a white terrycloth towel draped around his neck like a boxer after a fight. I waved and caught his eye. I waved again and tried to raise my voice above the music filling the festival grounds from another band. He raised a cup to salute us, and then turned away, thinking we were just fans.

"There's David," Suzanne said. He was sitting opposite a woman who took notes as he spoke. I waved but he didn't notice. Suzanne waved and he looked our way. He seemed to hurry through the interview, and when he was finished he walked over to the security guard, spoke in his ear, and welcomed us through the gate.

"You made it!"

"Yes! We were trying to get your attention during the concert," Suzanne said.

"I was looking for you. Thanks for coming."

David got us each a beer. He gathered two chairs, arranged them around his own, and invited us to join him. We talked about the concert, about The Hooters' next stop in Piteå in the north of Sweden. He asked about our campground and said it sounded more interesting than another hotel. I sipped from my beer. Suzanne sighed. David rubbed the palms of his hands against his jeans, looked into the sky, and then asked if we'd like to see pictures of his family. He disappeared inside and returned with a worn envelope of color prints. He sat down and smiled in anticipation, and then warned us that his wife and son were everything to him.

He extracted a picture by its corner to keep from smudging it. "Here," he said, and laid it in Suzanne's open hands. I leaned over to look at a picture of David in a swimming pool. His son, all of a few months old, was cradled in his sure arms over the water. "That was his first swim."

"My wife," David said after a long moment, and laid another picture on top of the first. She was a pretty woman with long brown hair, an adoring smile on a face canted peacefully to one side. "Beautiful, huh?"

He showed us more pictures, of his son crawling on the floor of their home, of David and his wife holding him close, of his son playing with a toy, in bed asleep. "That's the hardest time," he said. "At night, staring at the ceiling of a hotel room half a world away from home."

eight

Had the bike been a sailboat we could have run clear to Russia. A constant wind rushed across the landscape to the east. It came like swollen ocean waves rolling over us. We were better at reading the terrain now and better at anticipating the gusts before being shoved toward the shoulder of the road. Sometimes we could watch the waves move over fields of grain, see them part and press the tasseled heads toward the ground. At those times we could brace and lean, and just as they hit, I'd twist the throttle and power through them. But at other times the gusts traveled over the bare ground like a rock thrown in the dark.

We stopped often—at a gas station, beside a lake where we watched ducks being blown across the surface while others paddled to stay in place, and at a roadside cafe for tea. And yet we pushed on because each time we stopped we became crazy from the wind pressing into our eyes, sucking the moisture from our skin, and whistling through our ears. "Worse than the black flies in Africa," Suzanne said of it.

Around midday Suzanne began to sneeze behind me. "Allergies!" she yelled through the back of my helmet, and the word sounded like an alarm in my head. Back home she'd suffered terribly from them for years, and each spring and fall the symptoms began with a distinct sneeze. Within a few days her chest ached from all the convulsing, and she began to lose her voice. Her nose became raw from trying to keep it dry, and her eyes swelled shut. She became so exhausted that she slept through huge portions of a day. Medicines didn't work. She drank herbal teas until she sweat them. She considered acupuncture, aromatherapy, and hypnosis, but she finally decided on cortisone injections in the membrane of the nasal cavity.

"Guaranteed," the doctor told her. "Guaranteed to work with one shot, and you won't feel a thing."

I went with her the first time. The needle was three inches long, and as I watched it disappear up her nose, Suzanne's nails bit into my hands. But the shots didn't hurt, and for the first time in her life a change of seasons didn't mean misery. For two years she hadn't had a problem. We forgot about the sleepless nights of hacking and sneezing, the pain and fatigue, the wads of tissue that accumulated around our bed like mushrooms during the night. She thought she'd been cured and hadn't gotten the shots again.

Those first convulsions were like a shudder through all our plans, and I became angry because before leaving I had warned her of the flowers I'd read about and the pollens they produce. "They should be beautiful" was how she had responded.

As we rode through Hörby and Kristianstad I tried to concentrate on the winds and the road, and I tried to tell myself that each sneeze was the last, that they were caused by some flower or weed that only grew along this stretch of road.

We met the sea again at Sölvesborg and I hoped the air would be clear of pollens and dust, and that I'd feel Suzanne settle in behind me. But she continued wheezing and shaking. She signaled me to stop in Karlskrona, a small city on the edge of the sea, and I rode to the breakwater where the land began to dissolve into an archipelago of rounded granite islets. A lone sailboat moved starkly across the blue water, its mainsail full and listing heavily. Suzanne's face looked as though it had simmered inside her helmet. Her eyes were swollen and looked as if they'd been scribbled on with a red marker. Her nose was raw and her chin wet. She handed me her helmet and gloves, and without saying a word she disappeared into a restroom.

Her gloves were soaked, and the portion of her helmet that covered her face was wet. While she was gone I cleaned everything with water from a fountain and dried it with a cloth. I made a corner of the towel into a sharp spiral and worked it into the crevices of her helmet. I removed the visor and washed the surface with my fingers until it was clear. I rolled her gloves in the cloth to wring the moisture from them. I tried to make them perfect again, to have my efforts be enough to make her forget the discomfort of her allergies.

When she came out her hands were filled with a wad of toilet paper she was stuffing into the pockets of her jacket.

"When I get home," she began, "I'm going to buy a bed. It will be big enough so when I'm mad at you I can move to the other side. The mattress will be so soft I won't ever wake with aches. I'll have a down comforter of my own, and two feather pillows," she said, and she pulled her helmet over her head. She flipped the visor up and continued. "And I'm going to buy a new car, one with air-conditioning so I won't have to open the windows during the summer. And, I may never get on a motorcycle again."

That afternoon Suzanne went to sleep as soon as we'd set up the tent. She crawled into her sleeping bag with her clothes on, curled up in a ball, and asked me to leave her alone. I filled our collapsible bucket with water from the lake we were camped beside, and washed the fairing and windscreen of the bike. I picked at the tar collected on the rims, removed the luggage cases and cleaned the bottoms and sides where sand and mud had accumulated. I checked all the fluid levels, the air pressure of the tires. I checked that all the lights worked. Then I waited to get tired enough so I could sleep.

While waiting I remembered watching a cell divide. I was in a seventh-grade biology class and we were studying mitosis and meiosis. As an example of the process, we looked at onion tissue beneath a microscope. We cut the onion into thin strips and dyed them with India ink to stain the cells. I remember how some cells were occupied by pairs of chromosomes that were inextricably linked, while others looked like two pieces of dirty rope tied together in the middle. I found a set that was almost ready to divide, and I stayed late to see it happen. It felt like hours as I sat on a hard wooden stool with one eye pressed against the barrel of the lens. Finally, the pair did separate. I was struck by how quietly, how inevitably it happened.

~~~

Something was wrong with the bike as we rode toward Kalmar. I heard noises from the engine and transmission. There was a vibration I'd never felt before that worked its way up my legs and made my knees itch. I stopped three times on the side of the road, and each time I inspected different parts of the bike for a loose wire that could cause one of the cylinders to not fire. I checked for a fuel leak, a missing bolt. And each time I went over the bike Suzanne sat hunched on the side of the road and counted her remaining tissues.

We didn't talk much that morning. Suzanne hadn't slept well, and as she moved around our camp, it looked as if even walking labored her. Her coughing and wheezing had kept me awake, too, and as the night wore on I felt her frustration growing. Had we been at home this would only be a minor inconvenience, but everything is magnified on the road. A simple foot blister has led to the agonizing death of more than one explorer. I felt terrible, but there was nothing I could do but hope we would be through it soon.

I did my best to keep both our spirits up. While eating breakfast I said that I thought the good weather would hold, that we would arrive on Öland Island at the perfect time because the sea air would help her allergies. She turned and looked at me hopefully.

I cleaned our breakfast utensils, packed our clothes, and rolled our sleeping bags and tent while she sat against a tree in the sun dabbing at her nose and resting between fits of sneezing. Once we'd gotten on the road I was glad for the intimacy the bike imposed on us. I knew she was suffering, and I knew she was frustrated with me. But I needed to feel her against me. I pretended that her hands were placed on my hips because she wanted them there. I pushed back in my seat so I could feel her thighs, stomach, and chest draped around the curve of my body as we rode.

A few miles farther along we were stopped yet again. I was sitting beside the bike trying to divine the problem when she said, "There's nothing wrong with the bike, Allen. It's you."

She was sitting on a rock watching me. I sat up and looked at her. "What do you mean?"

"You're off," she said, and then sneezed. "You've lost your balance."

I turned back to the engine and continued my inspection. To have to stop and take the bike apart would be a relief, I thought. Maybe a gas station owner would let us use his garage and tell us about a cheap place to stay. Suzanne could rest while I discovered the problem and fixed it. In the meantime, summer would establish itself.

"We may as well go," she said from her rock.

She was right. Nothing was wrong with the bike. I put our tools away. We climbed back on and continued.

~~~

A long bridge over four miles long links the Swedish mainland to Öland Island, a stick-like strip of land eighty-five miles long and not more than ten wide. I'd been looking forward to our arrival, and now it seemed crucial that we get there. We had the bridge to ourselves, and as the island gained detail I recalled what I knew about it: the island has been inhabited since the Stone Age. Many wars had been fought there between ancient peoples. Cattle, sheep, cement, and tourism are the main industries. It's known for warm, dry weather. I'd also read that the island is inundated with tourists in the summer, that traffic jams can extend for miles as people wait for their chance to make the crossing on the bridge, and at such times traffic on the island's narrow roads is bumper to bumper. But we rode on Öland for an hour before we saw anyone, which made it hard to believe the island could ever become crowded.

On our way down to the southern end of the island we passed just two cars, and they were moving fast in the opposite direction. The land there is arid and stony and reveals the thick, horizontal limestone slabs the island is assembled from. They haven't been uplifted and torn like mountains, but have risen out of the water like submerged objects finally loosed from a captive force. We'd read how the entire trough that became the Baltic Sea was formed beneath the crushing weight of the last ice age, like a footprint in the snow. Since the ice receded the land has been rising at the rate of a few centimeters a year, and new islands and atolls will continue to appear with the passage of time.

We continued south along the edge of a crumbling plateau— an arid jumble of rocks and shale that had been blistered and peeled like skin by the ravages of wind, rain, and subzero winters. Beyond the plateau the land fell away to a narrow plain that was finally consumed by the sea. On the plain were heavily cultivated fields, a fertile band so tenacious it seemed to hold back the sea. I was struck by the abruptness of the transition between the two landscapes and stopped the bike. I walked toward the edge. Within just a few steps I moved from a desert to the beginnings of a fertile plain. I stepped back and forth between the two zones as though moving across a continent. Even the air was different between them. The one side was dry and smelled of hot, sage-spiced stone, while the other was heavy with the moist humidity of crops, wildflowers, the spicy scent of trees.

We camped below the plateau on the edge of the sea. A light breeze blew from it and was combed through a stand of pines behind us. Suzanne was able to breathe again there. Within an hour she was transformed. Her nose cleared and she was able to put her tissues away. The swelling in her eyes receded and she said she wanted to take a hike along the coast.

The shoreline was paved with flat spherical stones perfect for skipping across the water. Among them Suzanne found one with a node of pure metal ore that was being revealed as the surrounding stone eroded. She found the exoskeleton of a blue crab, a faded plastic bracelet with the name "Sophia" pressed onto it. I found the dry carcass of a swan curled behind a log, the vertebrae of its long neck laid out like a necklace. I found the skull of a ribbon fish, its teeth still sharp and menacing. And we found fossils, hundreds of them. The stones held their vague impressions like old snapshots. Behind us the sun swung toward the horizon as if it would land there. The early June days were growing extraordinarily long as we moved north. The sun now skimmed the tops of trees before setting just behind the horizon, but its light never fully disappeared, glowing like a dull fire throughout the night.

When we returned to camp we found a white Citrëon van with Dutch plates parked in the same clearing. An older couple sat in folding chairs beside it. Between them was a low table stacked with books, and each of them held one open. I said "hello" as we passed and the couple looked over the tops of their reading glasses as if we'd surprised them.

"Hello!" they said in unison.

"Nederlander?" I asked.

"Ja. Deutsch?" they asked of us in return.

"American."

"Ahhh, Amerikaaan!" the woman said, raising her eyebrows as she said the word, and then let them fall as she lingered over the last syllable.

"Beautiful weather," I said.

"Jaaa," the wife said. "So much rain before! Aach! So nice, this sunshine."

"Your motorbike?" the man asked. "Our daughter has motorbike. Ducati. She rides in front, her man in back!" They both laughed and asked Suzanne if she drove.

"Ah. Is too bad. Is better with man in back," his wife said.

"Coffee?" the woman asked. "You have coffee with us?"

Jan and Cory explained they were retired and spent as much

time as possible roaming Europe in search of exotic flora and fauna. On this trip they were after a particular orchid that grows only on Öland and Gotland islands. They had just arrived after driving straight from the Netherlands and would spend the next two weeks on their quest. Jan said it was their first time to the Swedish islands but that they'd been through a good bit of Scandinavia on previous trips, first back in the '50s when they were newly married, and later with their children. Jan said they liked the isolation, the endless forests, the mountains and sea.

While Cory heated water Jan showed us their books. One stack was written in Swedish, the other in their native Dutch. "Can you read Swedish?" Suzanne asked. "No!" Cory said, her eyebrows arching for emphasis. "We find pictures in this book," she said, pointing to the Swedish, "and write the Latin name. Then we open this book and change to Dutch. Jan does Swedish, I do Dutch," she said, and gave a turn of her wrist behind her husband's back as though she was driving a motorcycle.

Jan pointed out pictures of the orchids they were seeking, tiny purple things I tried to remember in case we saw them later. He took pleasure in pointing out flowers they'd found on previous trips around Europe. Their books were dog-eared. The pages were filled with marginal notes and hand-drawn diagrams.

"We find these today," Jan said, pointing to a small yellow flower as if it was a revelation. "Five kilometers from this place. Today!"

"Yeah?"

"Ja!"

"Sugar?" Cory asked.

Suzanne had been watching Cory as she moved through the van, and she said how she'd rather be traveling in such a vehicle. "Would you like to trade?" Suzanne asked.

Cory patted the edge of their stove and laughed. "We buy it with nothing inside. Jan make everything with his hands." She demonstrated her favorite features: the polished hardwood floor, a concealed sink beneath a pine cutting board, a hot water system that utilized heat from the engine. She slid open large drawers filled with canned food, onions, potatoes, beer, wine, pasta, and a set of sparkling pots and pans. And, for a finale, Cory showed us their bed and demonstrated how it unfurled from a small space in the back of the van. "And look at this!" she said, and slowly peeled back a down comforter so we could see the two feather pillows and crisp white sheets tucked beneath.

"Like home!" Jan proclaimed.

"Wow!" Suzanne said. "That's what we should have. It's beautiful."

Cory stepped out of the van onto a varnished pine stool Jan had made for her. She had four cups and a thermos to keep the coffee hot.

"Ach!" Cory said as she arranged the cups on top of their books. "Tomorrow we trade for bicycles."

"Bicycles?" Suzanne said, the surprise audible in her voice.

There was a pair leaning against the front of the van, identical to the ones we'd seen Danish farmers struggling to pedal across the landscape. They were old-fashioned, single-speed bikes, the kind of bikes someone would use to ride around town, but no more.

"Ten days," Jan said. "Ten days on bicycle. We have small tent like you, sleep sack, little food. We need no more. Is the best way."

"Where are you going?" I asked.

"All over!" he said, and waved his arm so wildly he could have meant the world. "Öland. Gotland. We search for flowers."

"That will be quite a trip," I said. "Several hundred miles."

"Ja. No problem. We pedal many, many places."

I ached to lean over to Suzanne and point out we were traveling in relative luxury. I wanted to say, "Look at these people! Their spirit should inspire us." But there was no need. We'd both spoken clearly through Cory and Jan.

~~~

The rush of the wind through the pines and the regular rolling of the sea against the shore woke me early the next morning. The sun was fully up at five, and the island seemed to ferment and

dilate beneath its warmth. Birds called frenetically, as if to an-
nounce that something important had happened. Behind their calls
and shrieks was another sound, a low humming barely audible but
omnipresent, like the droning of a ship's engine. It was the sound
of insects. When I began to look, I found them everywhere. I
walked down to the edge of the sea while Suzanne slept. It seemed
that each step revealed another colony of winged and crawling crea-
tures ravenously waking from under rocks and leaves, crawling
from the skin of trees and materializing from the air itself. As the
sun rose higher, its warmth brought out the smells of the earth.
There was the rich, vegetative salinity of the sea, the stench of mud,
the balm, civet, and musk of the trees, grasses, and flowers.

I went back to wake Suzanne and tell her what she was missing. I leaned into the tent and touched her shoulder. Her face was
covered by her jacket and she stirred beneath it. I told her about
the sounds and smells, the sun and warmth, and said this was the
day we'd been waiting for. I shook her again and she groaned. I
peeled her jacket from her face and stopped. It looked like an open
wound. Her eyes were swollen and red. Her skin was flushed, and
her nose was covered with scabs of dried mucus.

I washed her face with a cold towel and felt sick at being so
powerless. I wished for some equalizer between us. If I had a broken bone, I thought, it would be better. As I washed her face, I realized her allergies would only get worse as the weather improved.
And I, in contrast, never felt more alive.

~~~

We rode to the southern tip of the island, a point of land that
narrowed like a tail before it was submerged beneath the sea. At
the end of the point was a classic lighthouse, a tall, tapered cylin-
der crowned by a lamp, but there was no need for its light that
morning. There were no clouds in the sky, no clues for the eye to
gauge where the sea or sky ended in the far distance, just a
panorama of blue that extended to infinity.

The wind had all but died. The sea was as calm and flat as

water in a tub. A scattering of stones rose above the water's surface and we hopped from one to another to reach a slab of limestone some thirty feet from shore. We sat down and Suzanne
leaned her head against my shoulder. She began to cry softly.

I held her and kissed her eyes. I wanted to tell her everything
would be okay, but it would have been a lie. I could no longer
promise that good weather would bring the comfort and ease we'd
hoped for the trip. Instead, as we sat on that island of stone just
inches above the sea, I thought of the trouble we were in.

A flock of pelicans wheeled slowly overhead as they prepared
to land. I envied their smoothness, how the white plume of their
bodies so rightly occupied the sky. I closed my eyes and imagined I
was among them. I was gliding in slow circles behind the lead bird
toward the sea. I felt the wind over my wings and practiced leaning and turning by shifting my weight. By moving just the tips of
my fingers I could make the earth and sky revolve around me. As
we dropped closer to the water, I looked down to where Suzanne
and I sat on the stone and sensed so profoundly how awkward our
movements were.

I pulled Suzanne closer to me and watched the pelicans lose
altitude. They seemed to levitate over the water for the longest
time before they finally extended their bodies partially upright and
settled onto the sea.

~~~

Late that afternoon we found another place to camp beside
the sea. Suzanne was exhausted and cold and asked for my jacket
while I unloaded the bike. She'd gone through all her tissues on
the ride up the coast and had been using her gloved hands to wipe
her nose the last miles. She thought her allergies were exacerbated
by something on the island and we agreed to return to the mainland the following day.

She lay on the grass while I set up the tent, and then I
wrapped her in both our sleeping bags with her clothes on. Her
eyes were swollen and burned, and she let me bathe them with a

wet towel. She pulled a portion of it over her mouth and breathed through the fabric. I told her I understood something new about the importance of busy work and why, in old movies, extra hands would be put to useless tasks like boiling water and tearing sheets. I said I'd feel better if I had to walk five miles for the water or, better yet, a remedy. I got her to laugh, and she said she wouldn't want me gone that long, that I'd probably get lost and she'd have to come find me. After a time she began to feel better and asked that I take the towel away. But it was only a minute or so before she began to squint and blink involuntarily as if her eyes were filling with sand.

She fell asleep with her head on my lap in the tent, and I stayed with her until her breathing was regular and deep. Then I wrote her a note and set it beside her. I went out, zipped the door closed, stripped the bike of our cases and tank bag, and began riding north.

The northern half of Öland is a patchwork of woodlands, pastures, and orchards. The backs of fat sheep rose like stepping stones from the midst of dense meadows, and off to the right there was often a view of the sea. There was no traffic to trouble my mind, just an occasional slow-moving tractor I easily leaned the bike around. With nothing on the bike it felt light, nimble, and powerful, and when a turn revealed a straight section, I opened the throttle until the sides of the road became a green blur.

I'd always assumed Suzanne and I would just keep moving from one trip to the next. "Travel and die," she'd responded half jokingly to a friend who'd asked what our plans were after we'd spent the better part of a year traveling. Together we had assembled a reserve of great experiences that had sustained us through many dangers. That our reserve was running dry on this trip was as much a surprise to me as running out of gas.

I passed rune stones along the side of the road, stone tablets carved with line after line of bird's-feet script by the ancients millennia ago. I passed several of the peculiar windmills the island is famous for, small wooden structures the size of an outhouse mounted on a large stone that can be turned into the wind. I rode fast through a tunnel of trees that enveloped the road and was shot out the other side. And I kept riding through tiny villages named Uggeltorp, Kalla, and Böda, past farms and neat red houses, past an old woman pedaling her ancient bicycle with all she had, as if her job were to keep the world turning.

I rode until Byxelkrok, a small fishing village at the north end of the island. There were just a few buildings: a store, post office, a café. Toward the water were some weather-beaten buildings and fishing shacks, and farther still were boats tied along a wooden pier. There was also a small, informal group of people looking out to sea, a family, an older couple, and a taxi driver who leaned against his little car. They were all watching a ferry coming toward shore. I parked the bike and joined them.

For a while it looked as if the ferry would continue past us and dock farther down the coast, but then it made an abrupt turn toward the pier. Men appeared from town like members of a volunteer fire brigade and positioned themselves around where the ferry maneuvered to land. They handled ropes and cables and tied the ferry fast against the pier. They unloaded several palettes of cargo. They supervised the offloading of cars and a new tractor.

It was all over in ten minutes. The cars drove away. The cargo was loaded onto a truck and taken across the road into town. The tractor was left alongside the pier with the key in the ignition. People hugged and then vanished. Even the crew went away, leaving the small ferry empty and silent.

An old man was standing beside the bike. I hadn't seen him before, and he stood so still he startled me. He would have been the perfect image of the ancient mariner had he not been so old and bent. I could easily imagine one of the rotting boats lying on the shore to have been his.

He was bent over looking at the license plate on the back of the bike with a studied intensity. He was considering it as he would a strange new gadget. I walked up to him and said, *"Hej!"*

"Hejjjjj," he responded with a drawl.

For a while he didn't say anything more. He just kept staring at the license plate as if waiting for it to move. I was almost ready to put on my helmet and leave when he looked at me and shook his bent and swollen middle finger at the plate and mumbled something. I moved around and stood beside him as he pointed at the license plate. "Where from?" he seemed to be asking.

"California," I said, and let the word roll off my tongue as if it was something expensive.

He looked at me as if I'd just told him something unbelievable, but it wasn't me he was interested in. It was the bike.

"Kalafournya?" he asked.

"Ja. California."

He began shuffling around the bike, scrutinizing its many parts for signs of California.

"Kalafournya?" he asked again, as if to see if I'd understood his question.

"California," I confirmed.

He shuffled to the front of the bike and peered into the headlight. "Kalafournya?" he asked, pointing inside as though California were in there.

He worked his way back to the license plate and peered at it again. He prepared to lift his finger and ask once again.

"California," I assured him. "California."

He seemed to get it then and began to move away, periodically stopping to turn and take another look. Someone he knew drove up in a car and they stopped to talk. I watched the old man tell his story, watched him point to the bike, and I could see his friend's eyes follow and look, too. I could see the old man's mouth forming the word "Kalafournya" one last time.

~~~

The road wound beside the sea as I neared the northernmost point of the island. A strong wind blew across it, bending the grass over the edge of the road, and it sounded like rushing water as it broke through the trees. An identical lighthouse to the one in the south rose like an obelisk from the last portion of land. It was closed and the area was deserted. I sat down and thought of

Suzanne back in the tent. I wondered if she was awake and if she'd found my note. If she had, I wanted her to miss me enough that our trip together would regain its importance.

I once had a job that required I travel. For a while it seemed that I was passing through Chicago's O'Hare Airport every few weeks, waiting for a connection. I spent my time walking up and down the long terminals watching all the other people leave and arrive. In particular I watched the businessmen because I had received an invitation to become one of them. I watched them at the phones making calls, a fistful of business cards in one hand, a daily organizer in the other, and the phone receiver clamped between their head and shoulder, talking quickly so they could make yet another call before flying off again. It was from one of those phones that I called Suzanne and told her of my idea to sell everything and go away for a very long time. She asked when I was coming home and said she'd go anywhere with me.

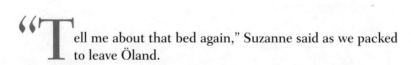

NINE

"Tell me about that bed again," Suzanne said as we packed to leave Öland.

I told her it was in a big room overlooking a flower garden. A bathroom with a full tub was attached, and the bed was queen-size with a down comforter and pillows. I told her she could sleep as long as she liked. But I reminded her I didn't know for sure whether we'd be welcome. Two years had passed since I'd last heard from my great-uncle Chester in Åseda.

I made a point of visiting him and his wife, Ingrid, at either the beginning or the end of my east European trips. They always had a bed ready for me and would immediately envelop me in their daily lives. I especially liked Ingrid's knowledge of the land and old country ways. We spent most days in the forest, where she instructed me in the uses of various flowers, leaves, mosses, and barks as dyes, herbs, medicines, and food. We picked bags of wild berries and mushrooms until our hands were stained.

Chester had always interested me. He was the first of two brothers to leave Sweden for the promises America held. He went first to Washington state, then south to San Francisco, where he met his first wife, Winifred, and opened an auto repair shop. During the Depression they lived off their earnings, and when those ran low, they'd drive north along the Eel and Klamath rivers, where they camped and lived off the salmon they caught. My grandfather joined them, and after the war they began to prosper. In 1948 Chester and Winifred moved their business north of San Francisco to Point Reyes Station, and they built a house to raise a family in.

Their only child was stillborn, and some years later Winifred died from complications with asthma. Chester married again and built a new house just up the road from the first, but after eleven years his second wife died from a stroke. At the same time his parents were getting old and needed care. After forty years away from Sweden, Chester moved back. He married Ingrid almost immediately.

I remember the last few years Chester lived in California. They're good memories of picking abalone off the rocks at McClure's Beach, cutting wood, barbecuing, and walking in the big field below his house to the base of a huge oak where an owl lived.

Chester visited California every few years, each time bringing with him a friend or relative he wanted to show the place he still called home. They were small-town people whom I remember being shy and childlike as Chester led them around the state. He took them to San Francisco and showed them the diner where he met Winifred and the location of his first shop. He described for them what it was like to witness the construction of the Golden Gate Bridge. He drove them to Yosemite and tried to explain how nature had made such a place. He recited from Walt Whitman's *Leaves of Grass* as he drove them north through the redwood forests in Humboldt and Mendocino counties. He tried to impress them with the size and age of the trees, as he had been impressed. And he always took them to Point Reyes and made them walk along the beaches until their feet ached and they were ready to go home. At night Chester continued his stories of how California had embraced him, and he explained the subtleties that made the land truly golden in his eyes. I can still recall many of Chester's stories, and in some respects my California is a child of his.

My letters to him had gone unanswered for the previous two

years. The last one from Chester was a long rant about demons and heathens, and he ended it by writing I was no longer welcome in their home. Perhaps it was because Chester was ninety-two years old and his mind was going. But I needed to find out.

~~~

We left Öland under a Mexican sky. The sun was so bright it bleached the color from the earth like an overexposed photo. And because it was so warm, the pollen and dust were suspended in the air. Suzanne's nostrils and eyes ran like small streams, and the tissue she used to wipe her face was used-up by the time we had ridden across the bridge to the mainland.

On the other side I stopped for gas and Suzanne disappeared into the bathroom to wash her eyes with cold water. I filled the gas tank, paid, and pushed the bike away from the pumps. I bought us cold drinks from a vending machine on the side of the station and sat in the shade. I watched cars drive past and scraped the dirt from beneath my fingernails. The sweat on our aluminum cans had run down the sides and stained the ground by the time Suzanne came out of the bathroom.

"How do you feel?" I asked.

"How do you *think* I feel? My allergies are raging, my back is sore, and I'm hot."

She sat an arm's length from me and began sorting the tissues she'd taken from the bathroom.

"Here," I said, and handed her a drink.

"Is that all they had?"

"You're hard to please."

"What do you mean by that?"

"Nothing," I said.

"Really funny," she said and opened the can anyway.

"I can't control the weather."

"Nobody's asking you to."

We finished our drinks awkwardly, got on the bike, and continued on.

While planning the trip I had spent a lot of time deciding which tools and spare parts to take. I could fix flat tires, fouled plugs, clogged filters, and shorted wires. I could adjust the clutch and cables and valves. I could replenish depleted fluids, and repair any burst hoses, but I could not fill the distance that existed between us as we continued down that road. Her hands weren't on my hips, and I couldn't feel her thighs or chest against me. It felt as though she wasn't on the bike at all, as if she'd stayed behind at the gas station.

We continued inland. The smell of brine was replaced by pine sap and road tar. Towns almost too small to notice slipped past. I was looking at a field filled with lilies of the valley when a turn came up fast and I had to lean hard around it. Suzanne's hands found my waist, and she didn't take them away.

I began looking for a place to pull over so we could talk. The road bordered a stream, and we came to a place where it had been dammed to form a small pond. A crumbling mill stood above the dam. Its roof was sagging, the walls were falling in on themselves, and the waterwheel had long since disintegrated into the stream. The pond was still and clear. I watched a school of fish streak from beneath a group of lily pads as I stopped the bike. A wreath of iris, buttercups, and lupine circled the pond. Bees and other insects fed noisily from them.

"Are you getting off?" I asked.

Suzanne sighed, and jerked her body to the left off the bike. "What are you stopping for?" she demanded.

"Look at that." I motioned toward the pond and all that surrounded it. "Beautiful, isn't it?"

"Yeah, yeah."

I walked across the road and over a small fence to the edge of the pond. I sat on a rock big enough for the two of us and waited for Suzanne to join me. A metallic blue dragonfly buzzed past me, then stopped to inspect the chrome islets of my boots. I looked over my shoulder for Suzanne. She was standing beside the bike, her helmet still on, staring at me as if I were doing something ridiculous and it would only be a matter of time before she simply wouldn't put up with it any longer. I turned back to the pond and listened for the sound of her footsteps behind me, but there was only the continued buzzing of insects.

"Okay. What is it?" I called out, but she said nothing from her place across the road. "What's the matter now? Look. I'm really sorry about your allergies, and I'm sorry about the weather. This is shaping up to be a long and difficult trip, and it's not going to help if we're battling each other. We've got to pull together and...."

"Can we go now?" she said from across the road.

"What?"

"I said, 'Can we go now?' I want to get going."

"*Where?* Where on earth would you want to be but here?"

She continued to stare at me through her visor. She didn't move. "You don't want to know."

From the way she said it I knew she meant anywhere but here. My mouth went numb. The inside of my chest became hot, as if something would erupt inside and burst through my skin. I stood up, looked over the pond, and restrained myself from yelling at her. I walked back across the road, pulled my helmet on, and was relieved that it concealed the emotion on my face. I started the bike. Suzanne climbed on, and we left.

～～～

We could have made it to Åseda, but I stopped instead outside the town of Alghult. I'd been there once with Chester to visit an old friend of his. I looked down the driveway where the man lived. It was overgrown with weeds and the windows were shuttered. We continued down a short hill to a lake. The road passed a swimming area for the local kids, and several of them waved from a wooden dock as we passed. There was a shack with a bathroom and a big open window where an old woman sold sweets and soda to the swimmers. She said we could camp beside the lake. I set the tent up on a patch of thick grass in the shade of some birch trees while Suzanne washed her face in the cold lake water. It took everything I had to keep quiet and not reignite our fight. I ached to tell her that something had to change between us, that I refused to travel like this.

Instead I took a long walk through the woods. I walked as fast as I could until my disappointment began to peak and I'd accumulated a long list of misdeeds and mistakes to present her with. Then I began to recite to Suzanne what I would tell her—how she was trying to change the terms of our lives at the very time when we needed each other most, how travel always held many surprises and not all of them were pleasurable. I wanted to tell her that if she would just open her eyes, she could learn a great deal from this trip and, just possibly, see its beauty.

A path through the forest led to another lake and followed its shore. I stopped at a point of land where a callous marked the spot where people came to fish. An old wooden boat was laid on its back in the brush, its ribs showing through the rotten wood of its belly. A swarm of bees worked through the flowering brush around me, and a fish leapt and splashed, breaking the smooth surface of the lake. I sat beside the boat and untangled a discarded nest of fishing line as I refined my argument.

By the time I was done it was both convincing and inspirational. I'd begin by sympathizing with her discomforts. I would say that I was as surprised as she was at the weather. I would remind her of past discomforts and trials and how they had become important lessons and the very stuff that made our travels important for us. I'd conclude by reminding her how she and I had dreamed this trip into existence.

As I was walking back I saw her sitting on a round granite stone beside the lake. She smiled and waved as I emerged from the forest. My speech and remonstrations unwound like that fishing line and lost all clarity. I sat beside her and she put her arm through mine. "I love you," she began. "And I'm sorry. You know, this really is the hardest trip we've ever done. Maybe you can't understand that, but it's true, at least for me."

"What can I do to make it easier?" I asked.

"You really want to know?"

"Yes."

A tear grew in the corner of her eye. She took a deep breath, and then said, painfully, "Sell the motorcycle, buy a cheap car, and let's go somewhere else."

Her words—sell motorcycle, buy car, somewhere else—were like three blows to my head. My heart stopped and without even thinking I said, "You know I can't do that."

"I know," she said. "But just understand I may not be able to do *this*."

As the sun hovered near the tops of the trees, we discovered a faucet with hot water behind the concession stand. The swimmers were gone and the shack was closed up. We peeled our clothes off and took turns ladling cupfuls of water over our bodies until we glistened. And in the long shadows of that still evening we built a fire and caressed the disappointment and sorrow from each other's skin until it seemed that, just maybe, we could fix everything.

～～～

For five days Suzanne's dream came true. We had a bed with a down comforter, and she had two feather pillows of her own. The mattress was soft. It was covered with thick linen sheets that smelled of cool water. "It's like the one I've been dreaming of," she whispered in my ear one night as she fell asleep.

For five mornings she woke with a smile on her face, stretched, and fell back to sleep again, as if she could store her comfort within her and take it on the road.

For five days she rode in Chester and Ingrid's car with the window up and a satisfied smile on her face. And for five days she didn't have to get on the bike, or put up the tent, or use our single-burner stove, or eat from our cook pots with her gray plastic spoon.

She let me know how she appreciated being in a room again where she could stand while she dressed instead of having to stoop and kneel. She hung her clothes neatly in a closet, left her toothbrush and comb on the edge of the bathroom sink, and left her towel to dry instead of putting it away wet with her things. She appreciated not having to pack and unpack every day.

And for five days she was the center of attention. Ingrid and Chester listened with great interest as she described our progress to Åseda, and several times they urged her to repeat her stories to neighbors and friends we met during our stay. Chester and Ingrid thought Suzanne was brave. They were taken with her charm and warmth, and they made a special effort to let her sleep and relax, to ask what she desired for dinner, and how she wanted to spend each day. Ingrid wanted to give Suzanne a favorite set of crystal to remember her by. She took Suzanne shopping for a new shirt, and she left Chester and me one afternoon so the two of them could pick wildflowers. Chester loved her smile and character, and each night before going to bed he sat beside her and sang, "Love Me Tender." He came alive around her. One morning I found them in the garden together and I overheard Chester promising her how, perhaps in another year, he'd come to visit us in California. I knew it was only a dream, though, and one morning while I was helping Ingrid put some of his tools away to clear some space in the garage, I realized he was dying.

Chester made murals, ornamental gates and railings, lamps, furniture, and sculptures from wrought iron, copper, stone, and wood. There were pieces in progress around the garage, pieces that, because I knew him, I could see the finished form in the parts. But he had let them all but go. As I helped him to the car one day he pointed to the rusting legs of a table, a covey of copper quail for a child's lamp, and the intricate detail of a handrail, and he explained how it would have all gone together, if he only had the time.

His work was now done. He reminded me of those pelicans on Öland and how they seemed to levitate over the sea until they found the perfect place to land. At ninety-two Chester was keeping tabs on the surface, the feel of the air, until he found his time to settle in and take leave.

He'd been ill for much of the previous year, and when I first saw him on the back porch the day Suzanne and I rode up, I was surprised at how thin he was.

"Water on the lungs," he said, and explained in great detail all he'd been through.

He was happy for Suzanne's fresh ear, and he spent hours answering her questions about his "three lives" in Sweden, then California, and again in Sweden. As I listened again to his stories I thought of him as a very rich man. His stories were his currency. They totaled the chances he took in life and the rewards he received.

Ingrid had also been ill. She'd had pneumonia and was diagnosed with diabetes after collapsing in the woods. During it all she still took care of Chester, their garden, and the house. She told me she still shoveled snow for several "older" people on their street. Her short, thick hands still made my chest echo when she reached up to hug me and clapped my back. One afternoon Suzanne and I helped her plant potatoes in the backyard, and I thought how some men must be envious of how much she could still lift and clear with them, how long she could bend over the earth as she pulled it up and turned it with a spade. I noticed, though, how her face was more ashen and dry than I could remember, and the color took longer to return after a strain.

"I am old," she told me one night after Chester and Suzanne were in bed. "Sometimes I am so tired."

She was born in that house in Åseda. She lived there with her parents until they died and then with her first husband until he drank their marriage away. Then Chester came and the house was filled with life again. Over the past years she'd been thinking of what to do when he was gone. She told me how she wanted to die with him, how she wanted them to go together holding hands.

Ingrid used to know everyone in Åseda, but most of her friends had died and their homes were occupied by people she didn't know. She believed the Chernobyl nuclear disaster in the Ukraine had something to do with it and, as proof, claimed her friends had been healthy until the winds carried particles of radiation over Åseda and heavy rains had brought them down and poisoned the earth. I didn't know how to respond, but I could almost see Ingrid worry her concerns like knots her strong hands should be able to take up and untie.

We spent a portion of each day in the woods, visiting familiar places like Stations of the Cross. I remembered many of them from previous visits, and felt I had a special insight into Chester and Ingrid's world. We drove great distances on dirt roads to reach their favorite places: a secluded dell where the elusive *Linnéa Borealis* thrive, a tiny bell-shaped flower that grows just inches above the forest floor and fills the air with a complex scent more alluring than most perfumes; a red-ant hill over six feet high that Chester said was a curiosity even in his childhood; past voids in the forest once occupied by small farms whose owners had abandoned them for the allure of America. We stopped for picnics beside lakes, and we stopped to pick chanterelle mushrooms and wild strawberries until our knees ached from crawling over the ground. We visited old friends who had known Chester and Ingrid since childhood. We visited the graves of other friends and relatives, and at each grave we washed the headstone with our hands until it was smooth. We pulled weeds slowly so the roots wouldn't break and raked the paths that surrounded the graves until the dirt was in perfect furrows and our footprints were erased.

During our last days Suzanne and I did chores while Chester and Ingrid thought of reasons for us to stay longer. We did things Ingrid had no time for, and which Chester could no longer do. Their washing machine needed a new belt. A door needed straightening. We unclogged a drain, rewired a lamp, cleared the garden of dead-fall, tuned their car, and scraped and painted the matching lamps mounted on either side of their front door. And then it was time to go.

"Russia. Why must you go to Russia?" Ingrid asked. "Suzanna. Tell Allen not to take you to Russia. I read in the paper so many bad things happen there. Stay with us."

We smiled, and finally Ingrid said no more.

"Just be careful," Chester cautioned, and translated for me a thoughtful article with recommendations on how to avoid road-banditry, kidnappings, and fuel shortages in the former Soviet Union.

I never discovered what had happened to cause the two years of silence between us. It was as if there never had been any problem, and in light of Chester's declining health, it seemed better to let it go. The morning we left he was sitting in his chair overlooking the garden with something on his mind.

"Good morning, son," he said. "Sit down. I have something to tell you."

I sat beside him and we silently watched the light change on the trees.

"Give me your hand. Now, look me in the eye." His lips trembled, and a tear slid the length of his old face. "There," he said, and squeezed my hand as if I was leaving forever. "I feel such love for you again."

ten

The road from Sweden's interior ran like a tunnel through the forest and then opened to the bare vista of the Baltic Sea at the port of Oskarshamn. The road had been fast, and we arrived an hour early for the ferry that would take us to Gotland Island. We paid for our tickets and wound our way past stacks of shipping containers to the foot of an empty pier where we were to wait. Four motorcycles were parked in front of us, two-by-two, and six riders leaned against a retaining wall and watched us as we parked the bike and dismounted.

"*Hej,*" I said as soon as I'd removed my helmet. We hadn't come across another motorcyclist since Kary in Copenhagen, and I wanted to ask them where they'd been and what they knew of Gotland. But the six riders said nothing. They only stared, and then turned from us. They spoke in a collective murmur with their heads down, and leaned toward each other as if we might overhear something private. There were four men, a woman, and a teenage boy, and they were all sheathed in color-coordinated leather riding suits and thick leather boots. The woman looked up at us, the boy's head followed, and I smiled and waved. They reacted like pigeons scared by a quick movement, and ducked back into their huddle.

"I guess we won't be camping with them tonight," Suzanne whispered.

We sat beside our bike and waited for the ferry. We got out our notebooks and I divided one of the sandwiches Ingrid had packed for us that morning. As we ate and wrote, the bikers stole occasional glances at us, and then, the oldest of them, a thick man of about fifty with close-cropped hair, slipped on a pair of dark glasses and began walking toward us. He pretended to keep his head turned toward the sea as if scanning the empty horizon for our ship. He whistled softly and scraped the toe of his boots along the ground. His friends watched him and remained huddled together like a clutch of street urchins.

The man moved past us, then stopped and bounced on the balls of his feet. He turned and began walking back, this time with his eyes on the ground as though looking for dropped coins. As he approached the back of our bike he looked over the top of his glasses, and I realized he was looking at the license plate to see where we were from.

His people created a place for him in their fold as he returned, and they leaned toward him as he reported his findings. I could almost hear him say, "Don't stare, but you won't believe what I saw...."

Two motorcycles with low-slung handlebars pulled up slowly behind us. The bikes' riders were bent low over the gas tanks and looked as though they were speeding even after they'd come to a stop. Both riders were wrapped in bright red leathers with yellow and black stripes that shot like flames off their shoulders. They dismounted, removed their helmets like fighter pilots after a particularly good run, and began laughing and talking with a giddy urgency. More riders pulled up behind them.

"Maybe it's a club," Suzanne suggested.

Ten bikes. Twenty. Forty, and they still came.

"Taller du Engelska?" I asked one of the guys behind us.

"Yes, of course."

"What's going on? What are all the bikes here for?"

"Big rally on Gotland. You didn't know?"

"No. We were just going to the island."

"Wow. Crazy."

"Yeah. Crazy," I agreed.

Someone whistled, and the whistle was followed by a cheer that announced the sighting of the ferry. We all watched it enter the harbor, a rectangular white monolith that looked more like a cruise ship than an inter-island ferry.

<center>~~~</center>

The belly of the ferry vibrated with the sound of racing motorcycle engines as we drove into it. A loading attendant motioned for us to park them like horses at a hitching rail against the side of the ship, and another came along and handed each rider a length of nylon packing twine that I wasn't sure what to do with.

"To tie the bikes!" the rider who'd parked beside us yelled above the noise. He reached for our twine and squeezed between the handlebars of our bikes and tied the front wheels to a metal ring welded to the floor of the ferry.

"Thanks," I said when he was done.

"No problem. It is ridiculous, this...how you say...rope? It is good for nothing, but they make us do it. My name is Niklas," he said, and offered his hand.

Niklas introduced us to his friend Conrad, and they invited us to follow them to the sun deck on the top of the ferry.

They led the way up narrow stairways and along corridors congested with leather-suited Swedes who acted as if they were departing on a vacation cruise. There were shouts and cheers as people met, kissed, and shook hands. Niklas and Conrad were greeted often, and each time they'd take a moment to introduce Suzanne and me. Suzanne said she felt underdressed in her denim jeans, worn jacket, and hiking boots. Most of the riders wore suits that appeared form-fitted and freshly oiled. They were multicolored with bright reds, blues, and stark whites in ornate patterns on their chests, arms, and legs, and most of the riders wore matching knee-high leather boots.

We found an empty table and dragged it to a place out of the wind that provided a view of the port. Conrad offered Suzanne a chair and he wiped it first with his leather gloves. "For you," he said as he set it down behind her.

"So, you really know nothing of this rally?" Niklas asked. "A surprise for you. Like coming from Mars."

Suzanne asked them both what the rally was all about. Niklas' round, boyish face brightened and a deeply pleasurable smile consumed it. Conrad laughed and raised his hands with a shrug. "Mine English," he said. "I have not the words."

The ferry began to pull away from the harbor, and as Conrad and Niklas laughed at our ignorance, Suzanne pulled at my elbow and pointed to the port. There we saw a long line of motorcycles racing for the ship. They were going so fast I wondered if they wouldn't make a jump for it.

"They come like that all day," Niklas mused. "And the next."

"But what's it like?" Suzanne asked again.

"I have come for, let me see...five years," Niklas said. "Every year is something different. It is very special. A big party. Competitions. Everyone has a great time."

"Many friends," Conrad said seriously, and he strained to find the words to say more.

"You must see for yourself," Niklas said. "It would be a great experience for you. A special look at Swedish culture."

"*Motorcycle* culture," Conrad corrected.

"You have these in America, yes?" Niklas asked.

"Yes. But we've never been to one," I said.

"Then it will be good for you," he decided.

"You can camp with us," Conrad offered.

I looked at Suzanne and she shrugged.

"We don't have any other plans," I said.

"Then you will come?"

Conrad was earnest and kind, with a fragility that was revealed in his pockmarked face and in his thin hands that shook like an old man's when he was searching for the right word. He had a thoughtfulness about him that made me think spending time with him could be very enjoyable. During the five-hour passage to Gotland he told us in halting English about his job as a bus mechanic for the city of Borås. He had begun as an apprentice doing odd jobs and grunt work in the garage, but he was now working on engines, unassisted. He hoped that in a few years he could take a trip abroad, perhaps to America. Either that or he'd buy a house.

Niklas, on the other hand, had bravado and a gregarious nature. His English was polished, and he explained in great detail his work with a computer firm and his many travels. Niklas had been to California three times and said he had once gotten to know a woman there. He asked us if we'd been to any of his favorite beaches between Los Angeles and San Diego. He knew all the best ski slopes in Austria, France, and Switzerland, and he was hoping for a better job that would allow him to travel even more.

"But," Niklas said, "there is something very special about Gotland, and I like to travel there. For the Swedish people, it is like the Grand Canyon in America. No, it's even more important. There is something, how do you say, spiritual about it. Almost every Swedish person goes there sometime in their life."

I'd heard that before. We met a woman in Åseda who went on at length about what we should see and do on Gotland. She told us about the beautiful walled medieval city of Visby, the stone churches, and the smell of the sea. She told us about the windmills, the pinnacle-like limestone formations along the north coast, the food, forests, wildlife, and a particularly inspiring field of wildflowers, which she gave us precise directions to. She spoke as if she'd just returned. I asked when she'd been there. She said almost forty years ago.

"For typical Swedish people, it is some kind of pilgrimage," Niklas explained. "Like a true pilgrim, he must do it the hard way. Not like us, on motorcycles, but with one of these antique bicycles you see the old people ride. They have one speed!" he said holding up the index finger of his right hand, and Conrad nodded in agreement. "Not like these fancy mountain bikes I see in California, with twenty-one speeds. The people rent them in Visby and then ride around the island. They ride from church to church, because wherever you are on Gotland you can always see the tower of the next church."

"How long does it take?" Suzanne asked.

"One week, ten days. Depends. These bicycles go very slow."

"You must be careful from them on the road," Conrad warned. "The rider...they gets so tired. Sometime they know not what they do...and ride right down the road. You can make a wreck with one. Motorcycle is better."

~~~

Gotland Island appeared on the horizon like a lush green encasement that held the gleaming gem of Visby. The limestone walls that surround the town were visible miles from shore and seemed all the brighter poised above the dark waters of the Baltic. As the ship drew closer I could make out the silhouettes of towers from within the city and turrets along the stone wall that surrounds it.

"A beautiful town," Niklas said. "Medieval. Can be very romantic."

"It looks Mediterranean," Suzanne said.

Like Öland, Gotland has been inhabited since the Stone Age and was a center of pagan culture. During the eleventh century it became a major international trade center of the Hanseatic League. Its power and influence grew until Gotland became an independent republic and, for a time, was one of the major powers of medieval Europe, rivaling London and Paris for influence and prestige. The town was host to thriving populations of tradesmen, pirates, clergy, merchants, farmers, politicians, and speculators. Despite the town's small size, its citizens built some of Europe's most impressive homes. Visby's port was one of Europe's busiest, and by the thirteenth century it grew to include sixteen churches and a major cathedral. And to protect it all, Visby was surrounded by one of the most formidable defensive walls in all Europe.

We followed Conrad and Niklas from the ferry and through a narrow stone portal into Visby. The cobblestone passages between the buildings were steep, dark, and narrow, and often doubled back on themselves like a maze. It was easy to imagine pirates, speculators, merchants, and clergy peering out at us from their shops and dens as we passed. In their place were hungry-eyed t-shirt and sunglass vendors, hawkers of seascapes, wool sweaters and sheepskin jackets, antiques, nautical equipment, and day-glo swimwear, all of them waiting for the first tourists who would mark the beginning of the summer season. We must have appeared like harbingers to them as they eyed us from their fat shops, but we didn't stop.

Niklas led us out of Visby, and just a few miles south of town we joined a phalanx of motorcycles headed in the same direction. We turned at a place named Kneippbyn, a small community of homes built at the top of a cliff with a wide view of the sea, and then we descended into a large area where a tent city was already under construction. We rode across a field to a remote corner and stopped.

"Beautiful, yes?" Niklas proclaimed. "From here we can see everything that happens."

"But *what* will we see?" Suzanne asked again.

"Oh, just wait," he said, and pointed to two women, supported by a man between them, who stumbled across the field below us. They were hollering and drunk and each clutched a bottle as if it were something essential.

"What are they yelling about?" I asked.

"No," Conrad said, his face flushing. "I say not with Suzanne."

"Well," Niklas said. "Let me just say it is about something the girls want from him in his tent."

Someone roared by on their motorcycle, the engine revved so high it vibrated my ears until they itched.

"Big surprises for you," Niklas said laughing, as if bringing us to the rally had been a joke and it was time to reveal the punch line.

Another motorcycle engine revved and the sound swelled across the camping area. It sounded as though the bike was going a hundred miles an hour, but it wasn't moving at all. Then the tire began to spin, creating a plume of gray smoke as big as a dream.

"Burn out!" Conrad said.

We watched the smoke rise, and then bend and break as a breeze rolled it across the field.

I looked at Suzanne. She was watching the scene with a look of astonished fascination. The palms of her hands were pressed over her ears. She nudged me with her elbow and tried to say something.

"What?" I asked.

"What have we gotten into this time?"

~~~

Niklas assured us our tents were in an ideal spot. "The others stay down there," he said, pointing to a multiplying cluster of people, tents, and motorcycles. "We camp here every year."

It was still early, and after setting up our tent, Suzanne and I left on the motorcycle to explore the island. Her allergies were better and she was buoyant in their absence. Perhaps the rest she'd had at Chester and Ingrid's helped, or perhaps the plant that produced the offending pollen had blossomed and died back for the year.

They were lanes and tracks, not roads, and we followed them along the cliffs above the sea. The water shone with a metallic sheen that made me think we could ride out across it, an illusion that was only broken by seabirds that fell from the sky onto fish like bullets through glass. We followed the roads through meadows of poppies, buttercups, and lupine, past lakes thick with lily pads in bloom, their flowers like small fires burning on the surface of the water. We followed them through ancient forests where the trees were thick and heavy with leaves and time. And almost always, somewhere on the horizon, we could see the steeple of the next church.

We stopped in Lau, a village of neat, single-story homes, farm buildings, and the oldest church on the island. The church sat unremarkably on the corner of two streets and was assembled from thick, off-white stones that had settled against each other over the centuries. The interior was still and close. It was cold and smelled of dust and wax. When the door closed behind us it was as though the world had been eclipsed and we were enveloped by an immense noiselessness.

The walls of the church were unadorned and the only objects inside were an iron cross fixed against the back wall, an old podium, and two rows of worn wooden pews that occupied a small portion of the floor. There was also a rope that hung from the steeple and ended in a neat coil on the floor. Just above eye level was a two-foot section so darkened and polished from the grasp and pull of hands over so many years that it shone like the skin of a snake. The church suddenly felt remarkably old and substantial as I imagined the number of times two hands would have to grasp a rope to polish it to such a rich luster. I could only imagine all the services, marriages, baptisms, deaths, fires, invasions, and harvests that had been announced through it. Suzanne and I sat beside each other in the front pew and watched a ray of light move across a wall marking the earth's revolution through yet another day. Neither of us moved for a long time, and we didn't speak. I was content watching the light, listening to the smooth cycling of Suzanne's breath, while contemplating time through a length of rope.

In an instant the ray of light was extinguished, and the interior of the church darkened as if the earth had slipped too quickly into night.

"Another storm," Suzanne said calmly.

We walked outside. A curtain of dark clouds had covered the sun, and the wind was building, rattling the leaves of the birch trees in the church yard. We got on the bike and outran the storm. We skirted its edge and moved beyond it as it invaded southern Gotland, but upon our return to the campground we discovered a different kind of storm was brewing.

~~~

It was as though a Hollywood producer had come and set up production for a Swedish sequel to *The Wild Ones*. The number of people and bikes had grown exponentially in our absence, and to reach our tent we had to ride through a maze of high-powered sport bikes, a neat line-up of customized Harley-Davidsons, and past riders encased in bright leathers and helmets with mirrored visors that reflected our image as we rode by. A large crowd was assembled around a billowing spire of smoke, and from its midst came a high-pitched scream as if some kind of Industrial Age sacrifice were being conducted there. Nearly everyone we passed had a drink in hand—a beer, a bottle of whiskey or vodka, a jug of something homemade. We had to ride carefully around three bodies on the ground, one with his face bent to one side so it looked as though his neck was broken. Out of nowhere someone passed dangerously close to us, riding a wheelie.

Niklas was smiling as we rode up. He looked happy, as if things were shaping up exactly as he had envisioned. He stood there like the producer of it all, and he seemed ready to turn it up a little farther.

"What do you think?" he asked us above the noise. "Great, huh? Here. Have a beer."

Conrad stood beside him, his eyes bright from alcohol and excitement. "They come all the day from the ship," he said. "They come all night."

Suzanne let her helmet drop to her feet and walked forward a few steps. "Who's that?" she asked Niklas, pointing to an early model American car with a Confederate flag painted on the hood. It was overflowing with writhing bodies, and though it was stopped, it bounced and hopped as if it was speeding over a very rough road.

"Groupies," he said. "They don't have money for motorcycles, so they come in that car."

Farther down the slope someone revved another engine and nursed the rpms before releasing the clutch and spinning the tire

on the asphalt. A cloud of smoke curled off the ground and consumed the rider. The spinning went on and on. The engine
reached a plateau and held steady as smoke poured from the tire
like a great fire.

"Oh, my," Niklas said. "She's crazy!"

"*She?*"

"Yes. I know her."

"It's going to blow up!" Suzanne said, and covered her ears.

The noise went on for so long that I thought it must blow up,
that the forces within the engine would impel it to fracture and
splinter and cause an explosion of metal and oil and body parts
that would be a kind of baptism for the cheering crowd. But the
engine didn't blow. Instead it backfired like a small cannon and
blew a flame out the tailpipe that illuminated the smoke. The engine slowed. The smoke cleared, revealing the rider intact. Then
she rode away as politely as she would from a stop sign in front of
a cop.

"Come on," Niklas said before the smoke had cleared. "You're
just in time for the competitions."

The competitions, he explained, were a series of games and
contests between the many motorcycle clubs that would last the
weekend, and the first were about to begin.

"The women go first," he said, with a mischievous smile.

Suzanne and I followed Niklas and Conrad to a sloping lawn
that served as bleachers for the gathering crowd. Below it was a
flat area with a bandshell and stage, and just beyond that was a
cliff above the sea. Paraphernalia required for the contests had
been assembled in front of the stage: two waist-high poles nailed
into the ground, two lines of orange road cones, and several lines
drawn with chalk over the grass. A man with a microphone
seemed to be waiting for a critical mass in order to begin.

We sat on the grass and I thought how the setting would be
ideal for a production of *The Valkyries of Odin,* or *The Hammer of
Thor,* something befitting the history of the island and the scope
of the sea and sky before us. But the crowd seemed primed for
something Roman, something with lions and slaves.

Most were drunk or well on their way to being so. Empty bottles and cans of beer seemed to multiply on the grass as we waited for the games to begin. Occasionally the crowd broke out in a spontaneous song or chant, or a group of men began wrestling, rolling down the lawn in an embrace of red faces.

The man with the microphone began to speak, but his words were drowned by cheers and whistling. Several women representing two of the motorcycle clubs assembled around him, and the first game began.

"What do they have to do?" Suzanne asked.

"Just watch," Niklas said.

Each woman positioned herself along a chalk mark and seemed poised to begin running over the cliff into the sea. Some of the women stretched or jumped like athletes. The man with the microphone blew a whistle and each woman began peeling her clothes from her body and laying the pieces on the ground. Niklas laughed and held his beer in the air in salute. Suzanne looked at me as if this were a bad joke.

The crowd cheered as the women removed their bras, socks, jeans, and underwear, and arranged them in careful lines that stretched over the grass. And when all their clothes were on the ground they rushed back to the beginning of the line and began to pull and stretch each garment between them to maximum length, and then rearranged them in as straight a line as possible. The man with the microphone called for time. The teams made last-minute adjustments and their supporters in the crowd chanted the names of their clubs. "Lille-bror! Lille-bror! Lille-bror!" "Lek-sand! Lek-sand! Lek-sand!" A whistle was blown and two men measured each line with a tape measure before declaring the winner. The two teams collected their clothes and regrouped as they dressed.

The second contest was a relay that required each woman on a team to guzzle a beer, then press her forehead onto the top of a pole and pivot ten times around it clockwise, and ten more times counterclockwise. Then each woman had to run through a slalom course of cones to her waiting teammates who were yelling and screaming encouragement. Most of the women crumpled and fell as they moved from the pole. They staggered dizzily, their eyes wide and desperate as their bodies began to list and fall to the earth as if they'd received a blow to the head. Many women crawled forward on their hands and knees between the cones, then rose sickly to their feet with efforts that seemed heroic, and then began staggering to their waiting teams. A stranger handed Suzanne a beer and slapped her on the shoulder. A woman passed out behind me and rolled against my back. Niklas fell backward and convulsed with laughter.

"God!" Suzanne yelled above the noise.

The storm we had encountered earlier spread over Kneippbyn like smoke from an oil fire. Golden veins of lightning shot from its darkness and probed the surface of the sea, and soon after the first drops of rain began to fall.

The games were hurriedly concluded and the crowd migrated beneath a covered area where food and drinks were served at picnic tables. A juke box played Bruce Springsteen's "Born in the USA" over and over, and it sounded as if half the motorcyclists joined the chorus. *"Booorn in the U-S-A! Booorn in the U-S-A!"* they sang and we couldn't hear the rain that pummeled the roof. Someone pulled the plug on the jukebox. A troll-like guitarist dressed like Johnny Cash took the stage and he began singing Swedish drinking songs.

The crowd became increasingly drunk and boisterous. People began to stumble into tables, fall into each other, and collapse. One man staggered from table to table and pulled people's hair. He'd shuffle up behind his victims as though he were trying to catch a fly on the backs of their heads. Then he'd grab a hunk of hair, give a sharp tug, and laugh hysterically. A boy so drunk that he drooled hovered around Suzanne and tried to get her to dance. She pushed him gently away and he became confused, as if he'd been pushed into another world. People passed out in their chairs, their heads laid like melons on the table. The guitarist began to sound like a toy whose batteries had run low. He began to have a difficult time holding his guitar and keeping his head up. Then he stumbled and fell forward off the front of the stage. He landed on his guitar, cracking the neck and smashing the body. Those who could cheered, and two men dragged the guitarist outside and laid him on the ground in the rain. Someone plugged the juke box back in. *"Booorn in the U-S-A! Booorn in the U-S-A!"*

~~~

I woke early the next morning and stepped outside our tent. The camp was utterly quiet. It looked abused. Cans and bottles lay everywhere. A motorcycle was on its side in the mud, and a jacket, several pairs of pants, and underwear were scattered across the ground like rude seeds. The quiet and destruction reminded me of the morning after a battle.

It wasn't long before others began to stir and crawl from their tents. They looked thick and beaten as they searched for places to pee. Someone turned on a radio and the easy rhythms of Glenn Miller softened the scene. One of the guys in the car painted with the Confederate flag swore and cranked up some heavy-metal. Suzanne groaned from inside our tent. Below us someone started their bike, revved it up, and did a burnout that woke the rest of the camp. A big blond man crawled from his tent naked. He snorted, and sucked something up from the depths of his throat and spit it on the ground. Then he inflated his chest and gave a piercing Viking yell that tore through the trees. It was like a signal because when his yell had faded it seemed that half the camp had started to drink again. It was only seven o'clock.

~~~

Suzanne and I rode north along the coast. After the rain the air was crystalline, washed and focused so every aspect of the landscape seemed to have an urgent vitality. The red tile roof of a house looked molten against the sky, and I was tempted to reach out and touch it. The sea simmered with convections that promised to part and let us glimpse a serpent if we just looked long enough. The coil of the road unwound before us in a way that made me wish it would never end, that we'd never have to stop again for fuel or food or sleep, and that the seduction of each curve would be enough to keep pulling us forward.

We rode fast along an empty coast, through woodlands and meadows that were void of human intervention. We rode to Farö-sund, a village with a small ferry that took us across a narrow sound to the island of Farö. *Farö* is the Swedish word for sheep, and it seemed an appropriate name because sheep were about the only thing the stony fields of the island could sustain. The soil was paper-thin, and often there was none at all. Stunted pines dotted the ground like cast-off bonsai, and grasses grew in sparse tufts like hair from moles. The landscape looked like an abandoned project, as if God had been called away from his work there and had forgotten to return. We turned onto a shale track that led to the sea, and there, along the shore, were coral columns called seastacks—the eroded remains of an ancient reef that once thrived when Sweden lay in a tropical zone. The columns stood as high as thirty feet above the beach, and from a distance they looked like melting Grecian columns.

"Like a Dali painting," Suzanne said, as we got off the bike.

The wind whipped off the Baltic and carried with it a charge of sand that blasted us from the knees down. We found shelter in the lee of a column and listened to the hiss of the sand as it abraded its way toward us. We sat down and watched the surf as it rushed and pulled at the beach, and we breathed the dusty brine of the air until the last traces of burned rubber were cleansed from us. Several black geese fed offshore, impervious to the wind. Among them was a clutch of some twenty or thirty goslings that scurried like crashing electrons around a nucleus. White gulls dove at any of them that were blown from their orbit, and each time they did one of the adult geese raised its long neck to pluck the gulls from the sky. I pictured the rest of our trip in my mind, the miles and countries and weeks, and they seemed too few.

~~~

When we arrived back at our campsite we had to step over the body of a young man who had passed out in front of our tent. His close-cropped blond hair was muddy from rolling on the ground, and one eye was partially open and rolled back so we could see only the white.

"Jesus!" Suzanne said. "Is he dead?"

A woman walked over and called his name, but when he didn't move, she laughed and staggered on.

Niklas and Conrad called us and we walked over to them. We had almost reached them when a drunken voice yelled, "Ayyyyy! Misser an Misses Ameriga!"

"Oh shit, Allen. It's that guy who was checking us out at the ferry."

I turned and recognized the man from the ferry, the one who'd scrutinized our bike and license plate but wouldn't talk. He was pushing through a crowd toward us.

"Ayyyy!"

We continued walking toward Niklas and Conrad, but I heard a rush of footsteps, then a press of clumsy weight against my back that nearly knocked me over.

"Where yew go? Stop! Mine nama Sven. Stop!"

I stopped and the man wrapped an arm around me to hold himself up while he caught his breath. I almost retched from the stench as he exhaled his words into my face.

"I be thinking...mine onkle...he leeve in Dee-troit. Yew knows him?"

"No," I said, and started to move away. His clutch of friends and the boy assembled around us, and Sven began relating something to them in Swedish. The group looked disappointed.

"No pro-blem," Sven decided. "Yew meet mine bea'iful woooman, Yoolianna!" Sven motioned toward an owlish woman with tight brown curly hair and a palette of green eye shadow around each eye. "Mine broder, Ro-ber!" Robert cracked a smile and saluted us with a half-empty bottle of Jack Daniels. "An Jan. He

be mine woo-man's lover! Ha ha ha ha ha! An mine sohn, Me-hail.
Now. Wha' be youse nama?"

"We have to go," Suzanne said.

"Stop!" Sven demanded, grabbing hold of a hunk of my jacket.

"Oh! Ah nudder woman," Julianna slurred and moved toward
Suzanne. "Zo many mans here, no? Come wid me," she said, trying to pull Suzanne away. "Stay wid me. Please."

"They'ss not 'ere to talk!" Sven yelled, and pushed Julianna
away. "'Ere! Drink!" From his other hand Sven produced a plastic
gallon jug and pressed it toward my mouth. It smelled of pure alcohol.

"No thanks," I said.

"Drink! Wha kinds of mans iss yew?"

"He iss no mans," Julianna sneered. "Even Mikail drink," she
said, and motioned toward her son, who couldn't have been more
than twelve years old.

"Ja! Eben Me-hail drink!" Sven declared, and then began
laughing so hard his body bent at the knees.

As he laughed I could see inside Sven's open mouth. I
watched with fascination as his thick, pink tongue scraped the
uvula back and forth against the roof of his mouth and thick
chords of saliva hung from his teeth. Mikail looked away from us,
saying nothing, ashamed.

"Isn't Mikail a little young to be drinking?" I asked.

"Hims?" Sven asked, and then handed his son the jug. "He be
juss like ees mudder...drink ever days an nights."

"Ach! He be not mine sohn," Julianna corrected. "He be mine
beer holder!"

It must have been a joke of theirs because they all began
laughing, except Mikail, and as they laughed Suzanne and I edged
away. The last I remember of them is the wet, pink insides of their
mouths, their tongues tucked behind their teeth like fists, their
bodies convulsing as they struggled to laugh and breathe at the
same time.

We found Niklas and Conrad beside what had become the burnout pit, a short stretch of asphalt that was reasonably flat. They were standing off to one side while a boy maneuvered his car into place.

"What's he doing?" I asked.

"He wants to blow up the engine," Niklas said. "Someone dared him."

"Too much spirits," Conrad said, and twirled his index finger around the side of his head to say the boy was crazy. I wondered if he meant spirits as in alcohol or that the boy was possessed.

It was an old car but in good shape. It looked like someone had taken care of it.

"He lives around here," Niklas said. "A farm boy."

I wondered if it was his parent's car and if he had come to see what was going on, gotten drunk with a bunch of guys, and started talking. He fumbled with a cigarette that had fallen from his lips and inhaled deeply. His movements were adrenal, his eyes dilated.

It seemed that most of the camp had gathered around as news spread of the boy's intentions. He got out of his car and walked over to talk with someone. His hands were shaking and for a moment I thought he was manufacturing an excuse, but I was wrong. He wanted people to move farther back and was asking for help. The crowd backed away and he climbed into his car.

The boy jammed the car into gear and began running the engine up in short bursts that were like steps. I watched his face through the window. He looked crazed, as if he were about to blast into space. His eyes were fixed on the dash, his teeth clenched, and both hands clutched the steering wheel as though he was holding the engine together.

The boy revved the engine still higher and then let out the clutch. The engine dragged for a second and the boy looked worried. I thought the engine might sputter and die, but the rear wheels began to turn slowly, then faster and faster as he nursed the throttle, and the air began to fill with smoke.

A look of hope washed over the boy's face, then satisfaction as the tires kept turning and the engine screamed. He lifted his eyes from the dash and looked out at the crowd. People cheered and the boy began to bounce lightly in the seat as if to keep the momentum going. He lifted his right hand from the steering wheel and waved.

The noise was deafening and the ground shook beneath our feet. People began to step farther back. Suzanne grabbed my arm and pulled me away. Smoke enveloped the car. The boy's smiling face seemed to dissolve into it, and then, as if he were about to die a heroic death, his fist rose in victory through the window.

We were devoured by a white-out of acrid smoke. It sounded as though the car was everywhere around us, and I remember thinking it couldn't last much longer. I remember thinking, *This has got to end. It's got to blow,* and each time I heard a tick, each time the engine sounded like it was coming apart, it didn't.

Then, finally, the engine seemed to yawn. It wasn't a loud sound but I knew something deep inside had come undone. It was followed by a heavy shudder, a strange and discordant racing that sounded as if half the engine was going faster than the other. There was a backfire, a series of pops, and then nothing. For a moment there was only silence, and then someone began to clap. The smoke cleared and the boy emerged, both hands raised above his head. He looked so supremely satisfied with himself that I wondered what could possibly happen during the rest of his life to compete with this moment. Someone handed him a beer. Another gave him a fresh cigarette. People clapped him on the back and shook his hand.

~~~

That evening the entire camp became a raging party that rose in pitch like the engine of the boy's car, and I expected it to explode in the same way. I expected a fight to break out between one of the yelling, thrashing mobs, or for someone to be run over by one of the careening motorcycles. Niklas laughed at me when I told him so and reminded me we weren't in America, and that I could relax. He said such things are almost unheard of in Sweden, and I was amazed to see that he was right. No matter how drunk and rowdy people became, voices were only raised in cheer and greeting and hands were raised only to embrace a friend or reach for another bottle. When someone did begin to get out of line, a friend gently pulled him aside and quieted him down.

But there was another kind of violence in the extent of the drunkenness. It was the abandon with which the party-goers embraced alcohol, almost to a man and woman. We were amazed at the carpet of empty containers that lay on the ground and the squads of near-zombies who staggered back and forth across the camp, and the fact that nobody was dead. We began to recognize the same people from the night before, not because of their faces, but because of their drunken posture and antics.

The boy who had passed out in front of our tent was still there hours later, still locked in the same poisoned state like one of the cemented bodies unearthed at Pompeii. Suzanne put her hand above his mouth and announced he was still alive.

"Look at that!" Niklas said.

A man from the Confederate car was crawling on his hands and knees through the mud. It was the first time I'd ever seen someone stagger while on all fours, and he looked mortally wounded, like a deer that had been shot in the gut. All of the man's attention was focused on the muddy earth and the excruciating movement of his hands over it. He seemed to be looking through the top of his head to find his way.

"My God!" Suzanne said. "This is beyond ridiculous!"

"Auf!" Conrad winced when the man tripped and fell on his left side.

"Where is he going?" Niklas asked.

The man pushed himself upright, faltered, and began moving again.

"Maybe to the trees to die."

"No. He goes to that tent."

Sloth-like, the man changed course and crawled toward a small orange tent. He steadied himself on one hand and blindly felt for a zipper with the other. While doing so he collapsed twice, and each time he pushed himself up. I found myself rooting for him.

"Left! Left!" Niklas directed. "No! Ahhh! He fell again!"

The man fumbled in his pants' pocket as if he had an annoying itch there. He pulled out a knife, opened the blade with his teeth, and began tearing at the side of the tent. He made a hole, crawled halfway in, and collapsed one last time.

Suzanne looked grave, as though she'd witnessed something so repulsive she couldn't respond.

"These people are missing an enzyme, Allen! I can't take much more of this."

Someone did a burnout. Suzanne rolled her eyes, and we waited for the noise to die.

"I feel like I'm on overload," she continued. "Like my nerves are fraying the longer we stay here."

"Everyone is leaving in the morning," I said. "We'll be on our own again then."

"It won't be soon enough for me. If they were all like Niklas and Conrad, that would be one thing. But shit, Allen, *look* at these people! It's pathetic."

"It's also pretty fascinating," I said.

"You don't get it. This is insanity!" she said and glowered at me.

"If this trip was a story you were reading about," I continued, "wouldn't this be a part you'd stop at and want me to read?"

"That's not fair."

"To be fair," I said, "we didn't come here knowing we'd see burnouts and drunks. We came because we were curious and all this happened around us."

"That's the problem! I just wanted to have a nice trip out here, and you're actually interested in this shit!"

"Allen! Suzanne!" Niklas called to us.

"Don't take it so personally," I said to her. "Tomorrow we'll be on to something else."

"Hey! Suzanne! Allen!"

Niklas waved for us to join him. He was smiling as if he had another surprise.

"Some fellow Americans to see you," he said, and then I noticed them, a couple in their late fifties standing uncomfortably to one side of Niklas. They were both fit, tanned, and their skin glowed with middle-aged vitality. They wore sturdy khaki pants, comfortably loose cotton shirts, and running shoes.

"Hi! We heard there were two Americans down here, and we just had to come take a look. I'm Bob, and this is my wife, Sharon."

"Allen and Suzanne," I said.

"My, my. What brings you here? Do you live in Sweden?" Bob asked.

"No," I said. "We're riding our motorcycle around the Baltic Sea."

"How wonderful!" Sharon said.

"Nothing like doing it when you're young!" Bob said.

"And you? What brings you here?"

"Oh, Sharon's relatives own this campground, and she's been doing some family research here on Gotland. Hey, if you'd like a break from all this chaos, come up and see us. We're staying in the villa over there on the hill." Bob pointed to a big California-style beach house with floor-to-ceiling windows overlooking the camp and the sea beyond. The place had been staring down at us all weekend, and I'd wondered who could possibly live there.

"We'd like that," Suzanne said.

"Please do. I'm serious now. It's just Sharon and me up there, and we'd enjoy the company."

~~~

From the living room of the villa I could see more of the sea than I could land, creating the illusion that I could step through the window and wade around in it. Bob and Sharon had four places set at a table in the middle of the room, and the view was as accessible from the table as the spoon and napkin set beside each teacup. From my place at the table I could look directly onto the camp and our place in it. I could see our motorcycle, our tent, and the body of the boy still passed out in front of it. The shabbiness of the camp was so apparent from the villa, and I realized that if I stumbled onto it, I would probably turn away. Smoke from several fires created a gray mask in the air. Groups of people swayed and staggered around tents, and a large group danced around the car painted with the Confederate flag.

"What's it like to spend time down there?" Bob asked excitedly.

"It's like being back in time," I said. "Reminds me of the pagan rituals I read about."

"How's that?" Bob asked.

"The equinox and solstice celebrations had this same kind of frenzy about them, the drinking and excess, and the motorcycles are good metaphors for virility, power, daring, and speed."

"It's pretty adolescent, if you ask me," Suzanne said.

"How so?" Sharon asked.

"It's just a big rowdy drunk. Too many hormones and big bikes," Suzanne continued.

"One woman I spoke with explained it as a celebration for having survived the long Swedish winter," I said, "which is what made me think of the pagan rituals."

"Doesn't it make you feel uncomfortable to be down there?" Bob asked while leaning forward. "Last night it looked like a bunch of Vikings getting ready to storm the castle."

"I was just thinking about how bad it looks from here," I said. "The fires, the bikes, and all the noise. But it also has a kind of innocence. There hasn't been a single fight, or even harsh words. Aside from drinking themselves into a stupor, there's a kind of reserve about them. Beneath the noise and leather they're almost docile."

"It's tiring," Suzanne said. "Last night we saw people so drunk they couldn't walk, and the same people were drinking again this morning. It's incredible!"

"We walked through the little village of Kneippbyn today," Sharon said. "Some of the older people asked if it was safe to leave their homes. They're very concerned."

"I don't think there's anything to worry about," I said. "If one of the bikers were to get out of hand in town, it wouldn't take much scolding to make them mind."

"It's how they look," Sharon said. "Dressed in those leather suits and big helmets, revving their engines wherever they go. I think it is kind of scary."

"Yes, but you should see them take their helmets and suits off," I said. "It's quite a contrast. I saw a kid yesterday who looked like a fighter pilot. He even had a swagger. Then he took off his helmet and he was nothing but a skinny kid with greasy hair and pimples. And under his leather suit he had on what looked like pajamas."

The whistle on the kettle blew and Sharon went to the kitchen for the tea.

Bob got up and walked to the edge of the window. "Look at that," he said just above a whisper, and Suzanne and I followed him. It was as though we were spying on an encampment of marauding soldiers. Off in the distant we saw a bonfire blaze high into the sky. "Are they throwing gasoline on it?" he asked. In the light of the fire I saw the illuminated bodies of frenzied dancers leaping toward the flames.

~~~

The camp emptied like a ragged circus leaving town. Motorcycles were packed like mules. Riders slipped into their leathers, pulled on their helmets and boots, and rode slowly away to the ferries. The car painted with the Confederate flag drove off, leaving behind it a trail of blue exhaust. Niklas and Conrad left soon after and we waved good-bye until they disappeared through the gate of the camp. We listened to the whine of the engines fade, and then we were alone again.

The camp was empty except for our lone tent billowing in the wind and the small orange one with the hole cut in the side not far away. Its roofline swayed as though in danger of collapsing. The hole in the side opened and closed like a panting animal. I walked over and looked tentatively in, as if it still contained something of the boy and what he'd been through. Inside was a crumpled sleeping bag, some clothes, and empty beer cans. The front zipper was zipped tight and toward the back was a big paper bag I didn't want to touch. Tomorrow the cleaning crew would take it down and throw it away with the other garbage left behind. Then, in a day or so, families would arrive to camp on the grassy slope overlooking the sea. Fresh grass would push through the earth and grow again where it had been trodden and burned. Children would come upon the rubber burns that were like crop circles on the pavement and wonder what had caused them. And then, I hoped, later in the year a troupe of actors would appear and set up a stage at the bottom of the sloping hill and recite from one of the old Scandinavian epics like the *Ynglinga Saga*, "...in this time the people of the land became richer, on account of peace and good seasons, than ever before."

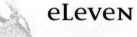

eLeveN

A popping noise woke me, and for a moment I wondered if it was yet another motorcycle trick, or someone beating a carpet.

"Hey, sleepyhead. You awake?" Suzanne said.

"What's that noise?" I asked her.

"It's just the wind popping the sides of the tent," she said, and brushed my hair from my forehead.

Suzanne was already dressed and lying on her sleeping bag, impatient for me to be up, too. The door of the tent was partially open behind her, and through it I could see a sky filled with bruised clouds of purple and orange. The air was cold, and the wind stampeded over the campground.

"We get to stay inside tonight," Suzanne almost sang, and pressed herself against me. "Peace and quiet. We'll be with friends. God, I hope they don't forget we're coming."

~~~

We had met Torbjorn and Jennifer three years earlier on Victoria Street in Sydney, Australia. It was late fall and the wet season had begun, bringing with it incessant deluges. After traveling for several months in the Outback, we had just sold our van to an Austrian couple and were looking for a place to park until they arrived to drive it away. Victoria Street was lined on both sides with the wheeled hulks that had taken travelers around the country. Most of the vehicles were patched and modified station wagons or delivery vans that looked like props for a *Road Warrior* film. The atmosphere was generally festive as travelers from all over the world waited to sell their vehicles, and while doing so traded stories of their adventures.

Parking space was at a premium on Victoria Street, and we asked a guy pacing in front of an orange Volkswagen bus if he would mind pulling forward to make room for us.

"I'm Torbjorn," he said, after helping us park. "And that's Jennifer."

Jennifer was sitting at the small table in the back of their van writing a letter, and she paused to greet Suzanne and me.

Torbjorn and Jennifer had been waiting three days to sell their van, and they were beginning to get frustrated. "But we had a great trip," he said. "Fantastic trip."

We began comparing notes on places we'd been. Suzanne and I knew that we'd made friends when we discovered Jennifer and Torbjorn had also suffered through the same plague of mice in the Outback, a bizarre experience that occurred in the middle of nowhere and included an invasion of mice into our van. For an entire night they ran along our bodies and over our faces in a frantic search for anything to eat.

Torbjorn was Swedish, Jennifer American, and they lived alternately in either Sweden or America while attending school and traveling. We met a few more times on Victoria Street before leaving Australia and, since they were also traveling north through Indonesia and Asia, we managed to meet them twice more before they left for home. Over the following years we'd kept in contact, and we promised to visit them in Stockholm. They'd invited us to spend Midsummer with them, the Scandinavian holiday that marks the summer solstice, on an island off the coast. It seemed like an especially valuable invitation as the clouds darkened over Gotland.

~~~

Our ferry swayed as the sea pushed and pulled at its mass as if trying to work it loose from the pier. Once we were inside, the ferry moved just enough to make it difficult for us to get off the bike and pull it onto its center stand. The corner we rode into was only dimly lit and it took a moment to join the rhythm of the ship's swaying movement. An attendant in grease-stained coveralls and high rubber boots came over with wooden blocks and a rope. He didn't speak English, and spoke Swedish with an accent we couldn't understand a word of, so he used his hands and he cleaved the air to form the sharp angles of words.

"Use these," he seemed to say. "Put them like this, here and here, and then finish it off with this rope."

We followed his instructions and the blocks fit perfectly. The rope, tied from the frame of the bike to a hook welded to the side of the ship, pulled the weight of the bike onto the blocks for support. I rocked the bike from side to side and it felt stable. I rocked it harder and the rope didn't budge. The attendant returned, checked our work, and said it would be fine.

Suzanne and I stood on the deck, sheltered from the wind by a lifeboat, and watched Visby lose focus as the ferry pushed away from the island. It became a splotch of color, and then just a speck on the horizon. We went inside where it was warm and still and smelled of food.

My idea was to buy food from the ship's cafeteria and sit at one of the formica tables beside a window and watch the sea pass as we ate. We each took a fiberglass tray and began sliding it along a metal counter. On the other side were stainless steel tubs containing bowls with fruit cast in gelatin and covered in cellophane, a bowl of tired looking apples and bananas, cups of yogurt, and cold cereals. There was a platter of open-faced sandwiches dressed with a lettuce leaf, slices of egg, and a thin fillet of herring arranged on the top. Other tubs, which leaked steam from around the edges, were filled with oatmeal, eggs, and meats in thick sauces. I was about to take some coffee, an apple, and a big bowl of oatmeal when Suzanne pulled me lightly by the elbow.

"Wait," she said. "Maybe we should treat ourselves. There's that restaurant we passed at the front of the ship. Wouldn't that be nice?"

"This is fine," I said. "There's fruit, oatmeal.... You liked Ingrid's oatmeal."

"But after all we've been through at the rally, Allen."

"But the food is so expensive here. We knew before we started this trip that would be the case." I thought of the two-dollar tennis-ball-sized heads of wilted lettuce we'd bought so we could have something green, the apples at almost four dollars a pound, and meat so expensive we could only salivate over it. "That restaurant will be outrageously expensive."

I moved toward the buffet again but Suzanne remained resolutely behind me. In my mind the most important expenses were fuel for the bike, fares, and equipment that would take us farther along our route. Suzanne and I had always traveled sparely, a little undernourished, and hungry for experiences. Food was one of the things that just didn't matter while we were on the road. For three months in the Outback we ate nothing but pasta and tomato sauce and oatmeal. Traveling in that way had an ascetic quality that appealed to us. We thought of our travels as pilgrimages. If we made sacrifices, we would be rewarded with experiences and insights. If we were true to the spirit of our pilgrimages, everything would work out. All of our needs would be met.

A tired woman in a stained white smock swayed with the ship and looked at us with impatience from behind the counter. She clutched a ladle and spatula in either hand and she seemed to suggest that we make our selections or move out of her cafeteria. I turned and looked at Suzanne. She'd put her tray back and clutched her bag to her side, and I knew she was going with or without me. I fumed as I put my tray on top of hers and followed her to the front of the ship.

Suzanne glowed as the attractive hostess led us through the dining room. I reluctantly followed them to a cozy table against a wall, but Suzanne asked if we couldn't have one beside a window overlooking the front of the ship and the sea instead. "You'll like that," she said to me and smiled.

The hostess pulled Suzanne's chair back and then tucked her in. Suzanne touched and inspected the crisp white cloth on the table, the sparkling glasses before her, the array of forks and spoons enveloped by the origami of her napkin. She unwrapped it like a gift and arranged it on her lap. The smile on her face was radiant.

"I'll just get something later," I said.

She finished smoothing the napkin on her lap. She was quiet as she arranged her forks and spoons, and then she leaned forward onto her elbows to speak to me. "You know," she said, "I realize you'd rather be down there with the motorcycle eating stale bread, but please don't spoil this for me. Don't give me any crap just because I want a nice breakfast and want to enjoy myself a little after eating out of cans for three days while camping with all those drunken idiots."

"We can't afford this food," I said. "And I don't like feeling railroaded into something like this."

"Allen," she said, and laid her hand on mine. "We can't afford *not* to."

I felt as though she had clenched my lungs in her fist. "What do you mean?"

The skin around Suzanne's lips and chin grew taut as she tried to suppress her tears.

"I mean," she said, and wiped her nose with her napkin. "I mean that I can't do this much longer. It's like you're outrunning me, and I can't keep up. I wonder sometimes if you want me to quit and go home."

We looked at each other and our rancor melted.

"Don't you start crying, too," Suzanne said. "The hostess is coming."

We wiped our eyes and tried to smile.

"Caf-fe? Tae?" the hostess asked, and punctuated each word by alternately raising the polished silver urn in either hand.

"Tea for me, please," Suzanne said. "Allen? What would you like?"

Suzanne smiled hopefully. The hostess waited patiently beside the table, her urns poised to fill my cup with whatever pleased me.

"Coffee," I said.

She filled my cup and left. Suzanne leaned back across the table. "That wasn't so bad, was it? And look." She pointed to a corner of the restaurant. "They have a buffet in here, too. You can have something simple after all."

I looked through the window into the storm and admired the ship's steadfast progress.

"I'm so sorry," I said. "It seems as though you don't want to be here, and the more that becomes apparent, the more I hold onto the trip. It feels like it's all I have."

"We have each other, don't we?"

I arranged my cup and wondered what would happen if I said, "no." We could split up and I could continue alone. Stockholm had an international airport. Suzanne could be home within two days. But I couldn't think farther than that. "We need to be in this together," I said.

Suzanne put her head in her hands and rubbed her eyes. "God. If it wasn't for the weather, everything would be different."

"We can't blame the weather, the people at the rally, or the price of the food. It's us. You were right when you said I'm fascinated with this stuff—all of it. I love the challenges this trip is giving me. I want to keep going. For good reasons you want something different. I don't know how to fix that."

The ship leaned heavily to one side and Suzanne steadied our cups.

"I love you, and I want to finish this together," I said looking at her intently.

Suzanne leaned back in her chair and looked at me.

"So do I," she said. "I don't know how, but that is what I want."

The buffet was formidable. It was arranged on several tables covered with silver platters, ceramic dishes, and bowls. There were baskets of warm rolls and thick slices of fresh bread. There were pastries and bowls of whole-grain cereals and dried fruit. Farther along were tureens of yogurt, mounds of fresh bananas, oranges, kiwis, strawberries, apples, and grapes. A platter of smoked salmon, garnished with fresh dill and lemon, was surrounded by plates of warm and cold meats, a nest of warm soft-boiled eggs, and pitchers of juices. We were on our second plate of food when I reached across the table and took Suzanne's hand.

"Thank you," I said. "I mean it."

~~~

Our ferry docked in Nynäshamn, a port thirty miles south of Stockholm. We gathered our things, went down to the bike, and rode north through the storm.

Halfway to Stockholm we stopped at a gas station and called Jennifer from a phone booth. Both Suzanne and I pressed into it to keep out of the rain and wind as we dialed the number.

"Maybe they've already left for Midsummer," Suzanne said. "We should have called sooner."

Midsummer Day, which falls on the summer solstice, is the biggest holiday in Scandinavia. In ancient times it was a solar ceremony that marked the apex of summer and the beginning of the slide back into winter's darkness. Formerly, it was the one night of the year when supernatural beings were about, and their presence was celebrated with huge bonfires that burned through the night, with dancing, drinking, and brazen abandon. In modern Scandinavia the presence of supernatural beings has been largely forgotten, but Midsummer is still, for many, a time of excess.

The prospect of spending it with Torbjorn and Jennifer appealed to us greatly. Torbjorn's family owned a summer house on a remote island in the archipelago off Stockholm, and every year they gathered there with friends. Jennifer and Torbjorn had spoken fondly of the communal feasts, the Midsummer pole they decorated with wildflowers from the island's meadows, and the dancing and music that lasted throughout the night. They'd spoken too of the island: its remoteness, the absence of roads, a small lake they used for bathing and swimming.

The phone continued to ring.

"Are you sure you dialed the right number?" Suzanne asked.

The storm beat against the phone booth. There was no reason to leave it, so we hung up and dialed their number again.

"Hello? Oh, Suzanne and Allen! You're here! Wait just a minute. I just got in. Let me dry off."

We waited, and when Jennifer picked up the phone again she told us her parents were also visiting. She said that it had been arranged for Suzanne and me to stay with Torbjorn's parents in Tyresö, a town just south of Stockholm.

"It's all set," she assured us, and then gave us directions. "I'll call them now. They'll be expecting you. But we'll see you tonight for dinner. You'll be coming to our place."

The rain and wind were ferocious, so we pushed the bike beneath the roof of the filling station and waited for the worst of it to pass. We watched in fascination as a layer of water accumulated on the road, filled the gutters, and overflowed onto the sidewalk in a matter of minutes. It fell so hard on the roof above us that we had to shout to talk. At one point Suzanne began to laugh and then did a little dance beside the bike.

"I couldn't care less about the rain!" she shouted tauntingly. "We get to stay inside tonight, and I couldn't care less about the rain!"

~~~

Tyresö is a suburb of Stockholm, a community of high-rise apartment blocks, and many smaller ones, that rise from the forest like a cluster of mushrooms. It's a place one wouldn't see in a tourist brochure of Sweden, and it reminded me that life can be ordinary anywhere. There are many communities just like it throughout Sweden, especially outside the larger cities and towns, the result of well-intentioned social engineering during the 1950s

and 1960s. It was as if the building of individual homes had come
to a halt for a time in Sweden and was replaced by planned communities that could be replicated quickly at little cost. Each
stands unto itself, with enough inhabitants to warrant a school,
medical facility, stores, a post office, library, playing fields, parks,
plots for gardens, swim center, and skating rink.

As we rode into Tyresö I became confused by the similarity of
the apartment towers. It was still raining hard. There was traffic,
and Jennifer's precise directions lost their clarity. I was about to
pull over to read through them again when I noticed a man waiting beneath the eaves of a building. He was looking into the storm
like a watchman and waving his arms. I knew the tall, thin frame
belonged to Arne, Torbjorn's father. He saw us, too. Then he
waved with both hands and we rode toward him.

"My God!" he said as we got off the bike.

Arne took half our luggage in his arms and led us to a
cramped elevator that took us to the eighth floor. Inge, his wife,
welcomed us at the door. She showed us our room, gave us towels, and pointed out the tub in the bathroom. We cleaned ourselves up, and when we were done, they called us to the kitchen,
where they'd arranged bread and cheese on a plate. Arne heated
water for tea and put milk and a bowl of sugar on the table. He
and Inge sat down opposite us and arranged themselves.

"So," Arne said. "Tell us where you been."

An hour passed. Our cups were empty, and the bread and
cheese were gone. The storm had picked up again. Inge looked
out the window and winced. From their eighth floor kitchen window we could see only the smoky-gray of the storm.

"A motorcycle!" Inge said.

"Uhmmm," Arne shook his head. "But, no more motorcycle
now. You come to Harö for Midsummer, yes?"

"Ahhh, yes! You must come," Inge insisted. "You need some
little vacation. I can see this."

"That would be wonderful," Suzanne said. "We'd love to go."

"Good! You have a wonderful time on Harö," Arne assured us.
"I loves it there. In one years I spend all my time on Harö."

"He retires," Inge explained. "Me, I have some years left."

Inge worked as a secretary in one of Stockholm's schools. Arne had spent forty years in the printing business, and he couldn't wait to get out.

"The economics," he said. "It be the same all over the world. So many changes I not understand."

"He is old," Inge laughed.

"Ja. Could be. But, in one year," he said, holding his index finger erect, "I be *finis!* No more. I go to Harö."

Arne pronounced it, "Haa-*ruh*." He said it slowly, the same way an Elvis fan I once met in Wyoming said, "Graceland."

Harö is one of more than a thousand islands that form the dense archipelago off the coast of Stockholm. The archipelago was once the home of fishermen and their families who supplied the city with food, but in the last decades it's become a land of summer homes. Inge was raised on Harö. Her mother went there as a young woman to work as a nanny for a well-to-do merchant family. She met the local customs inspector and married him. They worked, saved their money, and finally bought a place of their own.

Torbjorn had told us stories passed down from his grandfather about the storms that blew unimpeded across the Baltic from Russia, about trying to collect enough food for the winters, how he and Inge's mother would row their small boat for a day and a half to Stockholm to sell their fish and buy supplies, and how they'd make the same trip in the winter by walking over the frozen sea.

"Wonderful!" Arne said again. "You see. You love Harö, too."

~~~

At seven o'clock we all rode the elevator to the ground floor, ran through the rain past the bike, and climbed into Arne's car. Suzanne sat on the back seat and sighed. She'd put on the floral print dress and black shoes she'd wrapped in plastic and packed at the bottom of her bag. Despite the wrinkles in the fabric and her leather jacket she looked transformed. She'd added a hint of blue to the outside corner of each eyelid and stroked her lashes with a touch of mascara.

"Ahhhh! This is so nice," she said of the car. "I'm going to enjoy every minute of it."

"You like my car, Suzanne?"

"Yes! It's wonderful to ride in a car again, to stretch out, and not put my rain suit and helmet on. *This* is the life."

"I sell it to you," Arne joked. "You drive in back from Allen on the motorbike."

Suzanne absorbed the seat. She stretched out her legs and let her arms fall to either side of her body. She closed her eyes and her face relaxed. She could have been on the most comfortable bed in the world. I put my hand on her lap and she pulled me beside her.

~~~

Jennifer and Torbjorn lived on the north side of Stockholm, a half-hour drive that took us through the city. Arne called out the names of landmarks as we passed them: "Globen," he said of a huge golf ball-shaped building. "They play some sport there."

We crossed a bridge that spanned a body of water, and to either side were inlets, coves, and waterways. An ordered skyline rose along the shoreline on the opposite side. Suzanne and I sat up in the back seat to look out the windows as Arne pointed. As we drew closer I saw the city in greater detail. There were huge ice-breakers, ferries, and container ships tied along the shore. A light-blue subway train emerged from a tunnel and rushed toward the center of the city. I saw black church steeples, green copper roofs, and ochre- and rose-colored palaces.

"Is all built on granite," Arne said of the city. "Granite and water. That's Riksdagenshus, where the government lives," he said of an ornate and squat building beside the water. "Over there, opera."

I scanned the city for the buildings he named, but they were all ornate and formal enough to be operas and parliament buildings.

"Skeppsholmen. There," Arne said, and pointed across the harbor.

"Ship Island," Inge translated.

A sleek, white sailing vessel with three tall masts was moored against the shore.

"Gamla Stan," Arne said, and nodded toward the right.

"Old Town," Inge translated again.

Suzanne and I crowded against the right window to see the small island where the oldest section of Stockholm lay. As our car passed we were able to snatch a glance of the Renaissance facades, ornate entryways, and hairline alleys that ran between the buildings.

"Very beautiful. You must go there," Inge continued. "So old."

Our view of the city was eclipsed as the car entered a long tunnel that took us beneath the city, and as suddenly we were deposited in the middle of a busy intersection. Rain and wind lashed the streets. They were nearly deserted except for a couple hurrying along the sidewalk as they left a restaurant. They held their umbrella in front of them like a shield as they moved along.

The world outside was like a silent movie. There was no sensation of the gusts of wind or the blasts of rain. The interior of the car was still and warm, filled only with the murmur of our voices and the soft scraping of the windshield wipers. I opened my window a crack and the wind rushed in, carrying with it a drizzle of rain I felt on my face.

"Do you miss it?" Suzanne wanted to know.

~~~

Torbjorn and Jennifer's apartment was filled with a womblike warmth. It was the kind of warmth that invited us to remove our jackets as we walked into it, the kind that worked its way below our skin like a salve, a warmth I would never have noticed had we not been without it for so long.

Jennifer asked if we wanted a cocktail. The word sounded deliciously exotic, and I welcomed the tumbler of whiskey and ice she handed me. The liquid went down my throat like an abrasive cord, and then swelled and glowed in apology. We all sat around a low

table—Torbjorn and Jennifer, their parents, Suzanne and I. Rob
and Ginny, Jennifer's parents, had just completed a Jewels-of-the-
Baltic cruise that had taken them to Tallinn, St. Petersburg,
Helsinki, and Stockholm. I listened as they annoyingly described
long periods below deck because of the storms, the mediocre food,
the wreckage and squalor of Tallinn and St. Petersburg, and how it
wasn't a trip they'd recommend. Arne assured them Harö would be
different, that it was beautiful there, and it hadn't rained on Midsummer since before he was born.

"I'll drink to that," Ginny said.

Across the table from me Suzanne talked animatedly with Jennifer. She laughed and smiled, and it seemed that everything could
be right again.

twelve

Suzanne and I joined the Midsummer exodus that drained Stockholm and dispersed its inhabitants throughout the vast countryside. We took the subway into Stockholm to the central terminal where we met Torbjorn, and we stepped into a maelstrom of bodies and luggage.

"It's like they're fleeing the plague," Suzanne said.

We held hands so we wouldn't be separated as we navigated through the crush of people and their belongings. I tripped over a case of beer and almost knocked a woman and her child to the stone floor of the station. She yelled. I apologized, and we pressed on.

"Over there," Suzanne said, and pointed to Torbjorn.

Torbjorn led us through the terminal and outside to a line of buses. Groups of people surged for the door of each one as it pulled up.

"Where's Jennifer?" I asked.

"With her parents. We'll meet them at the ferry."

Torbjorn made himself as tall as possible and scanned the buses.

"Quick! This way."

Suzanne ran between Torbjorn and me, and we joined a crush of bodies at the front of our bus. The door opened and people shoved their way in.

"Don't lose your place!" Torbjorn yelled. "This is the last bus."

An old man with sad eyes coughed beside me. He was pressed between two women and a backpack. I thought he was choking and pushed backward to make a place for him. Torbjorn and Suzanne moved through the door and the two women followed them. The man thanked me, and then pushed me backward to let his wife and what looked like his grandchildren in before him.

Suzanne and Torbjorn climbed the steps into the bus and found a seat. They opened the window and told me to hurry. The old man and his family stepped on, and then I did too. The door closed behind me.

As we neared the coast the clouds began to fragment, allowing the sun to pour through the cracks. The air was drier and carried an essence of pine and birch. The inside of the bus became warm. Windows opened, and I took off my jacket. We drove beside a narrow stream that widened into a bay. It spawned boats, all heading toward the sea.

Jennifer and her parents were waiting at the ferry terminal. Our boat, a small inter-island ferry, was ready to leave. A young woman took our money as we boarded, and we were on our way.

Jennifer and Torbjorn led us to a bench on the sundeck overlooking the front of the ferry.

"An hour and ten minutes," Torbjorn said. "That's how long it takes to get to Harö."

Suzanne rummaged through her bag to find her sunglasses, and we settled in for the ride. The sea was busy with all kinds of watercraft that moved through the archipelago with us. There were ocean-going sailboats, yachts, and cabin cruisers, and sleek speedboats that impatiently wove through the armada. Kayaks and short dories hugged the shore as they rode a barrage of waves.

The bay widened farther, and the land began to fragment into granite islands. The stone changed color as we moved past it, from gray to golden brown, umber to rose. Slick, rounded bodies breached the surface of the water. They looked like seals, but I realized they were stones being washed with each passing wave.

"So many people," Suzanne said.

"It's the same all over Sweden today," Torbjorn said. "Everyone is leaving for the big party."

"You'll love Harö," Jennifer said. "The celebration is really nice. We decorate the Midsummer pole in the middle of a big meadow where a lot of wildflowers grow. We dance around it, and sing all these silly songs. We have a bit to drink. We eat a lot. And then, late in the evening, we climb a hill on the middle of the island and watch the sunset. It dips real low in the sky and barely disappears," she said, and made a skimming motion with her hand across the horizon. "It's the shortest night of the year, you know. It's wonderful sitting up there. The night's warm, and we laugh and talk. We save all our best jokes. Then, a few hours later, we'll watch the sun come up, at about three in the morning. Everyone knows winter is on its way after that."

The armada dissipated the farther we went. Boats disappeared between islands. Others pulled into coves and anchored. Our ferry stopped at seven islands before reaching Harö, the last stop.

"A village used to be here," Torbjorn said as we gathered behind him on the small pier. "But the Russians came and burned it down. That was a long time ago."

Arne was waiting for us with an old wooden rowboat powered by a one-cylinder engine. There was enough room for Jennifer's parents and our bags. Torbjorn suggested we walk to their cottages.

"The people rebuilt the village through there," Torbjorn pointed, and we watched Arne disappear through a narrow inlet hidden behind a veil of reeds and humps of raw granite.

"There are no roads on Harö," Jennifer declared. "Only trails. There's no electricity, either."

Torbjorn said that his grandmother's house was the only one with indoor plumbing, and that was because she was in her late eighties and still lived alone on the island year round.

"Going to the outhouse in a winter storm can be pretty miserable," he said.

We followed a trail that was just discernible as it crossed the stone, like the dissolving vapor trail of a jet in the sky. Strangled pines mutilated by the wind grew from cracks in the surface. Their roots clung like the arms of an octopus to the stone. There were taller trees as we moved inland. Grasses and pools of wild-flowers grew on deposits of soil. We walked through a swampy area thick with reeds, and we swatted our way through a cloud of ravenous mosquitoes. Suzanne was in front of me, and I could see how they set on her head and neck, on her back and arms, and I knew they were covering me, too.

"We can take a boat ride tonight," Torbjorn said, not noticing our flailing arms. "We can go out to the last island before the sea."

We walked over another short rise and into a cluster of cottages set along the edge of the inlet. Each was constructed on an exposed dome of granite, anchored in a way that mimicked the tenacious grip of the trees we'd passed. Each cottage was surprisingly small, almost miniature. They were painted a rich iron red with white trim. Arne saw us from a distance and waved. Inge walked over to greet us.

"So happy you came," she said, patting Suzanne's cheek. "So happy you came for Midsummer."

Suzanne and I were assigned the boathouse, a single-room structure built on stone pilings over the water. Old tools and fishing equipment hung from the walls and rafters. The inside was suffused with the sweet smells of pine tar and the sea. Inge and Arne had provided us with two metal cots that we pushed together and spread our sleeping bags over. Above us was a four-paned window that looked through a curtain of reeds to the still water of the inlet and the sky above. I went outside and picked some buttercups and put them in the mouth of a dusty bottle on the sill. We lay down together and listened to the sound of voices and laughter outside.

"Wonderful, isn't it?" Suzanne said after a moment.

"Perfect."

"Watch for rocks," Jennifer warned from the back of the boat. "They're just below the surface and hard to see."

She sat beside Torbjorn at the back of the boat as he piloted it through the inlet. Suzanne and I leaned over the gunwales and watched granite domes pass like mountains beneath us, and then fall away into dark canyons. We passed through the veil of reeds that hid the inlet, past the pier where we'd arrived. Then, Torbjorn turned the boat to the left and pointed the bow between two islands, toward the open sea.

We motored between them as if the islands formed a pass, and then we entered a great, limitless plain. I leaned over the bow and my face became the leading edge of the boat as we moved over the water. It felt as though we were flying. I could no longer hear the engine or any voices, only the mad rush of wind in my ears and the sound of the bow splitting the sea. I felt Suzanne's hand move up my back and felt her body slide beside mine. Her face appeared next to me and we rode together like two racing birds. At one point, I looked down at the water and saw her reflection staring back at me from the blue mercury of the rushing sea. She smiled, and blew me a kiss.

We were well past the islands when Torbjorn suddenly shut the engine off. The sound of its turning was swallowed by the void of the open sea. We coasted, slowed, and then the waves carried us aimlessly. I turned around and could no longer see the pier or the inlet of Harö. I didn't know if what I saw behind us was any longer Harö at all or one of the many other islands surrounding it. I turned back toward the open sea and imagined the point at which the coast of Finland lay over the horizon, and beyond that, the entrance to St. Petersburg, Russia. I had an incredible urge to take Suzanne's hand, step over the side of the boat, and walk to the edge of the horizon to see.

~~~

Arne looked worried as he picked at his Midsummer breakfast. "It never rains on Midsummer," he insisted as he nervously moved his cereal from one side of his bowl to the other. "It must stop."

Jennifer's mother sat across from me with a cup of coffee cradled in both hands for the warmth. "I can guarantee you it's not like this at home in San Diego," she said, and then bent to take a sip.

Sometime during the night I had awakened to the sound of metal clapping against metal. I sat up and Suzanne was standing in the open doorway of the boathouse. She heard me and turned.

"It's the roof," she said. "A corner of the roof has come loose."

I got up and stood beside her. The wind was cold, and a familiar stain was spreading across the pale sky. I put my arm around Suzanne's waist, and she leaned against me.

"Here we go again," she sighed.

We climbed back into bed and watched the curtain of reeds outside our window sway against the wind until we fell asleep again. I woke once more to the sound of the rain. It was coming down hard on the roof, and then I dreamed the water in the inlet rose and lifted the boathouse from its moorings. I dreamed I could feel the bottom drag across the tops of submerged stones in the inlet, and that we floated, turning on the current, out past the last islands and into the open sea. And I dreamed that I woke and joined Suzanne where she stood at the open door and watched the world spin gently out of control.

Arne got up from his breakfast and opened the door. He squinted into the distance and moved from side to side as if trying to look around something. "I thinks it must blow away soon," he announced hopefully.

Suzanne and I got up, stood behind him, and looked, too. The storm was entrenched over us. Suzanne looked at me and raised her eyebrows. I wanted to believe Arne, but we knew something about storms by then, too.

"It won't change by watching it," Torbjorn said. "Who wants to go get the Midsummer pole ready?"

Suzanne and I followed Torbjorn outside. He handed us two rain slickers, and then we went to a tool shed for sheets of burlap and rope with which to carry foliage to decorate the pole. He handed us a pair of clippers each, and we followed him across the wet meadow into a stand of trees.

"I want to show you something," Torbjorn said.

We put our tools down and he led us up a small rise to the beginning of a bare granite hill. The wet stone was as slick as oil, and as we climbed we used our hands and the edges of our boots to keep from sliding backward. Once out of the protection of the trees the wind assailed us. It got underneath my rain slicker and whipped the edges around my head.

We made the top of the hill, the highest point on the island, and set our legs against the wind. Torbjorn pointed out a small freshwater lake in the middle of the island and said that the year before it had been warm enough for everyone to go swimming. He pointed out the boathouse, the corrugated water of the inlet, and then he traced the ragged green circumference of the island with his hand.

"There's my dad," Torbjorn said. I was still looking past the rim of the island and expected to see him in the boat on the sea. But Torbjorn was pointing instead down into the meadow beside the houses. There, we could see a man furiously puncturing the earth with a tool as if he was trying to pierce the belly of the island and cause it to sink. "He's digging the hole. We'd better hurry."

We slid down the rock face and beneath the canopy of the trees.

"It's traditional to dress the Midsummer pole with birch leaves," Torbjorn said. "But there are only pine and oak on the island. Oak is best. Cut just above the ends of the limbs where there are the most leaves. Like this."

We gathered two bundles and carried them back across the meadow where Arne had made the hole. Off to one side was the Midsummer pole, a hewn pine about twenty feet long with a cross member like a crucifix two-thirds of the way up. We helped Arne place it on a set of sawhorses and he began wrapping the pole with twine to bind the oak clippings. The rain slowed, and then stopped. Arne looked into the sky and said, "You see? It blows away. Wonderful!"

Neighbors who had been invited to the celebration began to gather and pitch in. Inge and some other women wove two wreaths the size of bicycle tires from wildflowers. Their hands moved with the fluidity and speed of women who knit, and as they worked they sang a song about a girl who falls in love with a boy beneath her Midsummer pole. Someone fixed a long blue-and-gold streamer, the colors of the Swedish flag, to the top of the pole, and Inge tied the wreathes to each end of the cross arm. The base of the pole was positioned at the mouth of the hole in the ground. Ropes were attached to the top and Arne handed Suzanne and me one. Several people lifted the end of the pole, while those holding the ropes pulled.

"Heave!" Torbjorn coaxed. "Heave!"

It rose incrementally. The streamer began to swim in the wind, and I wondered how many thousands of poles were rising across Scandinavia at that moment.

"*Heave!*" Torbjorn yelled.

The base slid neatly into the hole. Torbjorn and Arne steadied the pole and Inge moved back in the meadow and gave directions to make it straight. I handed Arne stones to brace the base with. And when it was done everyone cheered and began singing a folk song, which Suzanne and I could only hum. And then, as if everything we had done was a call for rain, it began to rain.

It was relentless, a rain that should have washed the soil from the rocky island of Harö and stripped it clean; a rain that, once Inge had herded everyone inside the cottage, fell so loudly on the roof that I thought it would begin leaking and crash down on top of us. I went to a window overlooking the boathouse and inlet. The view ran in bright stains down the panes of glass, like water thrown on a painting. Arne came to stand beside me. "A summer rain. It goes for one hour," he said, as if it was just a cold and not the flu. "No more."

Suzanne put an arm around his shoulder. "It's okay," she said. "We're just happy to be here."

Inge called out instructions. A collection of tables was arranged in the middle of the room. Several bottles were placed on them. Chairs were gathered around. Torbjorn came to the window with four glasses and poured a measure of Aquavit, a strong liquor fermented from rye seeds, into each.

"Skol!" he said.

Torbjorn and Arne drank theirs neatly. I swallowed mine and traced its hot progress to my gut. I breathed and pulled the toxic vapors into my lungs and started to cough. Torbjorn laughed and clapped my back. Suzanne sniffed her glass and recoiled. She dipped the tip of her tongue into the liquid and winced.

"That's okay, Suzanne," Arne said. "Water is better for you."

We sat down and food appeared—plates of herring cooked in tomato sauce, herring in wine, herring fillets rolled into tight rounds, stuffed, and then baked; and smoked salmon dressed with fresh dill and thin slices of lemon, poached salmon with onions, Swedish meatballs drowned in thick gravy. There were bowls filled with sliced cucumbers, tomatoes, and onions; boiled potatoes that tasted like honey; and salad after salad. We ate and drank, and every few minutes someone proposed a toast, to the guests, to Inge and Arne, to Harö, to Sweden, for the rain to stop.

But it never did. It only varied in intensity, in how hard the wind blew and the angle at which the rain fell across the earth. We sang songs, told jokes. A card game began at one end of the table. We waited. I told Arne a joke. Instead of laughing, he looked out the window and said, "I *never* see it like this before." Suzanne showed him her only card trick, but he already knew how it was done. Then Inge announced it was time to go, despite the rain, and we all rose tipsily from the table, put our rain gear on, and filed through the door. She placed wreaths she'd made from wildflowers on Suzanne's and my head, and we joined hands in a big circle around the pole. Someone gave a cue, began singing a song, and the wheel of bodies lurched in a slow, out-of-kilter spin around and around.

It was as though we were on the bike again. Despite the rain gear, water ran along my face and neck, and under my clothes until my shirt clung to my skin. My pants became heavy with water from dancing through the meadow grass. People drifted away, our voices faded. Arne disappeared. Twice, somebody slipped and fell, pulling the wheel of bodies down as if it had broken. The wheel became smaller. We stopped dancing, and went back inside.

~~~

It was the absence of the roof's clapping that woke me. This time I went to the door and looked out. The sun was just rising in a sphere of bright promise. The sky was a deep royal blue, and the air was so still that the high whine of mosquitoes filled the air as they floated around my head.

"What is it?" Suzanne asked sleepily from our bed.

"It's beautiful," I said. "A perfect day."

We could have still walked to the top of the hill and watched it unfold, but we'd gone to bed long before midnight with everyone else. Arne had led the way by disappearing after the dance. "A headache," Inge said when we asked. "He goes to sleep."

The rest of us followed as the storm wore on, and gradually, the table emptied as guests stole away to their beds.

"At least," Suzanne yawned. "At least it will be a good day to leave."

As we packed Arne knocked on the door of the boathouse. He came in and sat on the edge of the bed as though he was our father and had something very important to say.

"Inge and me," he began. "We done some talking. You can stay here."

"Thank you, Arne," I said. "We'd love to come back again."

"That not what I mean," he said. "You stay now. Inge and me, we come back in two weeks. Stay here and fish, swim, and sleep so long as you like every day."

Suzanne and I had never refused such an offer. We made a point to remain flexible just so we could take advantage of such gifts. It seemed too good an offer to refuse.

"We have so far to go," I said, resisting the temptation to unpack. "It's a long way to the Arctic Circle. And then, we still have Russia and the Baltic States, and Poland."

Arne just looked at me as if I'd spoken gibberish.

"The weather," I said. "It can get even worse. And if we wait two more weeks, it could be snowing up north by the time we get there."

Suzanne stopped folding her clothes and looked at me.

"That is what I mean," Arne began again. "The weather, Russia...why you want that? Russia is a bad place now. Every day in the news we hear things. They kill people, they disappear, for nothing. They take your motorbike. Maybe they take Suzanne. Then what you do?"

I wasn't naive. I'd thought about those things. Plenty of other people had warned us, too, but I also knew that had I listened to people's warnings about places to avoid I would have never left my hometown. I knew people who were afraid to travel to San Francisco for the same reasons. Wherever you go in the world you can meet people who warn you about the people in the next town, province, state, or country. If you listen, they will describe in great detail the awful things that will happen if you go there. But I'd never found that to be the case. The next place was often better than the last. The people were usually just as nice, their hearts just as big, or bigger.

Suzanne began folding her clothes again. "It's okay, Arne," she said. "Allen and I will be fine. We do need to get going. There are some people we promised to visit a little north of Stockholm. Besides, we'll be back again."

Arne grudgingly accepted Suzanne's explanation. "Think about it. Change you're mind. Come back from Helsinki," he said, referring to the overnight ferry from Helsinki to Stockholm, and our last stop before entering Russia.

"Thank you," I said to Suzanne after he'd left. "I thought maybe you'd want to stay."

"We're in this together," she said. "Remember?"

tHIRteeN

Occasionally I have caught a glimpse of a place that betrays the veneer of distance, a glimpse of a landscape or building, or the inflection of a word in downtown Sydney, Tokyo, Istanbul, in the middle of Africa, that momentarily takes me right back home and makes me feel as if I've gone nowhere. It is as a friend of mine found in northern France, in a small village, where he had gone to live as an artist. He had his café of eccentric locals, his favorite shop for his morning baguette. He had the landscape and a rustic room above a bar where he painted into the night. Then, one day, after he had begun to understand the local dialect, after the architecture had lost some of its charm, and after the voices in the bar at night mutated from music to noise, it struck him he could have been in any of a hundred small towns on the flat plains of Kansas. You realize that ordinariness can be stumbled upon anywhere, and that even the places we dream of going, the places where we imagine our lives will change irrevocably, can be just as plain as the place we left.

Leaving Stockholm northbound on the E4 highway was like that. All indications that we were in the capitol of the Kingdom of

Sweden disappeared as we rode through stoplight after stoplight, past mega-car dealerships and giant retail malls with acres and acres of parking. As we passed neon banners proclaiming *"Rea! Rea! Rea!* (Sale! Sale! Sale!)," passed a Burger King and a McDonalds, it looked like the outskirts of any modern American town, and our journey seemed thousands of miles away.

Then, quite suddenly, the city was behind us. We turned northwest, away from the sea, and the flatlands began to give way to a landscape of gentle turbulence. Folds and mounds appeared on the earth and, gradually, hills took shape. The forest was less saturated with trees. They were taller here and grew farther apart. The air cooled as we climbed, and outside the town of Avesta we caught up with a slow-moving storm.

I'd never experienced anything like it before. The storm, a single cloud the size and shape of a huge dirigible, progressed slowly up the slope of the hills. It dumped rain as though unloading ballast to gain altitude and keep from crashing. Rather than riding through the storm, we took our time, rode slowly behind it, and stopped whenever we were about to ride beneath it. We watched it move steadily along, exhausting rain as it climbed.

After a while we stopped at a small roadside café for something warm to drink as we let the storm move ahead. As we removed our helmets and gloves, a white Volvo station wagon swerved suddenly off the road. It came too fast across the empty parking area, and the driver brought it to an erratic stop beside us. Suzanne pulled me by the arm to the far side of the bike. "Did we cut him off or something?" she asked.

A big man with dark glasses and thick, matted hair struggled to climb out of the car. His arms and torso moved awkwardly, as if he were stuck, or couldn't remove his seatbelt. His lips collapsed and yawned spastically, enunciating his struggle through the windshield. The man pushed the car door open and grabbed the edge of the roof as though he were desperately grasping the edge of a cliff. The man stood up and wheezed. He looked at me, then at Suzanne. "Heyza chow dammlink!" he yelled.

"He's drunk!" I said to Suzanne.

"Let's go," she said. "It looks like he wants to start something."

We took up our helmets and gloves. I quickly removed the tank bag, and we started to walk toward the café.

"Hey-za chow damm-link!"

I turned and stared hard at him. "*Jag taller inte Svenska!* (I don't speak Swedish), " I yelled back. "Leave us alone!"

"Just ignore him, Allen," Suzanne said. "Come on!"

"Heyy-zaa chooww dammm-link!" he said urgently, with a raised finger pointing at us.

"I said we don't speak Swedish!"

"Ack! Yeow iss ing-lish?" he slurred. "I sour-ry. I ass iff yeow iss care-ful on mo-tor-cyk-le."

"Of course," Suzanne said.

"Goooood. Me cal-led Tord. An-n I once drive mo-tor-cyk-le."

I then noticed a series of scars across his face and head, scars that looked like trenches only partially filled. And I noticed how half his mouth was paralyzed, as though he'd suffered a stroke. Then I realized he'd been in an accident.

"Did you crash on a motorcycle?" I asked him.

Tord closed his eyes, and for a moment his features convulsed and contracted. Suzanne relaxed and we walked toward his car. Tears ran from Tord's eyes, and he gripped the door and roof of the car for support as he seemed to relive the accident, the sudden realization that something had gone terribly wrong, the expansion of time that accompanies the moments of a crash, the numb concussion that enveloped his body.

"Ye-ess," he said. "I bee in mo-tor-cyk-le crash."

Tord explained that he had ridden mopeds as a child, then larger bikes as he'd grown older. He said he'd also been careful, but that one day he was trying to get home before a storm struck. He came around a turn and began to slide, and then flipped. The police found him one hundred feet down an embankment. He was in a coma for thirty-six days. Years of surgery and therapy followed.

"I stopp-ed when I seen youse. Tord hay-te mo-tor-cyk-le! Youse iss cray-zy," he cried, and pointed accusingly at me and then at the bike. And then Tord fought his way back into his car, slammed the door, and drove away.

"Jesus. That was bizarre," I said.

"I'm glad I don't believe in omens," Suzanne said.

"Don't start talking like that. He's just a little crazy."

"He's got reason to be, Allen."

~~~

Before leaving Åseda, Chester had given us the phone number of a relative, a woman he and Ingrid had once invited to accompany them on one of their California trips. Göta had gone with them, and one night they all went to my parent's home for dinner. Göta and I ended up on the sofa flipping through the pages of a National Geographic and talking. I remembered her owlish glasses, her attentiveness, an interest in Egypt. She told me about a book called the Koran. She and her husband Günner lived in Falun, a town fifty miles north of the café.

We called Göta from there not knowing whether she'd be home. She and Günner had a place in the mountains where they spent a lot of time, but she answered on the first ring. She said they'd been waiting weeks for us, that Chester had called and said to expect us a few days after leaving Åseda. "I keep a bed for you," she said, and as she spoke I mouthed the word "bed" to Suzanne.

Göta asked where we'd been and how we'd been getting along. She wanted to know if the Swedish people had been treating us well. I said we were fine, that the Swedish people were kind, and we would like very much to stop for a night or two. The coin meter on the phone sounded, and I didn't have any more change. Suzanne began going through her pockets, but Göta said not to worry, she and Günner would meet us in the center of Falun in an hour.

We found the storm trapped in the next valley. The hills were too steep for it to continue any farther, and the storm appeared to be trying to pry the valley walls apart. The road wound along the right side of the valley floor, just beyond the storm. I admired the swirling perimeter of the cloud bank. I admired its density, the way the black core seemed to absorb color, the way thick cords of rain fell onto the earth. I admired, too, the contrast with the calm, infinite blue of the sky above the road, and the way the sun healed the storm's wake. Then, the road made a broad, sweeping turn to the left, into the storm.

It began simply enough: drops of rain against the windscreen, a slight buffeting of the bike as the wind increased. Then the sky darkened appreciably and the temperature dropped. An explosion of light flashed inside of the clouds. It began to hail. And then the storm swallowed us. I hung onto the bike, and Suzanne onto me.

It reminded me of a movie I'd seen about storms in the second grade. There was a segment on hurricanes that showed a U.S. Air Force plane flying through one to measure its incredible force. The camera was positioned in the cockpit, behind the pilot and copilot's helmeted heads, so it was easy to imagine myself there, too. The plane began to shake as it entered the hurricane and the windshield appeared to melt. The pilot said, "Hang on!" and he hunkered down and took hold of the steering yoke as if the survival of the plane depended on how firm he gripped it. The sound of a thousand hammers beating against the metal skin of the plane filled my ears, and I thought the plane would surely come apart, as I thought the bike would come apart beneath Suzanne and me.

The road turned back toward the right side of the valley, and I saw a wafer-thin section of light that looked like a way out. I remembered how the pilot of the Air Force plane had seen a similar crack of light, and I remembered his staccato voice above the noise and confusion of the cockpit. "I see light!" he said with the conviction of a true believer. I accelerated the bike, and as we approached the edge of the storm, it opened like a mouth, and we seemed to speed off the tip of its tongue.

The air outside the storm was still and warm; the sky was an unblemished blue. I stopped the bike for a look behind us. The storm roiled as it compressed against the valley walls, and flashes of lightning hinted at the violence within. Suzanne peeled off her dripping helmet and gloves. She was shaking. "Jesus, Allen! You could have gotten us killed in there. Couldn't you have turned around?"

"It looked just like another storm," I said. "I had no idea."

"No idea? It was hailing! The wind was going to tear me off the bike!"

"We were already inside it," I said.

"Do you want to look like Tord? Do you want *me* to look like Tord?"

"Really," I said, and reached for her hand. "I didn't have any idea...."

"Don't touch me!" she said, and jerked away.

"Do you think I planned it? Do you think I woke up this morning and asked myself, 'What can I drag Suzanne through today?' Give me a break!"

Suzanne walked across the road and stared into the clouds. Minutes passed, and the storm's mass began to rise over the ridge and descend into the next valley. "I thought we were in this together," I called across to her. She ran her hand through her hair and squeezed it in her fist before letting it fall.

"I didn't mean to snap at you," she said, and walked back across the road. "It's just that every time things are going our way, something like this happens, and it scares the hell out of me."

"Don't look at me as the source of it," I said.

"I know! I know! Just be patient with me. I'm trying my best. But in some way I can't help but think you're looking for this stuff, that at least you're not trying to avoid it."

"Avoid what? That storm? The rally? We've been through much worse. Why now? Why has everything become so difficult on this trip?"

"Because I'm tired of slogging through the world like this! Can you blame me?"

"Yes, actually I can!" I said. "You agreed to this life."

"Well, I'm sorry that my tastes have changed. We've been traveling like this for a long time, Allen, but that doesn't mean we have to *keep* doing it. Not forever."

I didn't want to listen. I didn't want to hear anything more out of her mouth because as she talked I felt myself slipping again, felt my resolve and clarity begin to dissolve. I began to hear the voices

of people who thought I was crazy, who thought that my travels
were something I should have outgrown.

"Göta's waiting," I said. "We'd better go."

~~~

We rode down a hill, through an intersection, and into the
center of Falun. We turned into a large, cobblestone square in
front of an old church. The square was surrounded by a mix of old
and new buildings and had been turned into a parking lot. Göta
and Günner spotted us and waved.

"Welcome, Allen," Göta said, and wrapped her arms around
me before I could climb from the bike. "You become a man since I
see you. Wonerful you come. And this," she said holding out her
arms, "is brave Suzanne. Chester and Ingrid talk and talk and talk
about you. You are so welcome in Falun.

"And him," Göta said, "is Günner, my man. He speaks no English," she whispered. "But he knows what we say."

Günner smiled and shrugged. He shook our hands, and said
something in Swedish.

"He says we go home," Göta said. "He says you must be tired."

I pulled my helmet back on and saw Göta leading Suzanne toward the car.

"You follow us," she said to me. "Suzanne is safe with us."

I followed on the motorcycle as Günner drove through town,
by a stream and lake, and through some woods. I could see into
the back of the car, and I could see Günner's hands on the wheel
and the flash of Göta's glasses as she turned to say something to
Suzanne in the back seat. I watched the back of Suzanne's head
bob and sway with the car's movement. On a long straight section
of road I moved closer to the back of the car. I got close enough to
see how Suzanne's helmet had pressed her hair to one side. Beneath a whorl of black hair I could see the skin on the crown of
her head. I watched her hands race through the sky of the car as
she talked. Suddenly the woman sitting in the back of the car was-
n't Suzanne any longer. In an instant the car became just like all

the others we had ridden behind on this trip. I had a desire to lean into the oncoming lane, to twist the throttle, and disappear around the next turn.

fourteen

The foliage on the Midsummer poles had wilted. The leaves
had turned a pale green and curled like chips of old paint.
The flower wreaths hung in dull, tired bands from the cross-arms.
It would be autumn soon, and we should have already reached the
Arctic Circle, seen the midnight sun, and begun the long ride
south across Finland before the cold weather returned. But it did-
n't matter. The sun was out, and the sky was clear.

Suzanne and I stripped the bike before leaving for the day. We
removed the cases, the lock and tank bag, and the tent, and put
them all in Günner's woodshed. Göta packed us a lunch, and then
gave us directions to Sundborg, a small town in the hills north of
Falun.

We became pliable in the warm, still air of the hills as we rode
toward Sundborg. The air smelled of late summer, of grasses heavy
with seed, trees fat with sap, of pollen, and mushroom spore. The
air was congested with hives of desperate insects that looked like
beads of illuminated amber. Suzanne sat easily behind me as we
rode through the forest, past farms and meadows, and through the
occasional village.

The night before, Suzanne and I had lain spooned together on our bed. The glow of the polar night cast faint shadows on the walls, where old black-and-white photos of Günner's family looked down on us. We could hear the chatter of night birds as they ravaged Göta's berry bushes in the backyard, and once I heard a rustling outside our window that was a hedgehog foraging for food. Suzanne and I talked into the early morning hours, speaking softly so we wouldn't wake Göta and Günner in the next room.

It was one of those times we could say anything, when nothing was taken as a threat or slight, but was an inquiry between lovers. We talked about how the trajectory of her life with me had begun to shift in ways that were being amplified by this trip. She said the underpinnings of her assumptions felt shaken in ways she was only now realizing. At the worst moments of this trip she said her life seemed meaningless. She said she was often scared, and when she felt that way she just wanted to stop altogether. She said that our life of trip after trip had begun to seem pointless and overblown, that when she was depressed, she could only imagine it as a constant barrage of scenery, like looking through the window of a speeding car, and the only thing in focus was the reflection of her face in the glass. "But I thought everything had gotten better," she said. "I felt like I was getting back on my feet. I wanted this trip."

We held each other and grew sleepy as we listened to the pipping of the birds, to the mad bursts of their wings as they scrambled through the bushes and gorged themselves with an eye toward winter. The warmth of our bodies beneath the covers, the faint smell of promise on our clean skin, made me want to stay and talk through the fall and winter, stay and talk long enough for us to get things worked out. And then, perhaps in the spring, our sadness would melt away like the snow and we could try again.

We came upon Sundborg, a village much like the hundreds of others that appear regularly throughout the woods of Sweden. It had one main street, and from there the town—a bank, bakery, food and hardware stores, church, and post office—had only a slim hold against the interminable forest beyond. But at one end of town was the house of one of Sweden's most famous painters, Carl Larsson.

We walked along the dam of a mill pond to reach the Carl Larsson House, and a local girl dressed in a long, white cotton dress offered to give us a half-hour tour. She wore a sunbonnet and an apron of bright blue cloth tied around her waist. She said her name was Anika, and she explained how Carl and his wife, Karin, also an artist, had been given the home by her father when they were first married, how they'd added on, room by room, over the years, until their deaths in the early part of the twentieth century. Anika asked if we'd heard of Carl Larsson in America, and she was pleased we had.

"He is not so well known outside Sweden," she said. "But here, he is a kind of icon. Every Swede knows him."

Carl Larsson's work has been likened to that of Norman Rockwell and Degas. His most famous paintings include portraits and scenes of his wife and children, of the postman, local farmers and woodcutters, nannies, bureaucrats, military officers, and storekeepers. He painted their wives and children as they went about their lives in Sundborg. Those paintings have been criticized as being overly sentimental and saccharine. It's been suggested that he exploited the naiveté of country folk, that he idealized lives that were hard and oppressed by the rigid class system that existed in Sweden at that time.

I'd also read how Carl had grown up in extreme poverty, how his father abandoned the family. He'd struggled mightily as a young artist, lost his first wife in childbirth, and buried three of his children. He was a neurotic man racked by self-doubt, despair, and depression, and I found his efforts to create a sense of normality and joy both beautiful and encouraging. I wanted to believe that the children in his paintings were bright and happy, that the farmers were noble, and the military officer was a just man. I hoped that his wife loved him fully and that each of them was thankful and filled with grace.

Anika led us through the front door and pointed out the many windows that filled each room with light. She made sure we noticed how they looked onto portions of a large garden and a pond with ducks and geese. She showed us where Carl spent his time in the mornings, where the children sat for breakfast, and where Carl had painted portraits of Karin and the children on the backs of doors, on walls, windowpanes, and the ceiling of his studio.

"Carl and Karin traveled very often," Anika said, and pointed to the treasures and artifacts they'd brought home—Japanese screens and oriental rugs, books, furniture, and trinkets placed on mantels and sills. Anika took us upstairs and showed us the bedrooms, Carl's canopied bed. She showed us the library and the worn leather chair where Carl enjoyed smoking a pipe as he read.

I was drawn to the rich colors on the walls, the intimacy of the rooms and passages, the worn stair landings and polished handrail, and the smell of wood and smoke. The variety of pictures, sketches, vases, and walking sticks made me want to linger in each room. Suzanne kept running her hands over bedspreads and tablecloths, over the polished wood of the furniture and doors. I wished we could have remained in one of the rooms and let Anika go on without us.

I have a friend who rates movies by how he feels when they're over, by how his perception of reality is changed as he leaves the theater. When our tour was over, when we walked outside Carl Larsson's house and Anika wished us a nice day, I felt disassociated from my concerns about Suzanne and me. It was as if we'd been tinted with the light and ease of one of Carl Larsson's paintings. I didn't care if they were dead, mawkish muck and destroyed the truth of the lives they depicted. I didn't want truth or reality. I wanted instead to hold onto the feeling of goodness and possibility they portrayed. I wanted to take hold of a fistful of whatever it was and put it in my jacket pocket and zip it shut for the rest of the trip.

We walked slowly back along the face of the dam and found a place on the grassy edge to lay our jackets. The air was warm and the sky remained a simmering blue. We lay down beneath it and a languor covered us like a blanket, and we fell asleep in each other's arms.

~~~

Falun was built around an ancient copper mine. Discovered in medieval times, the mine flourished for seven centuries and only closed in the 1960s. Günner had recommended we take a look.

The most obvious reminder of those seven centuries of activity is a great red hill on the west side of town that, from a certain angle, has the look of a miniature volcano. Much of it has been subsumed beneath the sprawl of the town, and much of the rest has been reclaimed by trees and shrubs, but it's plain to see.

A scattering of wooden and metal buildings were set on the edge of an open pit as large as a stadium. It wasn't dug in the careful manner of open-pit mines I've seen before, ones with carefully terraced steps and roads to ease the extraction of ore. This one looked like a giant pock, the result of a cataclysmic explosion. Along the sides and bottom were strewn the rusted shards of heavy machinery, splintered wooden beams, lengths of gnarled cable as thick as my arm.

We entered one of the buildings that housed a small museum and a woman greeted us. We asked if we could have a tour, and she picked up the phone and spoke to someone. A few minutes later a young man in a yellow plastic hard hat and rain suit approached us. He said his name was Johan, and to please follow.

Johan told us he was Finnish, a student of languages, and was in Falun as a guide to perfect his Swedish. It was his second week on the job, and we were his first English tour. He asked where we were from and said he spent six months in West Virginia as an exchange student the year before.

"Did you like it? Suzanne asked.

Timidly he told us "No," and studied our faces to see if we were offended. "The people.... Well, it is difficult to explain."

"I'm sorry," Suzanne said. "Maybe you would have liked another state."

"Yes, I think so. I had a friend, he went to Florida. He wants to go back. Maybe I go with him."

Johan led us into a room lined with hard hats and raincoats, and asked us to please put one on. "The mine, it rains inside. Imagine that!" he said.

When we were dressed Johan led us into a large elevator car that lowered us below the surface. On the way, he began to recite the memorized text for all tourists.

"Imagine a trip back in time. The Falun Copper mine began production in the twelfth century," his voice boomed, as if the elevator was filled with tourists. "It became Sweden's first industrial company," he said, his eyes scanning the elevator to personally address everyone in the crowd.

"At this times, only pure ore was taken to the surface. In the early days of production the men used, uhm, primitives tools, and...."

The close formality was awkward with just the three of us in an elevator designed for fifty. Johan had positioned himself beside the door with his hands on the controls. Suzanne and I stood together in front of him, looking at the ceiling and walls, at his muddy boots, a stain on his hard hat, anything to keep from staring.

"We are descending one hundred and fifty meters below the surface...but the mine...it is much deeper," he said nervously. His eyes began to dart around the elevator. He began shifting his body from side to side. He seemed at a loss for words.

"We're going to Finland," Suzanne said.

Johan's eyes anchored on her face. "You are? When?"

"In a few weeks."

"You should stop in my town, Savonlinna. It is near the Russian border. You think you go there?"

"We really don't know where we're going yet," she said.

The elevator stopped with a lurch, and Johan opened the door with a press of a button. A wave of cold, damp air flooded the car, and we stepped into a black void. The shaft was lit by a string of lights our eyes adjusted to slowly. The rock walls glistened with water, and the floor, though paved with fine gravel, oozed a thin layer of mud.

"From here we will begin the tour by observing the ancient methods of ore extraction. Please watch your feet and follow me."

We followed Johan down a tunnel that opened into a large

chamber, and I asked how he liked Sweden. "It's okay," he said. "But, I miss my girlfriend."

"She lives in Savonlinna?" I asked.

"Yes. Maybe she comes to me this summer. I hope so. Okay. Gather round me," he said, and his voice swelled with authority again. "This is called the room of machines. Imagine using these heavy tools...."

But Johan's canned speech didn't last. He kept stumbling, and Suzanne and I kept asking questions about Finland and Sweden, and the places he recommended we go. We asked about the mine, too, but it became less of a guided tour than a stroll with friends. When appropriate, or when we asked, Johan explained mining processes, and interjected facts about himself as well. He asked if we knew how the early miners followed the ore through solid rock if they didn't have hardened steel tools to dig with? "I tell you," he said, and he described how the miners carried wood into the mine and built fires in the shafts that heated the stone. When the fires died, the men returned with water and poured it over the heated stone, cracking it. Then they carried the ore to the surface in baskets on their backs. "Imagine!" Johan said. "I never want to work so hard. Carry wood in...stones out...your whole life."

He said centuries later the miners used donkeys to move the ore, but the animals never saw the light of day, and they went blind because the only illumination was from the torches the men carried. Johan said he was bored in Falun, that there wasn't much to do, that he didn't make enough money anyway. In the middle of a long shaft he lowered his voice and said they paid him *nothing* for his labor, and that little had changed in the mine since the old days. Johan showed us what he claimed was the tallest wooden structure in the world, a hewn log shaft, down which the miners descended on a rope. He said it is perfectly preserved by the high level of copper sulfide in the air. In the next breath he assured us that this was only a summer job.

fifteeN

We followed a serpentine road back toward the sea. It meandered like a sprung coil across ridges and valleys. Occasionally, the forest parted and revealed the blue vein of a stream, a meadow of bright summer grasses, the silver skin of a lake. A pure sapphire sky enveloped us. As we rode along I was grateful for the thousands of miles still to go.

Despite our weight and the bulk of our gear, the bike felt more like an appendage of our will to move than a distinct machine. My hands knew just where to rest on the handlebars so I could coax the throttle with suggestions through my wrist. My feet were poised so the brake and gear levers were extensions of my toes. Each turn in the road was accomplished with an intuited shift of our torsos that sent us leaning toward the earth as we swept in precise arcs through them. The turning of the engine, the whirr of the tires on the road, the wind, were but the collective sound of our movement.

We rode through Furudal, Dalfors, and Voxna Bruk. Outside Arbrå a woman carrying an armful of wildflowers through a field stopped to watch us pass and waved. In the flatland around Karsjö we rode through a haze of mosquitoes so thick they made a paste on the fairing of the bike and our visors. And then, near Delsbo, we decided it was late enough to stop for the night.

We found a small lake outside town, and beside it a grassy slope used for camping. Some local kids were swimming there, their bicycles left in a careless heap along the shore. A small flock of ducks worried themselves in a far corner as the kids shrieked and yelled. Suzanne and I lay on the grass in the sun and watched them splash and dunk each other. They emerged exhausted and seemed to notice us with a start. The tallest of them, a boy with a taut, protruding stomach, asked in English where we were from. His face brightened, and he said excitedly that he'd never met anyone from California before.

"Hollywood?" he asked. "You have much money?"

The other kids pestered the boy to translate our answers, and when he did they looked let down.

Perhaps it was our tired clothes and scuffed boots that disappointed them, or our helmet-pressed hair. I think they must have expected more of two people from California, expected people who were flashier, better looking, a little more graceful. There was a moment of awkward silence between us, and then the oldest boy shyly said good-bye and they left.

Not long after, a station wagon pulling a house trailer drove slowly into the clearing. Three people were inside the car, their black hair and dark skin in stark contrast to most people we'd seen that far north. The driver, a man whose largest facial feature was a dense mustache that hung over his top lip, wheeled the car around on the grass. He tried to back the trailer onto a level area but kept turning the wheels too sharply, causing the trailer to veer toward a jackknife. A young boy was perched in the back seat, faced backward to watch the trailer turn out of control. He held one arm aloft in the cabin of the car, and his small hand waved helpfully. A woman sat impassively in the passenger seat, as expressionless as if she'd been riding the bus home at night. The boy's hand began to flutter as another attempt to park the trailer went awry, and the man swatted it away.

"Please don't invite them for dinner," Suzanne said.

The man gunned the engine, stopped abruptly, and shook his fists. He yelled something at the woman beside him, and she stepped obediently from the car. She positioned herself behind the trailer and began waving directions, but her husband couldn't see her. He searched the mirrors for her, turned his head violently back, and yelled. He gunned the engine and the trailer and car lurched backward. The woman jumped out of the way and waved harder, as if by doing so the trailer would respond. The man slammed on the brakes. He opened his window and yelled again. His wife walked around to his side of the car and she held her hands up, as if to ask, "What now?"

They tried once more. The woman made small rolling gestures with her hands. The man turned the front wheels of the car in quick S patterns, and the trailer shimmied slowly back until he stopped.

The boy climbed from the car and surveyed the camp, ignoring his parents' quarrel. He bounced a soccer ball a few times on the grass, then kicked it down the slope toward us.

"Nice motorcycle," he said in Swedish as he ran past us.

"*Tak!*" I said.

He came back with his ball, bouncing it from hand to hand, and surveyed the bike.

"Hey! You're not from California," he said in almost perfect English. "You steal this thing?"

"No. It's our bike," I said.

"Why is your English so good?" Suzanne asked.

"I was born in New York. Lincoln Boulevard. But now I live in Stockholm with my uncle and aunt," he said, and motioned back up the slope. "But I'll go home soon. Maybe two weeks."

"To New York?" Suzanne asked.

"Of course. Lincoln Boulevard. Where else? Sweden's too small for someone like me," he said.

"Too small? What do you mean?" I asked. He couldn't have been more than ten years old.

"There's a lot I want to do," he said impatiently, the ball bouncing like popcorn. "I've got big ideas."

"What kind of ideas?"

"I can't tell you," he said warily. "You look nice, but you might steal them, too."

"We didn't steal the bike," I said. "We shipped it here from home."

"What are you doing in Sweden?" he asked, and tossed his ball to Suzanne.

"We came to steal your ideas," I said, and made a face at him.

"No," Suzanne said, and tossed the ball back. "We're riding around the Baltic Sea."

"The whole thing?" he asked, bringing the ball to a momentary stop for the first time. "That's stupid. You should go to Austria, Switzerland. Even Italy. Somewhere nice."

His aunt called him from their trailer in a language I didn't understand, and he yelled something back.

"What language were you speaking?" I asked.

"Polish. I lived with them in Poland."

"And what are you doing here?" I asked.

"We sell things. We drive around and sell things," he said. "Hey. Can I sit on your bike?"

"Sure," I said. "What do you sell?"

The boy tossed his ball to Suzanne again and climbed onto the bike. He was a little pudgy and made little grunts of exertion as he threw his leg over the seat and pulled.

"Carpets, mixers, knives. Things like that," he said, and leaned forward to grip the handlebars. "We go door-to-door. During the day, when the woman is home. Nothing too expensive," he said as he surveyed the gauges. "Does this thing really go that fast?"

"Yes," I said. "Nothing too expensive?"

"Nope. Rich people won't buy expensive things at the door," he said emphatically. "But the woman, she'll buy a carpet...a knife. I pick out a carpet that matches the flowers in the garden so she likes the color, or tell her the knife would be nice for her husband. Every man needs a knife. And a little present keeps him off her back. You should buy him a knife," he said slyly to Suzanne.

"Is that all it would take?" she said smiling. "What's your name?" she asked him.

"Robin Williams, and I'm funnier than the other one," he said as he looked sharply down an imaginary road.

"You seem to know a lot of things," I said.

"I do know a lot of things. I know Michael Jackson," he said matter-of-factly as he climbed down from the bike. "And my dad knows the American President."

"Yeah? What does your dad do?"

"Mechanic. The best in New York. That's how he knows the President. He could fix your motorcycle if he was here."

"It's not broken."

"I bet he could find something broken."

Suzanne tossed his ball back, and Robin Williams placed it on the ground and sat on it beside us. He told us of all the places he'd traveled selling things with his family, to Moscow, Paris, Mexico City, and through most of the United States. He said that in a few weeks they would be back in Poland to pick up another load of rugs and knives.

"I thought you said you were going back to New York," I said.

"Oh, yeah! Well, maybe not."

Robin William's story became tangled, but he didn't seem to mind. At one point he lowered his voice and looked carefully around to make sure nobody was listening, but there was only the grass around the lake, the forest, and the sky. "Someday," he said softly. "Someday I will sell computers. And software. *That's* the future," he said, with the conviction of a prophet. "That's where the big money is. Then, I will buy a Lamborghini...a black one. It will be soooo shiny and fast! And then you know what I want to do? I want to take it to New York and drive down Lincoln Boulevard. That's my dream! Now you know my dream."

~~~

Robin Williams waved as we rode from camp the next morning. He was sitting at a table inside his housetrailer eating a piece of toast, which he used to salute us with. He was wearing only a t-shirt and I was jealous. Suzanne and I had on every bit of clothing we'd brought with us, and we were still cold.

Sometime during the night the leaves on the birch trees beside us began to clatter, giving the wind a voice that alternately whispered and roared. The wind flowed like a current over the tent and carried with it any warmth collected in the surface of the earth. The cold skin of the tent pressed against my side and I marked time as the warmth of my body wicked away. Suzanne and I pressed against each other as the temperature dropped, and we remained huddled until it was too cold to sleep any longer. As we debated whether to get up, Suzanne blew geysers of steam from her mouth that rose to the ceiling and then disappeared.

We dressed quickly, and carried our stove and pots into a shed beside the lake where we made a breakfast of oatmeal and tea. We held our hands over the flame of the stove and vigorously rubbed our arms and chests. We did jumping jacks and ran in place until we were winded. Suzanne held our rain suits open over the stove until they filled with warm air, and then we slipped into them.

I improvised a table from a narrow shelf below the window and brushed the cobwebs from it with my hand. Suzanne slipped out the door for a blood-red Icelandic poppy and pressed the stem into a crack in the window sill. She folded some paper towels we'd taken from a gas station so they looked like stars and set our spoons on top of them. "There," she said enthusiastically. "Better than a restaurant."

I poured water for our tea, and she took the steaming cups by the rims with the tips of her fingers and quickly placed them on our table.

"If I could, I'd make us pancakes," I said.

"Ummm. You read my mind," she said dreamily as I scooped oatmeal from our pot. "With lots of butter and syrup. And fresh blueberries to mix with the batter. We'll pretend."

We stood before the window looking over the lake as we ate and watched the wind skate across the water, leaving the surface agitated.

"Think it will warm up?" I asked.

Suzanne leaned her head against my shoulder and didn't say anything. The sound of her spoon scraping the bottom of her bowl was like a reminder not to say such things.

~~~

Our road through the mountains terminated at Hudiksvall, an old port set on the edge of the sea. Technically, it wasn't the Baltic Sea any longer, but the Gulf of Bothnia, an appendage shaped like a long, stout arm thrust defiantly northward, terminating just sixty miles short of the Arctic Circle. I had thought that our ride along it would be one of the more exciting parts of the trip. I had imagined the eternal days of sun as we neared the Arctic and the odd quality of light the midnight sun produces. I tried to guess what the people who lived in such a strange land were like, be they Swedes, Finns, or *Same,* the nomadic reindeer herders who sweep across Norway, Sweden, and Finland as though the region were still one big range. But as we were stopped alongside the road so we could change maps and cinch our clothes still tighter against our bodies, the Gulf of Bothnia looked like an obstacle we had to scale before falling down the other side into Finland.

As we rode north, I thought I detected an urgency in the air— a sense that summer, so short it couldn't be depended upon, was but a precarious truce arranged to accomplish essential tasks before winter began again. I saw evidence for this in the woolly coats of cattle and horses, in the streaks of gold bleeding into some leaves, in the accelerated pace of the harvest, the exaggerated size of wood piles stacked beside homes. We stopped three times that day for fuel and to get out of the weather and warm ourselves with coffee, and even in those settings people seemed impatient, as if to stand around serving us was somehow fruitless. I thought of the joke Hanne had told us on the ferry ride from Århus to Zeeland, the one about the Scandinavian summer that had happened on a Saturday afternoon. I began to think that we'd really missed it, that perhaps it was one of those years.

Midday the first pellets of rain ticked against my face shield. We had been monitoring an armada of precipitous clouds off the coast, and for a time I had convinced myself we were outrunning them. Then, just south of Härnösand, they moved inland. The wind picked up much as if we were about to be engulfed by the flames of a wildfire. The trees whipped and bowed. Leaves streaked through the air, and then the rain came down.

Perhaps it was only experience, but I sensed something had changed. The storm seemed easier to navigate, and I felt we'd learned a few of the tricks the wind and rain could play on us. We leaned competently against each gust and used their strength to hold us upright. I diminished the jolt of each rolling punch by incremental turns of the throttle. Almost intuitively our bodies shifted to trim the bike. Like sailors who grow used to storms at sea, we had learned that a storm like this was not likely to hold surprises for us. The wind subsided near Bjästa, and the storm softened to a gentle shower. But the day was not done with us.

Later we learned that summer is the only time for large-scale roadwork, the only time the frost-heaved roads can be pierced to their granite base, blasted, and scraped smooth again. Miles of churned-up roadway lay open as though a crude form of terrestrial triage was being performed. There were no detours or escorts. We were left on our own to pick the best path around the army of vehicles performing the work, around boulders freshly blown from the earth, through expanses of mud and rock, and ponds of muddy water. We rode slowly past a cranelike machine that shattered boulders as if they were nuts. We dodged the long, burdened arms of backhoes as they excavated craters. A bulldozer paused just long enough to let us pass before shoving a small hill of debris into a swale we had just ridden through. A team of drilling rigs spewed a choking cloud of granite dust as holes for additional charges were prepared.

The bike slipped several times on the slick rock, and it required all my strength to keep it from falling to the ground. In places the base rock had just been laid, hundreds of yards of six- to ten-inch shards we bounced over and slid across. Several times our tires pinched pieces of granite between their rounded edges with enough force that they shot away with a loud pop and twang. I flinched each time it happened and wondered if we hadn't popped a tire or torn a sidewall.

I followed in the compacted tire track of a grader until the driver suddenly stopped and flung it into reverse without looking back. I stopped the bike, honked the horn, but there was no way the operator could hear us above the roar of his machine. Suzanne recoiled behind me and I felt her legs scramble to get off the bike. I gunned the engine and we rode over a berm, and the grader passed safely to the side. I would have liked to have stopped but my legs shook so much that I wasn't sure I could hold the bike upright.

sixteen

We could have crossed the Arctic Circle that day. It was only another two hundred and fifty miles and everything was in our favor. Midday the rain passed as if it had been vacuumed away, leaving only occasional gray motes that drifted harmlessly overhead. The chill was replaced by a tepid stillness, and the many miles of road construction were behind us. We could have easily made Finland had we wanted to. But then, about thirty miles south of Luleå, I noticed a motorcycle parked on the side of the road. The rider was crouched on the far side of the bike inspecting the engine, and I decided to stop.

"*Hej,*" I said as I walked across the road. "Do you need any help?"

A woman pushed her head over the seat. A cigarette hung loosely from her lips and she took it with her grease-stained fingers.

"Ah!" she said. "Problem."

I walked around the bike to where she was kneeling. Her leather jacket was spread on the ground for her to kneel on, and a collection of clean steel tools were arranged on a canvas sheath beside it.

"I don't know how you call these," she said, and pointed into the engine.

"Points. What's the matter?"

"She dies. Just like that," she said, snapping her fingers. "Kaput."

"I'm Allen. That's Suzanne," I said, and waved for Suzanne to join us from across the road.

"Malin. Thanks for stopping," she said, and we shook hands.

It was difficult to keep from staring at the gentle angles of her face, her long auburn hair that hung in strands across it, her bare brown arms, and the way her thin hands moved as she pointed with a screwdriver. It wasn't just her features that attracted me, but that she was on the road alone, on a motorcycle with a duffel and sleeping bag tied to the back of the seat. She was broken down on the side of the road, and she knew how to take care of it.

"It is this thing," she said, and showed me how the screw holding the points in place had stripped, causing them to spring closed as the engine vibrated. Malin pushed at them, demonstrating how the bracket holding the assembly would slip closed with a flick of her finger. "You have a drill machine, and the other to make the road for the screw?" she asked. "I don't know how to say in English."

"A drill and tap? Afraid not."

"Hmmm. So I thought," she said, and smiled slyly.

"Do you have a longer screw?"

"I was looking," she said, and spilled a bag of parts onto her jacket.

I watched Malin's long, slender index finger sort through screws, washers, and nuts. She flipped a small container of fuses with a little kick of her nail and discovered two washers, which she moved toward the others.

"Here," I said. "How about that one?"

"The same," she said. "Same size."

I wanted to join her in her search, to move my own finger through the parts beside her own until I found the right one.

"Nice bike," Suzanne said, suddenly beside me.

Malin looked up and smiled. She wiped the hair from her eyes with the back of her hand. A strand fell back across her left eye. She pushed her lower lip out, shot a puff of air up the length of her face so she could see Suzanne clearly.

"She is an old thing," Malin said of her bike. "Swedish military machine from fifties."

Malin went back to her sorting. She pinched a screw between her nails and inspected it. She positioned the points with her left hand, set the screw, and carefully screwed it in. Her hands moved with the assurance of a mechanic's but with a woman's grace, and she held her tools with a familiarity that comes only from using them. It was all I could do to keep from reaching out and pretending to help.

"Ha!" Malin said as the screw bit into some remaining thread. The bracket holding the points flattened against the engine, and when she pushed them with her finger they remained in place. "There. Please stay," she asked the points. "About one hundred kilometers and I will be home."

"Where did you come from?" I asked.

"From Luleå," Malin said as she screwed a metal cover back over the points. "This road take you through. Not so far. Big motorcycle rally over the weekend. Crazy time."

"Oh, really? Allen and I went to a rally on Gotland. *That* was a crazy time. Is it over with?"

"Yeah. Everyone goes home," Malin said, and chuckled at a memory. She lit a cigarette, took a drag. She offered us one, and then asked where we were from.

"There is some American guy in Luleå you should visit. Really. Talk about crazy. He rides a broken Harley around the world. He comes from across Russia—alone. I think my bike goes farther," she said, and patted the engine.

"Do you remember his name?" I asked.

"No. Too much drink. But I can write my friend's telephone. He live in Luleå and will take you to him."

"You don't think it would be a problem?" I asked.

"No. Just say to him Malin sent you."

She wrote a name and number on a piece of paper and gave it to me. Then she wrapped her tools up, tied them with a leather strap, and stowed them in a metal tube below the seat.

"Okay," Malin said, and offered her hand to Suzanne and me. "I must go. Thanks for stopping. Go see that guy. I think maybe you like him."

"We will," I promised.

I watched Malin as she put on her jacket and helmet, and then kicked her engine over. It caught right away, and she waved before pulling onto the road. I waved back and listened as she shifted smoothly into second gear, then third. And then she disappeared around a bend.

"Come on," Suzanne said, and pulled at my arm. "That's enough looking."

An hour later Suzanne and I were standing in a phone booth on the edge of Luleå. The phone at the other end rang only twice, and then a man answered.

"Sven-Erik?" I asked.

I explained who we were, that Malin said to call, that perhaps he could tell us where the American was staying.

The voice on the other end was thickly accented and methodical. Sven-Erik sounded pleased that we'd called and wanted to know all about us.

He said he'd be happy to show us where the American was staying but asked if we'd mind going the following day. He made a point of stressing the weather would be especially nice the next few days, that it had been a long, wet summer, and that he was leaving work in just a few minutes to take a motorcycle ride through the mountains. Sven-Erik said something about a waterfall and that it would make him very happy if we'd go, too.

"What about the American?" I asked.

"No problem. I take you tomorrow."

"Just a moment," I said, and covered the mouthpiece.

"He wants to take us to a waterfall," I said. "Into the mountains. He sounds like a nice guy."

"Ask him how far it is."

I relayed the question. Sven-Erik said it wasn't far. Just enough for a nice afternoon ride.

"It's up to you," Suzanne said, and shrugged.

~~~

We heard Sven-Erik's bike before we saw it, a deep, throaty, high-revved roar.

"I hope he's not a Hell's Angel," Suzanne said and rolled her eyes.

Sven-Erik came into view around a long, sweeping turn. He saw us and slowed, then slid to a halt beside us. He wore a worn leather riding suit, and I took it as a good sign that there were no abrasions and tears from previous wrecks. He took his helmet off and offered his hand in greeting.

The first thing I noticed about Sven-Erik was his slightly mad, pale blue eyes. In the bright sun that illuminated that afternoon they seemed especially bright, almost a source of light themselves.

"A very special day," he said anxiously, and searched the sky as if he was looking for something. "We have not so many here."

Sven-Erik led us to a youth hostel on the edge of town and helped us carry our gear into our room.

"A wonderful ride I take you on," he promised as we passed each other in the door of our room. "You will see."

He was inspecting our bike when Suzanne and I joined him. "It is right for your journey," he said. His bike, an older model BMW, looked worn and tarnished in comparison. The paint was faded and the fairing looked as if it had been scrubbed with a wire brush. The short plexiglas windscreen was cloudy and yellow from weathering.

"I made it from three bikes," Sven-Erik said of his. "I have no money for a new one, so I bought the pieces from three, and made one. A little Frankenstein," he beamed.

He seemed to forget the urgency of our leaving as he explained to Suzanne and me all the modifications he had made to it. He pointed out the dampening on the steering, the four-valve heads, the stiffened suspension, tuned exhaust, a throttle linkage he'd machined himself at the local university where he worked as an engineer designing mechanized logging equipment. He explained in great detail the interior modifications to the valves, cam, timing, carburetors, and pistons. He got down on his hands and knees to explain the faults in the original drive-train, and how he'd corrected them. Then he was ready to go.

"Okay," Sven-Erik called out over the rumble of his engine. "How fast can you go?"

"Depends," I called back, not quite sure how to respond. "Depends on the roads."

"I like one hunred-forty," he said with a crooked smile.

"Miles an hour?" Suzanne asked incredulously.

"No. Kilometers. Something like eighty, eighty-five of your miles. Okay?"

I turned around to look back at Suzanne. She looked ready to get off but didn't. "We'll do our best to keep up," I said to Sven-Erik. "But don't worry if we fall behind."

He waved and roared off.

It was a wild ride into the mountains of northern Sweden, one that took us in a drawn-out loop halfway to Norway and back. At one point early in the ride, when I was still trying to catch up with Sven-Erik for the first time, I thought of all Suzanne and I were missing by riding so fast. I was tired, and eighty-five miles an hour on mountain roads I didn't know was too fast for me after a long day. And then I started to catch him, and I was able to slow to seventy-five. We swept cleanly through a turn that opened onto a wide valley. Sven-Erik sped up and we crossed the valley in a beautifully blurred moment. The road climbed steeply out the other side into a jade sky, then crested, and for an instant it seemed as if the world had fallen away beneath us.

We sped across ridgelines, beside rivers, through meadows and pastures. We raced through forests so dark the road became illegible. A reindeer bounced from the edge of the forest and crossed in front of us. A second slipped by before I realized there would have been little or nothing I could have done had it stopped in our path. I felt impossibly alive.

Eighty-five miles an hour became a dilated state of mind, one that created its own momentum and tempo, one that I became entangled in. Eighty-five miles an hour became a lean line scribed across the earth, and it was extraordinary. Eighty-five miles an hour became something I wanted to sustain.

We crested another ridge and rode down the other side into a long valley. The road ran straight before us, and Sven-Erik slowed until we were beside him. He was trying to yell something to us but I couldn't hear over the wind. He lifted the front of his helmet as if that was the impediment between us. I stole glances of his moving lips and tried to read them, but the words caught on the wind and dropped quickly behind. Then he pointed forward and began to pull away. I kept pace and noted the needle on the speedometer sweep past 95, 100, 105. The landscape became an adrenal rush of sapphire, magenta, fire-yellow, emerald, and saffron. One hundred-ten and the wind sounded as if it would crush us. One-fifteen and the bike was still surging as if this was just the beginning.

And that was enough.

I eased the throttle back and Sven-Erik rushed ahead. The needle on the speedometer fell back past eighty, seventy, sixty, and it felt as though we were barely moving at all. The world slowly regained its focus and I felt an elated sense of relief. Suzanne loosened herself from the knot she'd become behind me and uttered a giddy laugh. "My God," she said through the back of my helmet. "Why'd you do it?" She laughed again, punched me on the shoulder. She said, "My God! My God!"

Sven-Erik waited for us at a point where the road narrowed and the asphalt turned to gravel. He led us into a valley where a river hurried toward the sea, and we meandered beside it for several miles as we moved farther into the mountains. At some point I began to feel a percussive thrumming in my bones, a low-level vibration that could have been something in the engine of the bike.

"Do you feel that?" I asked Suzanne.

"Yes. Like a tremor."

We rode farther and the tremor became a rumble I also heard.

"It must be the waterfall," Suzanne said.

We rounded another turn, and while I was trying to avoid potholes and loose gravel, Suzanne tapped my shoulder and pointed ahead. I brought the bike to a stop.

It wasn't a waterfall in the sense of Niagara or Victoria with an abrupt cliff the water spilled over. Nor was it like the precipitous cascades famous in Yosemite and Hawaii. The fall was a wide hemorrhage in the mountain, a violent rent through which a great pressurized geyser had burst. The river thundered and roared over house-sized boulders as it fell several hundred feet toward the valley below.

"Well?" Sven-Erik yelled above the noise. He smiled at our reaction to the fall.

"Come on," he said after a minute. "We go up, to the edge."

We rode partway up the mountain and parked in a clearing of trees. The thrumming we felt on the bike was a pounding there, and the air was filled with a mist of atomized water carried on swirling eddies of wind. The three of us followed a trail through the trees, and then we were on the edge of the fall. We stood just where the river broke and quickened to transparent blue mounds that slid over the cold, granite bed, just where it shattered into a churning white rapids.

A narrow path led down the side of the fall, through an area of softly rounded boulders and polished nodes as smooth as hardwood. A drizzle fell, and multiple rainbows arced over the water. We walked to a point where we could look up and down the fall, to an impossible point where it seemed the ground must be frail, in danger of being eroded and consumed by the river. The three of us stood there anyway, perched on the edge of the current as though its force was pulling us in.

On a sliver of rock Sven-Erik told us about a friend he'd brought to the same spot a year before. She was going through a long, painful divorce, and her emotions had reached a crescendo that day. They too walked to the edge of the rock and stopped, as we had, just a few feet from the water. He described the way she stood, still and pensive, and I imagined a woman ready to dive, never to be seen again.

"And then!" he yelled over the rumbling of the fall. "And then she start to scream!"

She screamed as loud and for as long as she could. The river absorbed every decibel and sent them crashing over the rapids. Sven-Erik's eyes were wide and glowed as he told the story, and he seemed to hint at some secret power the place held. When he was through, a long pause enriched his stare, and I wondered if he'd brought us on purpose, if he had sensed we were troubled and needed to cast out our own devils.

Our return to Luleå was like a long doze in the half-light that was night. We were surrounded by an intermediary dusk our head-light did not help us through. The effect was a sense of time suspended. Each ridge revealed another in an endless series, and the rhythm of ridge, valley, ridge, valley, had a perfect tempo, a groove too good to escape.

Somewhere in the mountains, the clock on the bike pushed beyond midnight and it was sometime after that we arrived at the edge of Luleå. We said good night to Sven-Erik, and he promised to come for us around midday. Then he roared off, and we rode slowly through the night to our room.

At ten the next morning I was outside checking the bike and swatting mosquitoes when I heard the distinct sound of Sven-Erik's motorcycle through the woods. The tuned roar grew louder and I pictured him crouched over the gas tank as he swept through each turn, a knee extended for balance. I wondered what luck had brought him through so many years of riding. I could hear the quick pauses when he shifted gears, and the compressed rumblings as he slowed for turns. And then he came into sight, and because he had on the same helmet, suit, and scarf, it seemed as though he hadn't stopped all night.

"Tonight," he said after taking off his helmet. "We go to see the American. And today, I take you for something special."

"What?" I asked, hoping it wasn't another ride.

"Not a ride," he said as if he'd read my mind. "I take you sailing."

~~~

It was a small, yellow sailboat that Sven-Erik periodically borrowed from a colleague. It was moored at a pier filled with similar boats and a few fishing vessels. The water was flat and gleamed with reflected sun. The sky was breathless, a washed-out blue void of a single cloud. As we were setting the rigging, Sven-Erik apologized for the lack of wind but said the people of Luleå were thankful, that on such a day some businesses close their doors and let people go home to enjoy the weather.

"A sun day," Suzanne said, and Sven-Erik looked up at her wondering what she'd said. "Like a snow day," she continued. "When there is too much snow and the schools are closed."

"Too much snow?" he pondered.

Suzanne helped him string the foresail while I tightened a bolt on a loose pulley.

"The summer...it is so short here," Sven-Erik said, much as older people will warn that time goes by so quickly. "A day like this can be very important. You understand? And then winter comes, like closing a door. And it stays. Stays and stays."

We strung another sail, adjusted ropes, stowed our helmets and tank bag under the prow, and we were ready to go. Sven-Erik handed me a pole I used to push the boat from its slip and into the narrow lane between piers. He unfurled the mainsail and it barely rustled with wind, just enough to carry us at a slow walking pace through the marina.

We passed the last pier and slid beyond a low stone jetty into the open water, and Suzanne asked Sven-Erik what a winter was like in Luleå. He seemed puzzled as he searched for words that would mean something to Suzanne and me, words that would describe more than darkness and bitter cold.

"Some days in the middle of the winter, there are only fifteen minutes of sun. When I work, sometimes I miss it, and the night goes on and on. That is not good for me. But, the winter is a spiritual time. For me, it is like meditation, like a long dream. And to live through the winter here makes the spring and summer wonderful. Imagine life, flowers and animals, can live through such a time and be reborn with a little sun. It can be like a, how you say...like a miracle. Every flower and living thing becomes so precious."

Farther out into the bay the wind picked up. The sail filled and strained at the mast and Sven-Erik adjusted our course. The little boat leaned and we moved faster across the water.

"But the people think on winter different now," he continued. "The people, they know about warm places—Greece, Spain, Mallorca...Florida. We see picture of them on TV and video, and people go there in winter. *I* go to these places, too. But something happens then, something to the way we think about life here. Winter becomes a time to leave...and some of the magic leave."

Sven-Erik brought us about and asked Suzanne if she wanted to steer. They traded places and Suzanne skirted the edge of an islet. A flock of seabirds rose from the water with a clatter of wings and splashing feet. They rose on the blue of the sky, their black wings a blur against it. Then they fell, and brilliant white dashes marked their landing on the sea.

"Winter is important, like spring and summer," he continued. "It is an element...you understand? You must have them all—winter, spring, summer, autumn—for life here to make sense.

"In my grandfather's time, the people had mythology and ritual instead of vacation. You know Thor?" he asked as if he could be a friend we had in common. "He is the God of Thunder. There is Odin, Balder, Frigg, Njord, and many more. Everything made sense then. But now the people have Greece and Florida. Disney World. How can the life here make sense after that?"

We sailed for hours, tacking slowly back and forth across the bay in search of wind. Periodically the wind left all together, and we let the boat drift in slow, out-of-control spirals across the leaden water. Sven-Erik told us more about the gods, how Thor protected farmers and warriors. He watched over marriages and hearth fires. Odin was his father and the god of war, wisdom, and poetry. Frigg was his wife and queen of the sky. He told us how the world was created from two regions, one of fire and the other ice, and how a giant called Ymir was formed at the confluence of the two. The first man and woman grew from beneath Ymir's arms, and the first gods were formed from his feet. Ymir was slain by the gods, and all the world's water was formed from his blood, the land from his flesh. And all the while the wind blew and died around us, the sun shone and slipped across the sky, and the small boat carried us back and forth across the water until it was time to go.

~~~

We only knew what Malin had told us about the American: that he was staying somewhere in Luleå, that he was riding around the world on a Harley-Davidson, and that he might enjoy seeing Suzanne and me.

"He stays at the Aurora Harley Club," Sven-Erik announced as we were putting the boat away. "Outside town."

"There's a Harley club up here?" Suzanne asked.

"Sure. Why not?"

"How many members?"

"Mmmm. Three. Maybe four."

Suzanne and I followed him out of town, through a neighborhood of low-level apartments, a cluster of homes, and into the forest. We turned down a narrow lane that skirted a swampy area where the sound of our bikes interrupted a feeding moose. The bikes cleaved through clouds of mosquitoes that became a smear on the windscreens. We turned down a lane that narrowed as the limbs of trees hung over the edge like arms trying to snag us, and I thought the lane would soon dissolve into the swamp. Then Sven-Erik slowed and turned into an overgrown yard that surrounded an old two-story house.

It was properly dilapidated for a Harley club. The entrance to the yard was decorated with the rusted sculpture of a Harley created from an assortment of ancient parts and odd pieces of pipe. A layer of white paint peeled from the high walls of the house, like dead skin. The bare wood was discolored by moss and soot. Pieces of faded fabric hung loosely inside to cover the windows. The coming and going of people and machines had formed trails through the grass and weeds, and the trails were all that kept the forest from annexing the yard completely. We parked, and nothing moved. The house appeared deserted.

We removed our helmets and the distinct hum of insects filled the air. "Mosquitoes," Sven-Erik said looking around him.

Convective clouds of them tumbled through the air searching for a place to land. A haze of them rose from the shrub-clogged swamp behind the house like boils of smoke. They covered our clothes and hair, probed our jackets, gloves, and boots. I fanned the air in front of my face to keep them from landing, and I felt their soft bodies collide against my hand with each stroke. They were tenacious, ravenous, and Sven-Erik retreated under his helmet and closed the visor to protect his balding scalp. I felt mosquitoes on my head, parting my hair with their legs as they burrowed toward my skin. I swatted them off Suzanne's scalp, and I felt the sting of several along my neck and ears.

A curtain parted, and someone looked out at us. I waved, the curtain fell back into place, and someone opened the front door.

"*Hej!*" Sven-Erik greeted, his voice muffled inside his helmet.

A man with a shaved head, and wearing an oily sleeveless denim jacket, walked into the yard. He looked at us skeptically, as if our brand of machines and dress suggested we were from the wrong side of town. Sven-Erik lifted the visor of his helmet and introduced himself. The man looked annoyed, but then visibly softened as Sven-Erik spoke to him in Swedish. The man pointed once at Suzanne and me, and then rubbed his chin as if to adjust his expression. He looked again at Sven-Erik, and back at us. Sven-Erik looked our way, gestured, explained something, and the man laughed. His arms rose as if to welcome us, and then he went back inside.

Sven-Erik cleared the air around his head with one hand before closing the visor of his helmet. He assured us the American was still there, that he was asleep, but would be out in just a few minutes.

The three of us waited and swatted mosquitoes. Suzanne snapped the collar of her jacket around her neck and I helped her wrap a scarf around her head and neck so only her eyes showed. Sven-Erik looked snug in his helmet and gloves, and I thought of doing the same when the door opened and a ragged, road-worn man limped toward the steps leading into the yard. He looked like a mechanic, complete with black grease embedded into the crevices of his skin like tattoos. He wore a ragged pair of blue pants that were patched and frayed at the bottom of the legs, a shirt of indistinguishable color, and what looked like a Mao vest.

"Hi!" he said, not sure whom he should address. He walked heavily down the stairs holding the rail, and he kicked his right leg forward as if it was shackled with a heavy weight. "One, two of you, are from California?" he asked, and moved one finger like a pointer between the three of us.

"Us," I said. "I'm Allen, and this is Suzanne. Sven-Erik is a local. He showed us how to get here."

"David Barr. Pleased to meet you," he said, and gripped my hand with what felt like a rawhide chew-toy for a big dog.

"Someone told us you're going around the world on a Harley."

"Yeah, you could say that. Traversing all the continents actually, so it's a little farther than going around the world."

I looked down at his right leg, noticed the foot was made of metal, and realized it was a prosthesis. "Isn't it a little difficult riding with that?" I asked.

"I'm missing both," he said laughing, and reached down to pull the legs of his pants around his knees. David's left leg was an ordinary skin-tone prosthesis, but the right was created from an assortment of metal parts, welded and bolted together.

"What happened to that one?" Suzanne asked.

"I fell on it so many times the plastic disintegrated. I was in Colombia when it finally gave out. I went to a doctor there who told me a new one would cost seven-hundred dollars, but I didn't have that kind of money. So, I went to a welding shop and had a guy make me this one. This part here is made from a section of hydraulic ram, and this, the foot," he said as he lifted it for us to see, "is just a piece of quarter-inch steel plate with a piece of tire bolted to the bottom. It's not great, but it gets me around."

"Apparently. Where have you been so far?"

"Well, let's see. I began two and a half years ago. That was in South Africa. I first rode the length of Africa, crossed the Mediterranean on a ferry, and then rode through Europe to Nordkapp, the northernmost point in Western Europe. That's when I met these guys from Aurora for the first time. Then I rode to England where I did some work for the Leonard Chesshire Foundation. It's a group that helps people with handicaps. After a few months I shipped the bike to New York, rode to Washington State, up the Al-Can highway to Dead Horse Camp, Alaska. Then I turned around, headed south, and didn't stop until I reached Tierra del Fuego, in Argentina."

"Jesus!" I said, and felt all the grandeur of our own trip melt away like a wax monument. The place names spawned glorious images as David ticked them off like kilometer posts—the Congo, Sahara Desert, Algiers, Mediterranean Sea, Nordkapp, Anchorage, Managua, Pan-American Highway, the Amazon, Andes Mountains. I looked over at Suzanne and her mouth was hanging slack like a shoelace she'd forgotten to tie. She barely noticed as I picked a mosquito engorged with blood from her cheek.

"Why are you in Sweden again?" I asked.

"Well, that's part of the story," David said. "I shipped the bike to Hong Kong, rode across China, Mongolia, and Russia. I just came through Murmansk a week ago, and then rode to Luleå."

"Murmansk? That's a secret Russian naval base, a closed city," I said.

"Yeah, I know. But great people. I stayed with a retired subma-rine captain. The bike was on her last legs, again, and this guy and his buddies put me up and used a bunch of old equipment to help me get this far. At the border the Russians just let me through, wanted me out of there like I was a liability or something."

Sven-Erik poked me in the ribs with his elbow. He shot me a look of skepticism through his visor and rolled his eyes.

I asked David where he was going next.

"Back to England, and then I'll ship the bike to Australia. I'm planning to begin in Perth, ride around the country, then island hop through Indonesia, ride through Singapore, Malaysia, Thai-land, Vietnam, and back into China. Then the trip will be over, and I don't know what I'll do. I'll be broke."

"That's unbelievable," Suzanne said. "Where is your bike?"

"She's in the back, in a shed. Would you like to see her? I have to get a key from inside."

David walked toward the house, his leg making a metallic ratcheting in protest each time he kicked it in front of himself. I watched as he pulled his body up the steps and paused so he could right himself on his damaged legs before going in the door.

"He's *crazy*," Suzanne said in admiration.

"I think so, too," Sven-Erik said, believing Suzanne had been critical. "I don't think he did all those things. He is crazy in the head."

"I think he's wonderful!" I protested. "Can you imagine his journey? Across Africa, the Sahara, all the way to Argentina? China, Mongolia? That means he crossed the Gobi Desert! All the way across Russia."

"You think he did all those things?" Sven-Erik asked.

"Sure. You think he made it up?"

Sven-Erik looked bored and suggested it was time for him to go. The mosquitoes were getting worse, and he had things to do.

"You've got to at least see the bike," I said.

"Okay. We see the bike."

We followed David along a trail through the high grass, past an old wooden boat lazily concealed with a plastic tarp, to a shed behind the house. David unlocked a heavy wooden door and pushed it open. In the middle of the floor was his Harley-Davidson resting on its kickstand in the shadows. He turned on a light and we approached the bike.

The bike was as Malin had described it. It looked broken, as though someone had beaten it until the engine had stopped running. It was once a bright red Shovelhead model with a black frame and forks. There was a reminder of the chrome that had once highlighted the engine, rims, handlebars, and headlight. A greasy pillow was tied with a leather strap to where the seat had been. The area behind the rider had been transformed into a luggage rack with oilcloth bundles and leather bags tied to the frame. A wooden box, held together with wire and strapping, was set behind the pillow. The top was open and I looked inside. There was rope and wire, tools, plastic bottles of oil and tubes of grease. David explained how he tied on extra gas cans, his sleeping bag and tent, where he placed his small duffel of clothes and his rain suit. In front of the handlebars was another leather pouch that held additional tools, and below that a very small headlight the size of a bowl, which seemed inadequate for lighting David's way around the world. The gas tank was a log of his trip. On the right side was a painting of the world with an astral band surrounding it like a halo. The top of the tank revealed the true scope of the journey. The name of each country traversed had been painstakingly hand-painted in small white letters in columns that stretched from the top of the tank to the bottom.

"When the trip is over," David said, "she's supposed to go on display in the Harley-Davidson Hall of Fame. I hope that happens, so other people can see it and realize they can do a trip like this, too."

Small things on the bike attracted me: buckles and hooks, empty holes drilled into the frame, an upside-down Esso decal on the top of the air cleaner, a brass plaque fixed to the engine casing. I rubbed a coat of grease from it with my index finger and revealed a dedication from the Brazilian Policia Militaría.

"Nice boys," David said. "They helped me out of a big jam. Let me sleep on the police grounds and helped me get parts for the bike."

"But why are you doing this?" I had to ask.

"Well, that's a long story. If you'd like, we can go inside. Have some coffee, and talk."

Sven-Erik left, but Suzanne and I went inside and talked until one in the morning. Some guys in the club had bought David a big map of the world and had him trace his route. He spread it across a table and patiently retraced it for us, continent by continent, country by country, desert by desert, river by river. He told us about spending days in remote African villages, waiting for flooded roads to become dry enough to continue; of being blown off roads by gale winds and of falling off the bike twenty times in one day because of ice in the Andes; of having to wait hours in the middle of nowhere for help to lift the heavy bike from his body as precious gasoline dripped from the tank onto his clothes. He told us of crossing the Sahara, of the heat and endless sand, of getting stuck so many times he thought about walking away. He told us of his exhilaration of reaching Nordkapp in the middle of winter, of crossing the United States and reaching Anchorage exactly one year after leaving South Africa. We followed his finger around the world and listened to the long stream of words as he took us down the Americas, across China, Mongolia, Russia, and then, it finally came to rest in Luleå. "And here we are," he said.

A moment of reflective silence followed as Suzanne and I surveyed the scope of the map on the table. David took a sip of his now cold coffee and shifted his weight. The metallic ratcheting of his leg and the creaking of boards below his feet were the only sounds.

"That's incredible, David," Suzanne said. "But, once again, why are you doing this? It can't be easy for someone like you."

David explained how he was born in California, led a normal Central Valley life until the Vietnam War. "I did *time* over there," he said. "And when it was over, I just couldn't take any more of America. I've always been someone who had to act, and Vietnam was about inaction."

David said he went to Israel, worked on a kibbutz, did some

work with the military, but grew weary of the factionalism that diminished the clarity of the Israeli cause. He roamed from job to job in the oil fields of the Middle East for some years, and then the desire to act lured him to South Africa, where he fought against rebel forces in Rhodesia. He lost his legs when the personnel carrier he was riding in hit a land mine. After twenty operations and four amputations, David returned to active duty servicing heavy machine guns and training recruits in their use.

A year later he completed military service and returned home to California. As a way of putting his life back together he began restoring his Harley, and then struck upon the idea of riding it around the world. He planned, dreamed, and pored over maps. Then he went back to South Africa to work and took his bike with him. He saved his money and continued to plan the trip. One day it was time to go.

When his story was told, David said he had to get up early the next morning to begin his ride to England. He walked us outside and watched as we pulled our helmets on, mounted the bike, and rode away. I turned my head for a last look at him, and even through the semidarkness of night I saw him waving.

Suzanne and I levitated back to the hostel, floated on the tide of David's words. The roads were deserted, the night so still I imagined how the whine of our engine rolled through the quiet like the wake of a boat. We walked on tiptoe to our room, pulled our sleeping bags around us, and then whispered about our meeting with David until the sky began to brighten again.

~~~

I kept looking for David Barr the next morning. I hoped we'd cross his path before leaving. He had probably left at the crack of dawn and was well on his way down the coast by the time we left Luleå. He was on my mind though, was almost riding beside us as we turned onto the main route north and then turned again onto a narrow, frost-heaved road that led to the village of Jokk.

Jokk lay just north of the broken line that marks the crown of the globe, the Arctic Circle. We had planned to turn back from there and begin the long fall through Finland. As we drew closer I throttled back and downshifted to second gear. I wanted to sustain the moment and string it together into a clear narrative.

I didn't know why it was such an important point for me. After all, the Arctic Circle is just an arbitrary line drawn for the sake of convenience and administrative clarity; an illusive means of keeping the world neat and tidy. Lines and points have great significance to the world though. They're fought over and defended, scrupulously maintained and engineered. We spend years crafting our lives to one day get to the other side of one. Whether it be the Amazon Basin, the equator, India, or Ohio, who can really say where they begin or end exactly, but for many of us, it's important to get there. When we do, we pull out our cameras and take a picture, whisper a prayer, or get down on our knees and kiss the ground.

As Suzanne and I leaned over our atlas back home, I had gauged that the Arctic Circle would be the approximate halfway point of the trip. I'd imagined us arriving there seasoned and strong, in road shape. I'd imagined we'd spend the night there, light a bonfire, and sleep soundly through the Arctic night. I began to see the Arctic Circle as our apogee after the long vertical climb from Germany, a climb that would take us to the edge of a strange and enigmatic land.

As we approached the Circle a moose crossed the road in front of us and walked into a meadow, its rear legs rising exaggeratedly behind it like an awkwardly handled marionette. A herd of reindeer standing in the road parted to let us pass. Then the road widened to accommodate a narrow pullout and a big blue metal road sign that read:

POLCIRKELN
POLARCIRKEL
NAPAPIIRI
ARCTIC CIRCLE

I stopped the bike and we climbed off, removed our helmets, and I hugged and kissed Suzanne. "We made it!" I said. "We made it to the Arctic Circle!"

Someone had left a car battery on the side of the road, and I stood on it and looked south. It was as if I could see down the long expanse of Sweden, across to Denmark, and into Germany where we'd begun. I thought of all the miles and events that preceded this moment: the storms and islands, the people, the sea and forests; the clouds and the precious sun. And then I shifted my stance, looked toward Finland, and beyond that, Russia. I tried to imagine all that lay before us.

I jumped down and danced and spun in circles, and tried to pull Suzanne with me.

"But I'm cold," she protested.

"Cold? *Cold?* We made it! Aren't you happy?"

"Happy that we're going south where it will be warmer."

"But take this in," I said of everything around us. "We may never be here again."

"That would be fine with me," she mumbled as she swatted around her face. "And if you haven't noticed, the mosquitoes are worse than last night."

I hadn't noticed.

"Besides," she said. "I don't see what the big deal is. This looks just like Luleå, just like the last five hundred miles."

I took a look around, at the short, spindly trees and scrub brush, at the mosquitoes that moved like clouds of smoke, at the iron-gray sky above us, at some trash strewn at the base of the sign, and I became profoundly sad as I saw it through Suzanne's eyes.

"But we rode here together, you and I, on this bike, all the way from Germany. Doesn't that mean anything to you?"

She didn't say anything for several seconds. I should have let her alone, but I pressed. I was desperate to hear her say it was beautiful here, that the trip was a great idea, that she didn't want it to ever end.

"It means we have a long ways to go before we get back," she said icily.

"Please," I said, hardly able to contain my disappointment. "Please don't say another word."

seventeen

The history of Finland is a tale of survival and brief triumphs over the appetites of its expansionist neighbors, Sweden and Russia. From medieval times until the end of the Cold War, Finland was almost constantly invaded, fought over, and bartered away, with little regard for its native peoples. The Finns endured wars and rebellions, annexations and trumped-up treaties. They lived through the Great and Lesser Wraths, a famine that wiped out a third of the population, various disturbances, movements, wars, and depressions and somehow, the people always emerged again from the security of the forests and moved ahead. The demise of the Soviet Union and the end of the Cold War allowed the Finns to once again contemplate independence and freedom, though even that was but a brief euphoria. When Suzanne and I arrived a crippling recession had taken hold of the country.

The first thing I noticed about Finland was that the roads were narrower than in Sweden. They were pocked and patched with crumbling asphalt, and the yellow centerline wavered as if the painter had recorded a seismic movement deep within the earth. The cars were older than in Sweden, and the sturdy Volvos and

Saabs were replaced by nondescript and cheaper European and Russian brands. Many were patched together with gray primered fenders and doors. Fences around farms leaned and boards were missing. Homes and barns needed paint, and yards were overgrown with weeds and cluttered with old machinery and vehicles. On one farm a stack of fence rails had collapsed and spilled at awkward angles like pieces in a game of pick-up sticks. A barn door had fallen off its hinges, and a thin calf grazed on the overgrown lawn of a house, tethered with a frayed rope.

The Finns looked rougher than the Swedes. They looked like the kinds of people I'd see in a thrift store on a Saturday afternoon trying on old clothes, buying used bunk beds and chests of drawers. Unemployment was 20 to 30 percent in northern Finland, numbers reflected in bad teeth, out-of-date hairstyles, and too much make-up.

We stopped to change money in the town of Kemi, and afterward took some time to walk around its small and unremarkable center. We knew the language was an odd one, unlike any other in the world but Hungarian, but it became odder still as we looked at signs and eavesdropped on conversations. I'd tried to use a few words on the woman in the bank, but she only stared at me, then smiled, and tried to communicate in Swedish. Even simple phrases like *Puhutteko englantia?* (Do you speak English?) sounded terribly different than the way I'd practiced them at home. I wondered how we'd fare with greetings like *Hyvää päivä* (Good day) or simple requests like *Mistä lähtee saada juna maito?* (Where can I get milk?), let alone read *Leiriytyminen kielletty* (No Camping) on a sign and remember what it meant.

We walked into a store and I had an immediate lesson that *Työnnä* meant "push," and not "pull." The checker looked at me with an annoyed glare as Suzanne and I poked through a case of *juusto* (cheese), picked out some *leipä* (bread), and a bottle of *vesi* (water).

"Hyvää päivä," I said as best I could.

The woman said something under her breath, scanned our items, and then announced the total. *"Neljäkmmenta seitsemän."*

~~~

That night we stopped at the mouth of a river that emptied into the gulf. I set up the tent as Suzanne wandered along the river's edge, found a rock to sit on, and began writing a letter. When I was finished I joined her, and she moved over so there was room for the both of us on her rock. The temperature was almost warm and she'd stripped off a few of the layers of clothing she'd worn for crossing the Arctic Circle.

I listened to the tip of her pen scratch the paper, to the occasional pauses that marked her thoughts. I watched the dorsal fins of salmon pierce the air like small sails before disappearing, leaving tiny eddies that upset the surface. Three ducks flew down the river, almost touching the water as they went wide around a bend, their wings wheezing with each beat. Suzanne paused and stared after them.

"There's a reason why David Barr travels alone," she said.

I reached over and ran my hand down her arm. "Yes, I know."

A gull landed on the rock beside us, rustled its wings, and regarded us as if it had just occupied the seat beside us in a bus. Minutes passed as Suzanne and I watched as the bird preened, stiffened, and let go a teaspoon-sized excretion that ran slowly down the rock.

"You can travel like him, too, if that's what you need," she said carefully.

"That's not what I want. You know that," I said, trying to reassure her.

"You're getting pretty far out there, Allen. And I know what you'd really like is to be out there like David. I think what he's doing is great. It's wonderful. But I can only enjoy it from a distance. I couldn't do it."

"We've been traveling together for a long time. I can't imagine it ending."

"You used to have more patience. I had more tolerance. And it's never been as difficult as this trip," she said, and closed her notebook. "It's almost as though you're judging me through people like that woman fixing her bike, testing me by going so fast, and sizing up your possibilities through David's trip."

"I'd like to feel we both have the same goal in mind. And when we don't, when it feels like you can barely tolerate this, I admit I have to wonder how things would be different without you."

"What goal? What's our goal now?"

"To see this trip through."

She rubbed her face with her hands and I knew she was unsatisfied with yet another repetition of my story.

"It's like we're moving in different ways now," I said. "I'm always trying to get you to plunge in, and you're always trying to get me to take it easy. The result is that we're both fumbling. We're afraid to go at our own pace because we might just walk out of each other's lives," I said, and felt my eyes fill with tears.

The gull opened its wings and hopped off the rock, fell a few feet toward the water, and flew over the river. We followed it with our eyes until it disappeared over the sea.

We didn't say anything more. After a while Suzanne pressed her body against mine, and I slid my arm around her waist. Her head rested on my shoulder, and we watched the salmon swim patiently against the current of the river.

~~~

The next morning I had a long argument with our compass. We were riding south down the coast toward the town of Kokkola. The sky looked promisingly clear. Suzanne's hands rested reassuringly on my hips. The bike was running smoothly, and we were making good time through the tedium of the forest.

For months the compass had reliably confirmed our northward momentum. It had helped us through Bremen, Copenhagen, and Stockholm when the signs hadn't made sense. It had helped us find our way out of forests. But on that morning, as we rode almost due south, the compass doggedly maintained we were still heading northeast. It was as if we had been heading northeast for so long the needle had become stuck.

I tried to put it out of my mind, regarding it as a magnetic disturbance from the earth. We didn't even need a compass that day because the road was clearly marked. I wouldn't look at it for miles. I concentrated instead on the road, thought about what lay ahead of us. I calculated our fuel, the next time I had to change the oil. I wondered what riding in Russia would be like. But after a while not looking was like trying to ignore an itch, and I glanced down to see if anything had changed. But each time I did the compass insisted we were still heading northeast. We stopped for gas and I pulled the compass from the map case, turned it over, tapped it, and spun it around. The dial moved freely, but always settled back in the same place. Suzanne looked at it too, shrugged her shoulders, and told me not to worry.

I checked our map to confirm we were in fact heading in the right direction. I unfolded the whole thing on the ground and traced our path from the Swedish border. I even asked the gas station attendant, but she didn't speak English, and my phrasebook Finnish only muddled the matter.

As we continued I noted the towns we passed, the mileage between them, and confirmed that Helsinki was somewhere farther along the way. But still, the compass persisted unwaveringly. I poked it with my finger through the plastic cover of the tank bag where it rested on top of our map, but the dial only wobbled, and then resumed its position.

I thought of the endless stories of pilots who had crashed their planes because they hadn't trusted their instruments, how they'd been upside down instead of right-side up, or sideways, or heading north instead of south, and despite their compass, horizon, and altimeter, they'd flown out to sea, into the side of a mountain, or straight into the ground. Perhaps, I fussed, the compass had been wrong from the very beginning and was working properly now. Perhaps we weren't anywhere near where I thought we were. Perhaps I'd led Suzanne into this despite her better judgment, despite her pleas and patience. I slapped the compass with the palm of my hand and shook the tank bag, but the needle on the compass persisted. Then I forgave it, said I was sorry, smoothed out its resting place on the map so it lay perfectly flat.

Miles passed. Forest, sea, fields, forest, forest, forest. The engine turned precisely, smoothly, and I became hyperaware of something about to go wrong. I tried to ignore the compass again, but the small round dial was like the pupil of an eye staring up at me. Each time I looked, it was there, suggesting I was wrong, off the mark, foolish, suggesting Suzanne had been right all along. *What kind of a stunt are you trying to pull, Allen?* a voice that sounded like my father's asked. Just one little slip, and *bang!* It would be all my fault.

But we had just passed Pyhäjoki. Yppäri was down the road. Or was it? Yes, there was a sign, and I checked the spelling. It *wasn't* me. I hit the compass with my fist and tried to pull it from the map holder by the piece of strong nylon string I'd tied it with so carefully back home. We swerved and Suzanne pinched me with her thighs, yelled through my helmet, *"What's going on?"*

I pulled over and stopped. Suzanne jumped off and stood in front of me, her eyes blazing with alarm. "What is it? Are you okay?"

"The compass," I said. "It's all wrong."

"The *compass?* I said just ignore it."

"You don't understand," I said, and got off the bike and began untying the string.

"Don't understand what?"

"It's telling me we're going the wrong way. All morning long it's been telling me we're going the wrong way."

"So? Ignore it."

"And almost since the beginning of this trip you've been telling me the same thing." The knot came apart and I pulled the compass free of the string. I stepped off the road and put the compass on the ground.

"What are you doing?" Suzanne asked.

The compass was still mockingly pointing northeast as I smashed it with a rock. The face cracked and the inside filled with champagne-sized bubbles. I hit it again and the plastic body shattered. The liquid inside stained the ground and smelled like kerosene. I smashed it once more and the small black pupil disappeared into the mud.

A silent minute passed, and I would have given almost anything to hear the sound of Suzanne's feet moving toward me, to feel her arms slide around my neck, to hear her whisper in my ear, "There, there, my love." A truck passed in a rush that sounded like a waterfall and then the silence returned.

I walked back to the bike. Suzanne looked at me, and rather than getting mad, her face softened, as if she understood. She handed me my gloves and helmet and we left.

~~~

Rain and wind hurried us down the coast of Finland. It was just as well. The land was as featureless as the sea, and the green of the forest became monotonous. Even the towns had nothing to offer us. They were single-purpose places—ports, an oil refinery, terminuses for the millions of logs harvested from the surrounding forest—and were as Spartan as outposts. They felt like obligatory settlements thrown up to lay claim to the land.

At the seacoast town of Vaasa we turned inland and rode across the lower portion of Finland toward Helsinki. The land there began to roll uncertainly, and any sections not saturated with forest were taken over by fields of electric-yellow mustard blossoms.

We entered the lake district, the swollen, soggy middle of Finland. These innumerable lakes comprise a third of the country, and many are connected in a seemingly endless chain of sounds, canals, rivers, and streams. We decided to spend the night on the shore of one outside the town of Valkeakoski, a town just a hundred miles northwest of Helsinki.

The camping area had a municipal quality to it, as if people used it for a convenient getaway from the capital. There were barbecue grills and picnic tables, spigots with running water between sites, and trash cans with plastic liners. A paved road wound through the camping area with pull-outs where families had sprawled as though they'd been there for weeks. Clothes hung from lines stretched between trees and tent poles. Children's toys were littered around campfires. The shore of the lake was blocked by a wall of house trailers parked bumper to bumper to take maximum benefit of the view. We were about to leave when we saw a trail that led to a secluded corner beside the water. Some canoes were parked there, and a small stream emptied into the lake. I drove the bike over the trail and parked beside an old gazebo.

We set up the tent, and then Suzanne sat on the shore of the lake. I rode back into the camp and parked beside one of the water spigots so I could wash a layer of dead insects from the bike. A gang of children rode up on their bicycles and watched me. They were shy and squirmed when I tried to talk to them. I spoke some Finnish phrases that made them laugh. One of them, a little boy, tried to teach me to say something phonetically. When I'd succeeded he smiled, and quietly asked to sit on the motorcycle. Once in the saddle the boy underwent a transformation. He growled and twisted the throttle so many times I thought the engine would flood. He clenched his little teeth and made squealing sounds to mimic the wild spinning of tires. The other children got on their bicycles and pretended to be racing alongside him. But there was no keeping up with the boy on the motorcycle. At one point he looked quickly over his shoulder at his friends as they fell far behind, and then he sped out of sight.

A commotion began off to one side that brought the race to a halt. A family of Gypsies was camped there, five men, three women, and so many children that I wasn't able to count them. I'd noticed them earlier because they were so out of place in the camp. The men sat at a table drinking from dark glasses and playing cards. They were all heavy, with dark skin, greased black hair, and mustaches. They all wore matching short-sleeved pullovers with bright horizontal stripes, pressed slacks, and shiny black shoes. The women were magnificently odd. They had long black hair tied with bright ribbons, and they wore pale blue chiffon blouses covered with glittering silver sequins the size of coins, and long, black velvet skirts that draped over their vast hips. Their children were all stripped to the waist and barefoot.

The Gypsy kids had been chasing each other around their camp. They were having a good time as they shrieked and eluded each other. Periodically one of the men yelled, as if to quiet them down. He had done so several times while I was cleaning the bike, his voice raised so it carried through the entire camp. It was one of those yells, a prolonged wailing cry, that broke up the race. The children on the bikes and I watched as the Gypsy man pushed himself up from the table and began chasing the children. The Gypsy kids stopped their laughing and scattered. Like a predator, the man closed in on the slowest child. He raised a switch above his head and began whipping the child across his bare back. The boy fell to the ground and writhed and screamed in the dirt as the man beat him. Then the man took his place at the table, picked up his hand of cards and resumed the game. One of the Gypsy women, who hadn't moved during the fracas, walked quickly over to the boy and pulled him by the arm across the road to a cinder-block bathroom. The boy fought her the entire way, but he was no match for her bulk. His tortured screams echoed from inside the bathroom. The boy on the motorcycle climbed down and whispered something urgent to his friends, as if to avoid angering the Gypsy man. Then they climbed on their bicycles and slipped away.

The screams from the bathroom finally subsided. The Gypsy men continued their game, and the women brought food to the table. The children emerged from their hiding places and began to play quietly in the middle of the camp with a ball. Then the child who'd been beaten was led across the road and let loose to rejoin them.

All seemed right again. The Gypsy men played cards and ate, their children played with their ball, and the women stood in a bright huddle beneath a tree. Then the ball went wild. It landed on the table, disrupted the cards, and knocked over a drink. The man who'd done the beating bellowed. He climbed from his seat and whipped the same child a few more times with his switch. When the man was done he resumed his seat, smoothed back his hair, and said something like, "Damn kids!" As if it was her task, the same woman pulled the child from the ground and dragged him across the road to the bathroom, but this time her grip was not strong enough. The child broke loose and ran to the table. He grabbed the switch and gave his tormentor several whacks across the shoulders and head. The man curled for a moment to protect himself and then rose in a quick fury. He screamed as he ran and kicked at the boy's legs until he tripped him. Then the man tore the switch from the boy's hands and began whipping him as if he was a poisonous snake. The child wailed and spat and jerked along the ground.

Again the man took his place at the table. He filled his glass and took a drink to refresh himself. The man on his right shuffled the cards, and the one across from him scratched the inside of his ear. This time two women pulled the child from the ground and led him screaming into the bathroom where they remained for a very long time.

~~~

Suzanne and I sat on the shore of the lake and watched the sun fall toward the horizon. The trees on the far shore lost their detail and became like a blunt wall, and the water acquired a dark steel-blue sheen. We realized we'd fallen far enough south to experience night again. The darkness made us tired, and I think it was I who suggested we go to sleep early.

I fell into a deep sleep, as if someone had concocted a special opiate for me. Through it I remember hearing a bird sing from a tree above our tent in long weeping notes, followed by three shorter bursts that rose in pitch at the end like a question. I dreamed the Gypsy boy was the source of the song, that he was crouched on his haunches, sitting on a tree branch high above camp where no one could touch him. His chest worked like a compact bellows to create the wind for each note, and his little mouth worked furiously to form each one just so. Another voice intruded, a deep smoker's voice that resonated and settled in the bottom of my ears. The Gypsy boy stopped his singing. He jumped to the ground and ran awkwardly into the bathroom revealing long red streaks down his back that looked like plumage. The voice became louder and was joined by another. Someone laughed for a long time, and then I was awake.

"What is it?" Suzanne asked sleepily.

"Some people in the gazebo," I said.

"Great. Right beside our tent. Out of the whole campground they had to come here."

"They're just talking," I said.

We lay still and tried to fall back to sleep. It sounded like three men and I pictured how they were sitting on benches built on the edge of the round floor. I'd sat on one of them earlier that afternoon. The wood planks were scarred with initials and names, and so many instances of the English word "Fuck."

The men spoke in short, low sentences that were broken by barrages of laughter that lifted us farther from sleep. A while later some women joined them, and their higher voices added range and wholeness to the noise. For a half hour it was only a dull droning like the hum of insects in the background. A while later the voices began to rise and warble like out-of-tune instruments.

"They're drinking," Suzanne said, and I guessed that the gazebo was the one out-of-the-way place in the camp for people to go. In an ironic attempt to be polite to the other campers, they'd gone there.

"They'll go away soon," I said hopefully. "They'll get drunk and go to sleep."

"But they're Scandinavians."

What felt like an hour passed and the party only got louder. A woman began singing the Beatles' "Sergeant Pepper's Lonely Hearts Club Band," and the others joined in. The woman got the words wrong, and because she was leading, the others stumbled, too. They laughed drunkenly and began again. Another woman started to yell as though she'd suffered some slight, then began to cry, and Suzanne hissed, "This is ridiculous!"

I got our flashlight and discovered the batteries were dead. I lit matches and opened our phrasebook in search of the right combination of words to ask that they please keep it down. The book contained detailed sections for shopping and sightseeing, public transport, accommodation, doctors, and dealing with customs officials, but nothing for unruly drunks.

I found *Anteeksi* (excuse me) and memorized it as I looked for other words to string into an intelligible sentence. "*Olkaa hyvä* (please). *Oklaa hyvä*," I practiced.

"Don't forget to say *kiitos*," Suzanne said.

"What?"

"*Kiitos*. Thank you. Remember? But only if they quiet down."

But I couldn't find words for "quiet down," or "we'd like to sleep." I burned my fingers on several matches and decided to just wing it.

I opened the door of the tent and was struck by the total darkness outside. I couldn't see the gazebo, though I knew it was only about twenty feet away.

"*Anteeksi*," I said into the black. I heard a bottle tip over and roll across the floor of the gazebo. Their voices continued undiminished. "*Anteeksi*," I called again, and someone said "Shussshhh," and the others became silent. "Hi. We're trying to sleep over here," I said in English, figuring at least some of them would understand, "and we'd really appreciate it if you'd keep your voices down, or move somewhere else."

My appeal was followed by silence as if they were trying to decipher the words. A man whispered. A woman began to sing again. Someone burped.

"Oh, God," Suzanne groaned behind me.

I pulled on my pants and boots and walked toward the sound of their voices. I saw the glow of cigarettes, recognized the outline of the gazebo, and walked to the base of the steps. I stepped on the soft, relaxed meat of someone's arm and they didn't move.

"*Anteeksi!*" I said, and had their attention. "Hi! We're trying to sleep right over there. It's pretty late. Maybe it's time you all went back to your camp."

I saw the outline of faces staring at me. The ember of a cigarette rose to someone's mouth and flared.

"Yah, right," a man sneered.

"Excuse me?" I asked.

"Yah. Fuk'in right."

Someone turned on a flashlight and pointed it into my eyes. I expected to feel the sting of a bottle off my head and moved back. A woman let loose a repressed giggle that sputtered from her lips, and the others followed.

I lay in the tent and seethed. I fantasized about all the evil I could unleash on them. I thought of spraying them with a fire hose, of following them back to their camps and slashing the tires of their vehicles, of throwing gasoline on their tents and saying, "Yah, right!" before I set them on fire.

Eventually the sky brightened and each of the voices slipped away. Suzanne and I fell asleep for a while, and when we woke, we packed and left for Helsinki.

eighteen

For three days the bike remained parked. I covered it with a plastic tarp and threaded the lock through both wheels and the frame, as if to keep it from continuing on without us. And for three days Suzanne and I slept on a bunk bed in a youth hostel dormitory on the north end of Helsinki.

The hostel was set beneath the bleachers of the 1952 Olympics stadium. A long corridor paved with squares of brown linoleum followed the outer curve of the building, and off it were doorways that led to dormitories, several small bathrooms, a dining area, and a communal kitchen we had to stand in line to use. There was a large sitting room with several ragged chairs and mismatched formica tables, the tops of which had been branded by smokers despite the dirty, plate-sized ashtrays on top of each. In the corner of the room was an oversized color TV that flickered intermittently when it was in use.

Our room was lined with bunk beds upon which an ever-changing tide of travelers briefly slept. Most of them remained anonymous, but a few stuck out. One night there was an Asian couple in the bunk beside ours who slept with all their clothes on and with their backpacks placed on the end of their beds. Before going to sleep they both tied a string from their wrists to the frame of their pack. They were gone when we woke up the next morning. Another night there was a German couple with three small children. The woman snored loudly all night. The next morning a rail-thin English woman complained and rudely told the woman there was a hotel down the street. "But Finland is so expensive, so we *must* sleep in hostel," the German woman explained on the verge of tears.

On each night of our stay a young woman occupied the corner bed. She was alone, and I always saw her in the sitting room, where she claimed the same chair, her legs curled protectively beneath her as she wrote furiously in a notebook. She was there each morning when we left, and she was there when we returned at night. She never smiled or looked up from her paper.

In the small kitchen we met Charles and Alan, two young men from South Africa whose aim was to remain abroad for as long as possible. We shared adjoining burners on the stove one night as they made an elaborate curry with fresh vegetables and a pile of meat. Charles and Alan had been out about six months and still glowed with the enthusiasm of discovery. "Nuthin betta," Alan proclaimed. "Sha beats tha chang'in a tha gawd beck home," he said, in reference to the transition from white to black rule taking place in South Africa.

"Cood bae civil wah," Charles added, as he cut vegetables into precise squares and rounds. He then explained the differences between the major political factions in minute and clear detail, and outlined several possible scenarios that spanned the gap between all out war and the beginnings of a Pan-African confederation of brotherhood.

"But at tha end a tha day," Alan concluded, "me an Chaels hev ta ate this pot-a curry, dan't we Chaels?"

There was Don, a soft-spoken guy from Los Angeles, with a sharp goatee and a ring on his thumb, who had been churning through Europe in search of the ironic and profound. I first met him in the bathroom standing at the urinals and thought he was

French because he had such style for someone on the road. He
wore trousers, a matching shirt, and nice leather shoes. He had on
a long brown overcoat, and his hair looked freshly styled. I said,
"Hi," and he said, "Nice bike. I saw you ride up. Looks like a cool
way to travel."

Don joined Suzanne and me in the sitting room, and he told us
he'd just come from Berlin where he could barely tell the city had
once been divided by the Iron Curtain. He seemed disappointed, as
though he'd missed something.

"But," he said hopefully, "I'm going to Russia after this."

And there was Jim, an eighty-three-year-old retired merchant
marine from New York who ticked-off the countries he'd traveled
to like a birder reciting his life list.

"Finland makes one hundred-two," he told me proudly just
after we met. "Before this trip I only had ninety-eight, but Finland
makes one hundred-two."

Jim was short and bull-strong. He looked more like sixty than
eighty-three, but the first time I saw him I thought he was dying.

It was our first morning at the hostel, and I was waiting for
Suzanne in the lobby. Jim was sitting on a plastic chair, sweating
and staring horrified at the wall before him as if he had just remembered something terrible. He was panting and working hard
to unzip his jacket. After it opened he sat very still as if to keep
from upsetting something fragile. I stood up and asked him if I
could help, but his hands pleaded with me to stay where I was.

I sat back down and pretended to read a tourist brochure titled
This Week in Helsinki. I watched him struggle out of his jacket as
if it weighed a hundred pounds. We eyed each other as he labored
for breath. I looked over at the receptionist once and Jim knew
what I was thinking. His eyes filled with worry and he seemed to
say he would rather die than raise a ruckus.

Suzanne came out and said she was ready to go. I whispered
what was happening and we sat and read the brochure. In the middle of page two, after reading a glam article about harbor tours,
Jim's body began to relax. He wiped his sweaty face with a red ban-
danna and coughed. I read to the middle of page three when he

pulled himself heavily from his chair and stood up. He steadied himself, and then shuffled toward the corridor that led to the rooms. He walked past Suzanne and me and he smiled weakly, like someone who was nauseous. Then the fingers of his left hand rose from where they hung at his side and gave a kind of wave. "Thanks," he whispered as he passed. He never mentioned the event again.

~~~

Suzanne and I began each day by making the half-hour trek to the harbor where the city began. From there we could look out toward the countless islands of a vast archipelago. Behind us the flanks of the peninsula that Helsinki has grown across were apparent, and in the distance we could see where the forest regained its primacy. The weather was unusually fine except for a few showers and cold winds we escaped by ducking into a shop or café, and from those shelters we observed the weather dispassionately, like watching a storm on TV.

Our copy of *This Week in Helsinki* informed us about the devastating fire of 1808 that consumed most of the city. It told us how the city had been rebuilt on an efficient grid pattern of wide boulevards and how the new city center had been modeled after the Empire-style buildings of St. Petersburg. The glaring white dome of the Lutheran cathedral dominated the city center, and our brochure told us we would find the cultural heart of Finland in the streets surrounding it. We only found other tourists, antique shops, and bland cafés. Our brochure urged us to visit the Government Palace, the House of Scientific Estates, the Theater Museum, and Uspenski Cathedral.

Instead we discovered the shipyards west of town where a freighter and two cruise ships were under construction. A perimeter fence kept us away, but the flying bridges and upper decks of the ships rose above it. Against the sky and clouds they looked like the foundation a mountain would be built upon. Immense cranes fed slabs of steel to the men we couldn't see working below.

Through a hole in the fence I was able to see the raw sculpture of an enormous hull taking shape. A small army of men clung to a scaffold built against its side, their task so huge they didn't appear to move. Showers of sparks fell like golden rain to the ground as the men welded the skin of the ship together. The heavy clang of hammers against steel suggested the ship was being beaten into shape. Had they given tours of the facility we would have spent time there, as I wanted to see how the construction of a ship was managed. I imagined the patience, the long view of time the people who built them must take, and the small ways they measured their progress.

We stopped and studied the main train station several times, a building I had wanted to see since I first discovered a picture of it in an encyclopedia as a boy. The exterior facade was what had struck me. It was a handsome art nouveau building of buff-colored stone that was made extraordinary by the pair of massive sentinels guarding the entrance. They looked like the strong citizens depicted in old Soviet propaganda posters, people who became monolithic by the clarity of their dedication. Each sentinel held a large glass and copper globe that illuminated the front of the building at night. The light hardened their features in a way that made them ominous, like ancient totems that kept spirits at bay. It was as if the station were something holy, a temple, and that all who entered were blessed.

And we walked through every neighborhood that surrounds the city center, and when we went through them, we put our map away and just walked until we became tired, or until something caught our eye. It was usually something small: a cat pressed behind a pane of glass that appeared to be melting on a rainy afternoon, a young couple washing rugs by hand in the water of the sea, or a poster of Jimi Hendrix that grinned at us from inside a garage stacked with bicycles and skis, a dusty sports car in pieces on the floor. We stopped for the paint on a door, a deep blue with red trim and a polished brass knob in the middle that made me want to knock and see if we would be invited in; and we stopped for a toothless drunk with lips like peeling paint. He held his hand out in a way that made me question if he wanted money or a hand up. I gave him a few coins, and we moved along.

In the evenings after dinner Suzanne and I organized our passports, visas, motorcycle registration, insurance, and letter of passage from the Russian Consulate in San Francisco. We went over our maps and decided on an alternate route to St. Petersburg that bypassed an area where road bandits had been reported. I studied a legend of Russian road signs, and Suzanne and I practiced translating Cyrillic letters to English. I tucked away several five-dollar bills, the preferred denomination for bribes. We washed all our clothes and packed freeze-dried soups and vegetables, oatmeal, and an extra water bottle for gasoline in our luggage cases. I went outside, uncovered the bike, and checked bolts that were already tight, fluids that were clean and full, and double-checked electrical connections and tire wear. I went through our spare parts—filters, fuses, spark plugs, extra bulbs, electrical wire, patch kit, air cartridges, oil, and tools—and realized we could never carry enough.

After our chores Suzanne and I migrated to the sitting room where we wrote and read. The woman who slept in the corner bed was always in her chair, writing, and I decided she must have left someone and was trying to explain why.

Invariably we'd also see Don, Jim, and the South Africans, and we'd drift into conversation. Jim told us about his years in the merchant marine, of traveling to the same ports year after year, how it wasn't a very glamorous job after all, but the pay had been good, and it beat years in a factory and a house in the suburbs. Jim said he was married once, but that his wife died in childbirth. "I was at sea at the time. Don't remember where.... And the child, a boy, he died shortly after. We hadn't even picked out a name."

"You never remarried?" Suzanne asked.

"Almost," he said. "Years later. A wonderful woman. And rich. But she didn't like to travel much, and she was used to having her way. Wanted me around all the time and, well, I didn't want to lose my independence. It's all I have left."

Suzanne and Don usually fell into a private conversation. It was oddly pleasing listening to them. They talked of things

Suzanne and I had talked about when we first met: where they were born, where they went to school, parents and siblings. Suzanne told Don about the dog that bit her lip as a child, how she wouldn't eat tomatoes unless they're in sauce. She told him about her parents' divorce, and cried, and Don touched her arm. Don said his parents were divorced, too, and he made her laugh when he spoke about growing up in Los Angeles. Suzanne told Don about our trip to Indonesia, and said that she'd like to see New Zealand again. And he told her about the heat in Morocco, how he was constantly hassled by men and boys to be his guide, how small Venice is. Watching them from my place across the table made it easy to imagine them together.

"Good news!" Alan and Charles announced one night. "Wer goin' ta Russia!"

They'd applied for visas on a lark and got them. They'd already booked passage on the train to St. Petersburg and reserved beds in the same hostel as us. They were leaving the next morning, and Charles said they'd be looking for Suzanne and me. "It'all bae a pawty, mun!"

"Too bad I have to leave in a few days," Jim said. "Russia would make one hundred-three."

"Hundred-three w'at?" Charles asked.

"Countries," Jim explained.

~~~

One hundred and twenty-five miles to the Russian border and the road was no different than the others we'd traveled across Finland. The same forest grew on either side of the pavement. Brief clearings meant yet another farm. Prosaic little towns were spaced with a calculated regularity. Occasionally we were rewarded with a glimpse of the Baltic through the trees.

As we approached the border I looked for signs of the terrible disintegration taking place in the former Soviet Union, of the violence of the Russian mafia and of the road bandits lurking on the other side, anything that would confirm even one of the rumors and warnings we'd heard. I looked for police, a military presence, but the people in the towns and fields looked like all the others we'd seen, and they seemed to go about their business with the same ease.

Outside the town of Hamina I saw a long column of camouflaged troops working their way along the road ahead. There were about a hundred of them on green military bicycles. Perhaps, I thought, this was an elite unit that could silently dispatch themselves to remote sections of the forest, crack troops trained to hold off a battalion with just a few bullets from the cover of a tree. They were riding toward us at a good rate, their heads down to help slice through the wind, their polished black boots pumping like machines. I slowed to pull over so we could ask the commander the latest information. The lead man lifted his face when he heard the bike. His cheeks were flushed, his red lips parted in a smile as he noticed us. He waved and I saw that he was not much more than a boy. Down the line one of the riders broke ranks and swerved onto the road. He pulled the nose of his bike up and began to ride a wheelie. Another leaned lower over the handlebars of his bike and worked his right hand like a throttle. They were all boys despite the machine gun each humped on his back. They smiled and waved to us. I honked the horn and one of them waved so enthusiastically he lost his balance and fell.

And then we were there.

The border was less substantial than I'd imagined. There was a twenty-four-hour diner and truckers' store stocked with alcohol, cigarettes, small appliances, condoms, cassettes, t-shirts, and other duty-free items. There was a gas station, and just a little farther on, a concrete-and-glass building with a Finnish flag hung from a pole above it.

I filled the tank until gas began to overflow and gave the bike one last inspection. Suzanne spent the last of our Finnish money on a box of crackers, a square of cheese, two chocolate bars, and a cola. We packed the food away, and then I asked Suzanne if she was ready to go. She opened her arms as if to ask me the same question.

There was just one transport truck in line to cross the border before us. We parked the bike behind it and entered the border post. The truck driver held a stack of papers, which he exchanged one at a time with an official behind the counter. The trucker was a heavy man whose bulk was exposed by the thin cotton t-shirt he wore. It wasn't quite long enough to conceal his bloated kidneys and the patch of matted hair on his lower back. With each exchange of papers the trucker shifted his weight, causing his pants to fall and reveal the crevice of his buttocks. The trucker and the official chatted about what could have been the weather or the score of a soccer game. Another official, a woman who was typing into a computer, added something that made them both laugh.

"Maybe the road's just fine," Suzanne whispered. "This guy looks like he's going across town, not running a gauntlet."

The truck driver gathered his papers, said good-bye, and then it was our turn.

I handed our passports and papers over and watched the man's expression. He flipped through the pages, found a blank one, stamped it, and then did the same with the other. He didn't even bother to look at our other papers.

"How's the road to St. Petersburg?" I asked.

"Not so good," he said casually in English. "You must be careful. Between the towns you must be more careful."

"Have there been problems?"

"Things happen," he said dispassionately, as though commenting on a place very far away.

"And petrol? Is there petrol along the road?"

"Sometimes, yes. But this petrol is not so good. You have motorbike?" he asked, and then looked past us through the window toward the bike.

"Yes."

"I once have one...but then I crash. Be careful."

Beyond the border inspection was a high wire fence and a swath of shaved earth that stretched as far as we could see on either side of the road. We rode over a convergence of Finnish and Russian asphalt and began to bounce along the uneven surface. A stone on the right bore the letters "CCCP," the Cyrillic abbreviation of the disbanded Soviet Union. We passed a small guard shack where a Russian soldier with a machine gun hung across his chest flashed us a peace sign and toothy grin.

We rode for almost a mile and saw the beginning of a line of trucks waiting to clear Russian customs. A quarter mile farther was an old wooden building that looked like a fruit stand. A soldier put up his hand for us to stop.

The building was constructed of weathered plywood painted a dull brown. The inside of the building was almost dark and we knew where to go from the path worn through the linoleum. The air was heavy with the smell of sweat, tobacco, steamed cabbage, and sour meat.

Suzanne and I stepped up to a small window. Two young men sat at a tiny desk on the other side and shared a single wood chair. Their faces were red and pinched as if we'd caught them in the middle of a joke. They tried very hard to look official, but I smiled and they giggled. An older officer led a muzzled German shepherd through the room and the two boys hid their faces in their work until he passed.

"Pass!" the one on the left side of the chair demanded in a high voice.

Suzanne handed him our passports.

"Auto? Autocar?" he wanted to know.

"*Nyet*. Motorcycle," I said, and handed our registration and insurance papers to them, which they regarded like hieroglyphs on papyrus.

"Auto?" the boy asked again. "Auto!"

"Car," the other said to help. "You come in car?"

"No. We have a motorcycle," I repeated, and Suzanne held up her helmet for them to see.

They looked at each of our papers very carefully as if searching for something. They occasionally pointed to a sentence and whispered. A woman in an identical brown uniform looked briefly over our shoulders, gave an order, and then moved on. Soldiers passed in and out of the building carrying papers from the trucks waiting outside. The boys seemed stuck on a particular page.

One of the boys picked up the handset of an old crank telephone and waited. Someone answered and the boy referred to the document as he spoke. The other boy interjected, pointed to our letter of passage and held up Suzanne's passport. The boy on the phone repeated what his colleague had discovered, and then hung up. Then they spread our papers and passports on their small desk, stamped each with a bright orange emblem, and handed them back. "Please," one of them said, and motioned for us to continue through the building.

An older woman dressed in a faded blue smock motioned Suzanne and me toward her. She had us step through a metal detector and held her hands out for our papers. She looked through them quickly, handed them back, and motioned us along the trail on the floor.

The thudding of heavy boots filled the room and the woman's hand pulled my elbow. "Moment," she said. I turned around and an officer leaned through the window the boys sat behind. His voice was raised as he questioned them and I could picture the two boys squirming on their shared seat. The officer looked our way, and walked quickly toward us. The alarm on the detector sounded as he stepped through it, sending the woman into a panic.

"Pass!" he demanded above the machine's buzzing.

"Do you speak English?" I asked him.

He snapped at the woman who fiddled nervously with her machine until it was quieted. "Little. Pass!"

"Is there a problem?"

The officer said nothing as he shuffled through our papers. I pointed out our insurance and registration, our letter of passage, the fresh stamps on our visas.

"Everything is in order," Suzanne offered.

"We see," he said, and walked back through the detector with our papers. It began to buzz again and the woman reached to turn it off.

"What's the problem?" I called after the officer, but he disappeared into an office and closed the door.

"What's that all about?" Suzanne asked.

"Probably just a mix up."

I asked the woman operating the metal detector if she spoke English, but she only shrugged. I started to walk across the room to ask the boys what had happened but she put her hand out for me to stay.

Twenty minutes passed. The office door remained closed. I asked the woman if she could check what was going on but she ignored me. It was as though the matter had already been settled and they'd forgotten to tell Suzanne and me what we were supposed to do.

A half hour passed. Forty minutes. Finally the door opened and the officer reappeared with our papers in hand. The woman rushed to her machine and turned it off before he walked through it again.

"You have big problem," he said, as if the situation was terminal. "Big, big problem."

"What is it?" I asked. I'd heard the same refrain many, many times before while traveling through Eastern Europe, and it almost always meant that a fee was in order.

"No Russia. You go back."

"But why?"

"You have not the right paper," he said, and handed them back to me.

"Which paper?" I asked.

"The right paper."

"But we have the right papers," I said, and began to display them. "We have passports and visas. We have this insurance paper. It says right here it's good in Russia. We have our registration...a letter from the Russian Consulate, and it's even stamped," I said, and offered them all back for his inspection. "We *have* all the papers."

"You have not the *right* paper," he said, and clasped his hands behind his back.

"Yes we do. You can see here that the Russian Consulate, *your* consulate, in San Francisco, California, has approved all these documents and given us their permission to enter Russia."

"No!" he said, getting angry, and I noticed the rest of the soldiers in the room had stopped what they were doing to watch us.

"What paper do we need then?" Suzanne asked.

"The *right* paper. I say you needs the *right* paper."

"Show us the right paper," I said. "What does it look like?"

"How can I show? You have not the right paper."

"But in San Francisco...."

"Those Russians know not what happens. I say those papers is no good," he said, and began to walk away.

"Look. Can't we pay you for this paper?" I said and opened my wallet. "Isn't there a fee we can settle on? We have dollars."

He turned quickly around and looked me in the eye. "No!"

"But we met this American guy who just rode across Russia on a motorcycle, alone," Suzanne explained. "He even rode through Murmansk, your secret naval base."

"It is done! The visa is kaput."

"What do you mean?" I asked. I looked at our visas and saw heavy black lines scratched through their middle. I opened my passport and the line was replicated there as well.

~~~

Early the next morning we parked the bike along a busy street near the Russian Consulate in Helsinki. From there we could see a long line of people already assembled outside the gate. A strong wind blew between the buildings and picked up dust, leaves, scraps of paper, and whipped them into dervishes the size of children that clattered against the sides of cars and buildings as they ran down the street. An old woman loaded palettes of bread into the back of a delivery truck and stopped to watch us as we parked. She was stooped and thin, but she lifted two palettes at a time with a mechanical precision. Sweat ran down her face and collected on the end of her nose in a translucent ball that shone like a jewel. She sniffed as though trying to pull it back inside her body, but it finally broke free, fell onto a loaf, and was absorbed into the crust. The woman stopped for a moment more and smiled at Suzanne and me as we talked and gathered our papers, then she wiped her face with her sleeve and went back to work. She hefted the palettes until they were all in the truck, then she called to someone. A fat little man with a bushy mustache appeared from inside the building. He said something sarcastic and the woman replied with what sounded like, "Piss off!" The man laughed, waved his hand to dismiss her, and climbed into his truck and drove away. Another truck took the place of the first. Two men wheeled a new stack of palettes from inside the building and left them on the sidewalk. They greeted the new driver and ushered him inside. The woman wiped her brow, took a deep breath, and resumed her work.

"This could take a while," I said to Suzanne.

"I know."

"An hour or more," I said.

"That's okay. I have my book," she said.

While waiting to cross the street I looked back at Suzanne sitting on the bike. She was facing backward, her back reclined against the tank bag, her feet stretched comfortably over the seat. Behind her the old woman was still loading palettes into the truck as another waited in line.

The line outside the embassy stretched half a block down the street and I walked to the end of it. The man in front of me was Russian and he could speak a little English. He said he'd been standing in line every day for a week trying to get through the gate for an important paper that would allow him to remain in Finland a while longer. He said most of the people in line were also Russian, and that they too were there for the same reason. When he discovered I was American he told me there was no reason to wait a week, that I should go to the front of the line.

A crowd of people pressed against the gate, all of them holding their red Russian passports above their heads as if they were bidding on something valuable at an auction. A suave-looking thug with greased hair, a mauve suit, and pink shoes stood guard on the other side of the gate. He looked bored and sucked greedily on a cigarette. Occasionally a voice squawked over the walkie-talkie he held in his other hand. Then he would scan the crowd of raised passports outside the gate, point to someone, and allow them to enter. It took a half hour for me to catch his eye, and I frantically waved our papers in a fan so he couldn't miss our blue-and-gold passports. His gaze continued past me and I thought I'd lost him, but then he pointed at me to squeeze through the gate.

I walked up a set of stairs and into a small room where five lines had formed. At the beginning of each was a bank-style window with thick glass and an opening beneath for passing papers. Several women worked on the other side, collecting and distributing documents and passports. I joined the shortest line and waited.

It was the third trip to the embassy for the old Russian woman in front of me. She'd come to Finland to visit a cousin she hadn't seen since World War II, though they only lived a few miles on either side of the Russian-Finnish border. She was sad to be spending most of her time trying to get her exit visa extended. A middle-aged Russian man and his son were in Finland to buy used bathtubs, pipe, sinks, electrical wiring, and anything else they could take home and sell, but they needed something stamped first. They took great interest in my case. They looked solemnly through our papers but only shrugged when I asked if they thought I could get the matter resolved.

I smiled at the unhappy woman behind the glass when it was my turn. I asked if she spoke English, and she responded with a string of Russian words. I asked her again and she bent down to speak through the hole in the glass and repeated what she'd said in Russian a little louder. She then waved me away and waited for me to leave. I passed our papers beneath the glass to her and watched as she briefly looked through them. Then she pushed them back through the glass to me.

"I need some help. I have a problem with these papers," I said, and pushed the papers back through to her. I smiled. She frowned, and shoved them back to me like a change machine that doesn't like your dollar bills.

I leaned down to speak through the glass. "Look," I said. "I've got a problem with my papers and I need to speak with someone so I can explain." I stood back up and faced her. The woman looked past me as if I no longer existed and waved the man behind me forward.

"Wait!" I said and cut the man off. "I've been waiting a long time."

The woman behind the glass stormed off. The man behind me began to chatter angrily as if to say, "Now look what you've done!"

The woman didn't come back, but after a few minutes another came to the window. "You want something?" she asked brusquely.

"Thank you. I have a problem with my papers," I said, and related what had happened at the border the day before. I pointed out each of our documents and explained that I needed some authorization, a certain paper, to get back into Russia.

"Moment," the woman said, and disappeared with our papers into another room.

Several minutes later yet another woman returned with our documents.

"This is no good. Cancel. You see?" she said, and pointed to my visa.

"I know it's been canceled," I said. "I need to know why it's been canceled, and what I need to do to get it uncanceled. We just want to get to St. Petersburg on our motorcycle, but we were turned away when we tried."

"Who turn you way?"

"The Russian soldiers."

"They turn you way? Why they do this?"

"I don't know. That's why I'm here."

She reluctantly looked through the papers in her hands. She sighed. "Moment," she said, and disappeared.

"You can go with train, or autobus," she announced when she reappeared behind the glass. "No motorcycle."

"But we must go on our motorcycle. These papers say we can go on our motorcycle."

"You have big problem with this."

"What is the problem?"

"These papers is not right papers."

"Okay. Could you please give me the right papers?"

"No," she said. "This paper does not exist."

"Doesn't exist? How can I need a paper that doesn't exist?"

"This is not my problem."

"But look at *this* paper," I said, and pointed to the one from the Russian Consulate in San Francisco. "The people there said I could go to Russia. They stamped this paper. See? Those numbers are for my passport and my visa. And that one is for my motorcycle. It matches the number of this paper, this paper, and this paper."

But the woman wasn't looking. For her the matter was concluded. "You must go," she said.

"Go where?" I asked.

"Away. Go home," she said. Several people around me murmured.

"No!" I said. "I have nowhere to go but Russia. Just please tell me which paper I need, or where I can get it."

The woman glowered at me, then snapped the little door through her window shut and stormed away. The people behind me quickly dispersed to other lines and I was left standing at the window alone. I, too, got into another line and began to wait.

Other people in line looked at me, pointed, and whispered to each other as if speculating what would happen next. The women on the other side of the glass were looking at me as well, and then I noticed one shaking her head. She picked up a telephone and dialed. A moment later the guy with the mauve suit tapped me on the shoulder.

"You have problem?" he asked, exhaling smoke into my face as he talked.

"As a matter of fact, yes," I said, and then explained very calmly what had happened.

"Nothing to be done," he judged as he twiddled his cigarette. "You must go."

"Look, we have come a long way to visit your country. We have all these papers," I said, and showed them to him. "The woman over there tells me we need just one more. Isn't there someone I can talk to?"

"Not possible," he said.

"Are you sure? There is no one?" I asked again and laid a five-dollar bill on our papers. He saw it, snapped it up between his fingers, and put it away.

"Moment," he said, and left me in the line.

A few minutes later a young man appeared beside me. "Hi," he said. "Everyone is talking about you."

He was about eighteen and his accent was only slight. He wore a new pair of tennis shoes, new blue jeans, and a New York Yankees t-shirt. His hair was fashionably cut and his mouth was filled with a wad of gum.

"I'd be happy to leave if someone would help me."

"What's the problem?"

I told our story yet again. The young man listened. He interrupted me several times for details. He shook his head when I told him about the officer at the border and laughed about the women behind the glass, and when I finished he said, "Wait here. Maybe I can help."

Time passed and I began to wonder if either the thug or the young man would return. My line was moving and I'd be up against the glass again. I was composing our story for another try when I heard the snapping of gum behind me.

"Well, maybe," the young man whispered, "I can arrange it for you to see the head man. But it will take some time."

"How much time?" I asked, and wondered if a few more dollars wouldn't hurry things along.

"I don't know. Some time," and he offered me a cigarette.

He took me to a corner of the room and we leaned against the wall there. "This door," he said pointing to one nearby, "the head man...he comes this way for lunch."

The young man said his name was Ivan and that his father worked for the Russian consular service. Ivan said he was on his way home to Moscow after a year in the United States as a guest of the Rotarians. He said he had lived in Little Rock, Arkansas, and that he had traveled to many other states as well.

"Did you like it?" I asked.

"Was okay," he said, as though he'd been many places in the

world and was still evaluating the experience. "Lots of money in America. Lots of opportunity. I made many contacts there. I met your president. I think we can work with him."

Ivan told me he was thinking about going back to America for college. He said he'd go to an East Coast school because he could make many contacts there. "That's where the power is," he explained. "You have to know the people with the power."

His expression changed when he talked about going to Disney World. "Was wonderful," he said and suddenly became boyish. "Epcot, Haunted Mansion, Pirates of the Caribbean, Tower of Terror! I buy these shoes there," he said, and lifted one of them for me to see. "The best."

The guy in the mauve suit came over and spoke with Ivan in Russian. Ivan nodded, gave him a cigarette, and he left.

"Some kind of guy," Ivan said after him. "He only wants my cigarettes. But he says the head man is coming."

"I gave him five dollars," I admitted.

"Him?" he said, and laughed. "Bye-bye to that!"

The door opened and a knot of men rushed through. Ivan stepped forward and called out as if he'd just seen a cab headed to Moscow.

The head man was short and bald. His eyes drooped as though they'd been used up a long time ago. He was moving very quickly but Ivan's call stopped him. Ivan introduced us and I shook the consul's hand. Ivan began telling my story in Russian and the man asked a few quick questions. He appraised me with a few glances and then asked to see our papers. He shuffled through them quickly and then asked a question in Russian.

"He wants to know where your invitation is," Ivan translated.

I pointed to our letter from the San Francisco embassy and to our reservations at the youth hostel in St. Petersburg.

"Do you have something from a Russian organization?"

"A what?" I asked.

"A kind of invitation...from a club, from a society."

"No," I said. "I didn't know I needed one."

Ivan reported back what I'd said and the man shook his head.

"But what about David Barr?" I asked desperately.

"Who?" Ivan asked.

"This American guy we met who just rode his motorcycle across Russia. He showed us a picture of himself on it in Red Square. He rode through Murmansk about a month ago."

Ivan translated again and the head man spoke for the first time. "Impossible!" he almost spit. "Impossible!" and he began to push past me.

"Isn't there some fee I can pay," I asked, and stepped in front of the man. He looked incensed, as if I'd just called his wife a whore. I stepped out of the man's way and he pushed past.

"Nice try," Ivan said.

"What do I do now?"

"You don't go to Russia on your bike," he said.

Ivan walked me to the gate. "You know," he said. "It may be better this way."

"What do you mean?"

"Personally," he said and leaned close to me. "Personally, I don't think you would have made it."

"Why?"

"Guys like him," he said, and lifted one eyebrow in the direction of the guy in the mauve suit.

~~~

"How'd it go?" Suzanne asked.

The old woman sat on a wooden box beyond Suzanne and the bike. There was a delicate ceramic tea cup and saucer between her feet on the sidewalk.

"Not good," I said, and told Suzanne what had happened in the embassy.

"What do we do now?" she asked.

"Maybe we can apply for new visas, find out about a sponsor in Russia. We can ask the American Embassy for help."

"But that could take days."

"I don't know what else to do," I said, and watched as the old woman rested her face in one hand as she sipped tea and watched us.

"Let's just take the train," Suzanne said, and climbed off the bike. "It'll be a nice break from riding."

"We've just had the last couple days off. I'd like to get back on the road."

"The train is the road," she said. "Besides, we deserve it. The train would be a nice break."

"But going on the bike is the whole point," I said. "The idea is to *ride* around the Baltic Sea."

"Oh, come on, Allen. They just told you we can't do it. We've ridden back and forth to the border, spent half a day here. Let's just move on."

"We can try again. David Barr had to wait quite a while before he was allowed to ride across China, remember?"

"We're not traveling like David Barr," she said sharply.

The old woman perked up as though eager to witness a dispute.

"It's not a matter of traveling like David Barr," I said. "It's a matter of accomplishing what we've set out to do."

"But I don't want to fight it anymore. I'd like to enjoy myself a little, and from everything we've heard, riding through Russia may not be a good idea."

"Let's not give up so easily. It will be worth the extra effort if we do get through."

"And what if we do get the papers. What if you push so hard they say, 'Fine! Go!' And then we get robbed, killed, or maybe I just get raped? What then? Will your pushing have been worth it?"

My resolve suddenly faltered, and Suzanne recognized it. The woman winced a little and looked away.

"Well?" she persisted, and the old woman cupped a hand around an ear to listen.

"Oh, come on," I said. "If we listened to every warning and fear, we'd never go anywhere."

"Well maybe this time it's serious. Maybe this time someone is looking out for us."

"How will we get to Estonia? Where will we store the bike? We can't just leave it on the street," I said. "We can't take it on the train."

"We'll come back here and take the ferry across to Estonia. We can store the bike in a garage. There's one right down this road by the harbor," she said. "I saw it when we drove up here."

Suzanne moved toward me and put her arm around my waist. "Let it go," she said. "If we hurry, we might catch a train today. We can be in St. Petersburg tonight."

The woman stood up and leaned back to stretch as if bored. Another truck pulled up, and she sipped the last of her tea as she watched it back into place.

"But Suzy, we came to ride around the Baltic. We'll miss Russia if we take the train."

"We'll miss nothing," she said. "Please. Do this for me."

Two men climbed out, opened the back of their truck, and walked inside the building. The old woman began unloading palettes, two at a time, onto the sidewalk.

NINeteeN

I hoped something would happen as Suzanne and I walked across town from the garage. I hoped we'd miss the train, or that we'd discover it wouldn't leave that day. I hoped there wouldn't be any more tickets available. Instead, I wanted time to go to the U.S. Embassy and talk with someone there who would give us a copy of the missing paper and help fill it out, someone who would say the road to St. Petersburg was just fine, that going on a motorcycle was a wonderful idea; someone who would spread a map across their desk and show Suzanne and me the turn-off to a little-known village beside a lake, a place of beauty and pleasant memories that was especially beautiful at this time of year.

Suzanne buzzed with happiness as we waited in line to buy our tickets to St. Petersburg. "Cheer up!" she told me. "We tried our best. And the train will be so nice. Like a ferry through the countryside. Maybe they'll even have a buffet."

"Two tickets to St. Petersburg," Suzanne said to the woman across the counter.

"Two ticket. St. Petersburg," the woman mumbled as she filled out our tickets. She wore thick, cloudy glasses and a big onyx broach that looked like a lozenge. "What train?" she asked without looking up.

"The next train," Suzanne said. "Are there still seats?"

"Plenty seat," the woman said, and handed us our tickets.

~~~

When it was time, Suzanne and I collected our bags and walked through a set of tall glass doors at the back of the station and found our train. It was made up of five worn Russian carriages painted a dull blue. We were the first ones there and the doors were locked. We set our bags down and waited.

"I'll be!" someone called from behind us. I turned. It was Don, and he was with two other men. Don looked as regal as ever. His clothes looked laundered and pressed. He wore a black turtleneck under his overcoat. His eyes were covered by small, dark round glasses with silver frames. "What happened?" he asked.

We told Don our story, and when we were finished he said he was sorry and that he'd been rooting for us. "It was nice thinking about you two out there, on your way to St. Petersburg," he said. Then he introduced us to Mitch and Doug.

Don said that he'd met them both at various times during his trip through Europe, in Morocco and Germany, and they'd just happened to be in Finland at the same time.

They couldn't have been more different than Don. Mitch wore a second-hand beret he'd bought in a military surplus store, a black leather jacket with too many zippers, a pair of green shorts, and scuffed tennis shoes. He stood with his knees and back bent a little, as if he was ready to jump out of the way. "'Sa pleasure," he said with a thick Southern drawl as he shook our hands.

Doug was taller than us all by several inches and was dressed as if he'd just come off a shift at the shipyard. He wore a pair of worn army boots and a green-and-black flannel shirt that hung loose over his blue jeans. His blond hair was cut close on the sides but a shock of it hung over his brow and into his eyes. He kept wiping it away and held his head a little high so he could look beneath it. "He's from California, too," Don said, as if it would explain something about him.

"City of Orange," Doug said as he lit a cigarette.

A conductor unlocked the doors of the train and we climbed in. While looking for our seats we discovered we'd all been assigned the same compartment. We crowded in, put our bags on the overhead racks, and sat down.

Doug, Don, and Mitch got along well. They joked and laughed easily together, and Doug especially made an effort to include Suzanne and me in their banter. They particularly liked Suzanne, and she instantly became part of their group as she told them a few details of our trip; about some of the storms, the difficult camping, our trip to Russia and back.

"My gawd, woman. Y'all deserve this train efter what'cha been through," Mitch said, and Suzanne poked me in the side to make sure I'd heard.

Doug said that he had a motorcycle back home, and that next time he traveled he'd take it, or a car. "Go where you want. Do as you please. No more waiting like this," he said looking around our compartment as if it should be moving.

Then the three of them spoke of the inconveniences of their own travels, how they always seemed to be waiting for trains, trains that never stopped exactly where they wanted. They spoke of the crowded hostels, and all the cities, museums, and monuments, one after another, until they began to blur together.

The train crew arrived, two women and a man dressed in stained, pale-blue uniforms that were stretched so tightly over their stomachs that you could see ellipses of skin between the buttons. They had a cart full of bags and boxes that bulged with food, tools, and used machine parts that they pushed onto the train. The man busied himself at the front of the train as he lit the samovar, a complex machine made of pipes and valves and a fat steel urn used for heating water for tea. The two women noisily stowed their cargo in the compartment in front of ours.

Just before the train left, one of the women came into our compartment and asked for our tickets. She was out of breath and her pudgy face was coated with a sheen of oil. She coughed, cleared her throat, and then quickly checked our tickets and passports before hurrying back to her compartment.

~~~

It was seven hours to St. Petersburg. For the first three we all talked and watched the landscape pass. Suzanne and I pulled the food we'd bought at the Russian border from our bags and set it on a little table in the middle of the compartment. Mitch contributed a package of syrupy pastries wrapped in cellophane. Don had some apples, and Doug offered a large bottle of water and a knife.

Ours was a fortunate group. Between the jokes and stories, the idle chatter, our talk edged toward intimacy and revelation. Don told us how his mother had come to visit him in Spain, and how he'd experienced her as a great friend. Mitch said he had worked in the film and music industries and had become caught in a whirlwind of drugs and alcohol. He'd been sober for a year and this trip to Europe was a gift to himself. Doug said he'd been in the Rangers, an elite unit of the U.S. military that conducts special operations. He said he was traveling to clear his head before deciding what to do next. And I alluded to the troubles between Suzanne and me, that the winds and rains were not the only kind of storms we'd weathered. I settled back in my seat and felt an ease come over me. It was as if the weight of Suzanne's and my troubles had been distributed between everyone in the compartment.

The train slowed, stopped, and then we crossed the border into Russia. The forest and the slow progress of the train were hypnotic. One could get lost in them, in the gentle sway of the cars and the endless green, until you could, like Suzanne and the others did, fall into it, asleep with what appeared to be the feeling of never needing to wake again.

Sometimes the train passed a small village and I thought how they were similar to the villages Tolstoy, Dostoyevsky, and Chekhov wrote about, little villages hacked from the forest, with muddy streets and pine-board houses sinking unevenly into the earth and held up only by the columns of smoke that issued from their chimneys. They were occupied by big, round women, rail-thin men, and doll-like children who waved at the train as we passed. They were the kind of villages I would have liked to have ridden through, stopped at, and stayed in. While the others slept I fantasized that I'd walk to the back of the train, quietly open a door, and slip away. I could do that and never be found again, I thought. I imagined how I'd climb down and close the door, how the train would begin without me, and for just a moment I'd realize I could jump back on if I changed my mind. Then it would pull away, pass out of reach, and my decision would be cast. I imagined how the sound of the engine, the turning of all those wheels, would fade before the train itself grew faint and was lost in the distance.

Suzanne and the others woke as the light was falling, and the car filled with the smell of cooking cabbage, spiced meat, and the laughter of the three attendants in the next compartment. I walked past them as I went to the bathroom and stopped long enough for a look. A pot was boiling between them and their window was clouded with steam. A half-empty bottle of vodka and three glasses lay scattered across their table. The man was talking animatedly and his eyes bulged with the urgency of his words. The two women laughed like little girls. Their lips were pulled taut, their teeth gleamed, and their faces glowed with perspiration. The woman who had checked our tickets had her shoes off, revealing fat, gnarled toes and bright red nails. She leaned back to laugh and slid down in her seat. Her skirt slid up, revealing her dimpled thighs, bright green underwear, and a patch of pubic hair that looked like weeds taking over an abandoned wreck.

~~~

We were all at the window as the train rolled into St. Petersburg. The attendants had already changed their clothes, turned off the samovar, and were the first at the door with their bags and boxes. I walked forward for a closer look at what they had and saw slabs of meat wrapped in plastic, cartons of cigarettes, tins of coffee, and a cardboard box with bandages, needles, and syringes. There were bags of disposable diapers, boxes of videocassettes and music tapes, a roll of insect screening to cover windows, and several boxes of automobile shocks, headlights, sparkplugs, and anti-theft devices, things I realized they were bringing back for family and friends, and to sell.

The train came to a stop beneath the cavernous roof of the station and we climbed out. The station was almost deserted. The lights were dim, and we wondered how to make it to the hostel. Mitch found a metro map, but the Cyrillic names were like worn puzzle pieces we were too tired to assemble. I walked through the front of the station and onto the street where a man stood beside an ancient taxi. For five dollars he agreed to take us all.

The driver raced down wide boulevards and swerved often to miss the larger potholes. He couldn't speak English so we left him to his driving. His car didn't have a meter, but in its place was a small religious icon illuminated by the dashboard lights, a sad Holy Virgin crowned with a golden halo. A cross swung irregularly from the stub that once held the rearview mirror. Outside I watched as legions of poorly lit two- and three-story buildings passed in a blur. There were very few other cars on the road, and only occasionally did we glimpse the shadow of someone walking. We crossed a long bridge and the sky opened to reveal stars.

The driver dropped us outside the hostel, but the door was locked. Doug knocked and we waited. He knocked again and we waited some more.

"It's eleven-thirty," Don said. "They may be closed for the night."

"I hope we don't have to sleep on the sidewalk," Suzanne said.

Doug pounded the door and Mitch called for someone to please open up.

Another car drove down the street and stopped to watch us. The driver rolled down his window and began shaking his fist as if he was either mad or wanted us to knock harder. When there was still no answer he began honking his horn in bursts that filled the space between the buildings. A light came on above the door. The driver of the car nodded and drove away.

An old woman opened the door. She was annoyed and mumbled as she led us up two flights of stairs and showed us where to sleep. Charles and Alan, the South Africans we'd met in Helsinki, came out of their room and welcomed us. Charles had a bottle of vodka and held it out for us. He said it only cost two dollars. His eyes shone as if he'd discovered gold.

~~~

My face, neck, and arms were swollen and itched when I woke that first morning in Russia. I rubbed my hands over my face and felt a colony of bites. There was a particularly large bite on my left eyelid that made it feel fat. There was another on the edge of my lip that caused the corner of my mouth to feel numb. Mosquitoes hung sated from the ceiling. I used a cleaning rag to flick them down and left little brush strokes of blood against the paint.

Suzanne was still asleep and I lay carefully back down beside her. A moist sheen covered her face and I kissed the bites there. She didn't stir. I kissed my way across the plain of her cheek to the ridge of her nose. I kissed the lids of her puffy eyes and her lips. I smoothed the rush of hair that fell over her ear, and noticed the rhythmic plumping of the vein along her neck. I wondered what dreams it fed.

A while later her eyes opened and she smiled. "You again?" she asked hoarsely.

"Good morning."

"Oh, more mosquitoes," she said, and ran her hand over my face as if to heal it, and then over her own.

"I'm okay," I said.

"I can't believe we made it to Russia," she said. "After everything, we made it."

"Yes, we made it after all."

"I'm sorry about the bike. Really. It's too bad. But you'll have a good time here, won't you?"

"Of course. We'll have a fine time here."

Breakfast came with the price of the bed and was served at a single narrow table covered with white plastic that just fit in the dining room. Folding metal chairs were pressed tightly against each other and each guest had to wait in the hall for someone to leave before sitting down. Each guest was handed a plastic bowl, a tin cup, and a set of aluminum utensils by the woman who'd let us in the night before. In each bowl was a cold hard-boiled egg that rolled around the bottom. A basket of stale white bread was passed up and down the table, followed by a large plastic bowl filled with a coarse cereal, the Russian equivalent of Cheerios. There was a kettle of hot water, a jar of instant coffee that tasted like acid, a jug of milk, and a plate of glistening jam.

A babel of languages rose from the table. Don, Doug, and Mitch sat at the far end beneath a window that looked onto a small paved courtyard and the back of another building beyond. A couple got up and left across from them. Suzanne and I were issued our bowl, cup, and utensils, and sat down.

"How's the food?" Suzanne asked.

"Better'n back home," Mitch said sarcastically. "Don' get much better 'an this."

"It's shit," Doug said. "But it's a little better than the military, which means you won't die."

"I don't recommend the cereal," Don said. "I think it's made from sawdust."

"I've got splinters in my tongue," Doug said, and stuck it out for us to see.

Suzanne poured herself hot water and added a little sugar. Mitch passed us the bread, and then the jam. "They don' have butter," he said. "Must be a shortage."

I cracked and peeled my egg, taking most of the cooked white with it. Inside was a tiny golden yolk that I spread over a piece of bread. I added a pinch of salt from a bowl and ate.

Two young women, Spanish I guessed, sat down with their bowls and cups and looked lost. They whispered to each other as they guessed the purpose of each plate and bowl moving up and down the table. Someone passed them the cereal and they peered over the lip of the bowl, sniffed, and passed it on. They asked for the bread, took several pieces each, and then turned them over in their hands like archaeologists inspecting site finds. One of them, the more adventurous of the two, mixed a spoonful of instant coffee with water in her cup. She sipped as her friend looked on. The one drinking winced, covered her mouth with a napkin and coughed while her friend laughed. The old woman doing the serving looked on disapprovingly, as if the two young women were just fooling around.

~~~

Moving off as a group was a spontaneous thing. I remember Mitch asking aloud, as though to the entire hostel, who was going where. Suzanne was talking with Doug and Charles about things they wanted to see, and I heard each of them say, "Yes, me too." Then Don asked me what our plans were.

"To walk," I said. "Down Nevsky Prospekt to the Neva River. We'll see what happens from there."

"I think that's what we're going to do," he said.

"Ya mine if we come along?" Charles asked.

"That would be great!" Suzanne said.

I'd never traveled in a group like this before, even for a day. My way of seeing a city or country was to jump in alone or with Suzanne. A group created a barrier to the rest of the world. In a group you generally aren't approached out of someone's curiosity. You're not as likely to have to ask directions, ask for a map or place to stay, or fall into a conversation and be invited home for dinner or a weekend away. You're not as likely to ask for help and come to trust a stranger, or be told something about a place that no guidebook could ever know.

It seemed natural that the seven of us gathered on the sidewalk outside the hostel. The sun was still low enough that the street held the night's cool air, and the air, in turn, held the muted smells of the neighborhood. It smelled of diesel fuel, bread, urine, and dust, the smell of poverty and decay. Third World smells.

The far end of Nevsky Prospekt, the city's main thoroughfare, was two blocks from the hostel, but we heard its pulse before we arrived. We heard the car horns, the whine and hiss of buses, the rumbling of heavy trucks as they pounded over the loose pavement. When we were one block away we saw the stream of people walking along it, and then we joined them.

A young city by European standards, St. Petersburg was founded in 1703 by Peter the Great on a swampy river delta on the edge of the Baltic Sea. He conceived it as a kind of national telescope for the Russian people, one that would focus their attentions on the culture, science, and economies of Europe, and away from the conservative and archaic traditions of the Orthodox church, nobility, and peasantry. In just nine years the city was on its way to becoming one of the world's most stylish and influential, if only for a time.

Six lanes wide and three miles long, Nevsky Prospekt is one of Europe's most impressive boulevards. It began as a log-paved road through Peter the Great's swamp, linking his governmental offices with a monastery. Over time cathedrals and mansions were built along it, and the city grew out from it like a fertile belt along a river. By the early eighteen hundreds it rivaled the Champs-Élysées in Paris.

The curvature of the Earth seemed to hide the end of Nevsky from my eyes. It was lined for as far as I could see with the immense facades of buildings familiar to me through countless pictures. The people around us looked like characters from the pages of Chekhov. A woman dragged her feet along the sidewalk as she hurried past us. Behind her she pulled a large plastic bag that was full of other plastic bags. With her free hand she waved at a bus to wait, but it didn't. She yelled and stamped her feet, then muttered something to herself as it pulled away. When she turned to look back down the Prospekt for another bus, I saw that part of her cheek was missing, revealing the few teeth she had left, and the wandering white orb of her eye. A middle-aged matron with a platinum blond wig walked her toy poodle in front of us. She wore a pink sweater and a white miniskirt with black polka dots that exposed the soft white flesh of her thighs. We passed an old man who leaned against the side of a building as if waiting to be absorbed by it. His clothes and skin were the same filthy color of the stone. He began to plead with us as we passed and held a small pad of paper with both hands for us to inspect. It was blank and I realized it was for sale. His mumbling quickened to a stuttering whimper, a sales pitch gone awry.

Only a little traffic competed for the six lanes of the broad Prospekt. There were thin horses pulling ancient wooden wagons filled with coal, wood, and equipment. There were overcrowded buses, and tiny Russian cars that left lines of smoke like a spider leaves webbing. Occasionally, a brand new Mercedes or BMW flashed by, swerving dangerously in and out of the slower traffic.

"Reminds me of something I read," Mitch said, "that more Mercedes are sold in St. Petersburg and Moscow than all the rest of Europe combined."

"Mafia," Alan concluded, as if he'd been in Russia a long time.

We passed some of Russia's most famous buildings and monuments, ones with wonderfully grandiose names like the Cathedral of the Holy Virgin Icon of Kazan, the Church of the Resurrection of Christ, and the House of Books. Some were obscured by scaffolding, which promised a renaissance of the city after decades of neglect.

Between and around them all were clusters of tables covered with nesting *matrishka* dolls painted with the likenesses of Yeltsin, Gorbachev, Brezhnev, Stalin, and Lenin. Other tables offered amber necklaces and bracelets, lacquer boxes that, individually, were stunning with their intricately painted scenes of pastoral and mythical life, but seen together became gross in their overabundance. There were t-shirts that mocked the failure of the communist system. "The Party is Over!" declared one. Another bore the Communist red star and sickle with the international circle and slash sign for "No" superimposed over it. Still other tables offered jars of caviar, bottles of Russian vodka, beer, and champagne, night-vision field glasses, military uniforms, and combat medals. I'd read of places where live grenades, machine guns, mortars, even tanks, could be bought for a little cash, and I had the feeling I could have asked someone where.

Near the Griboyedov Canal, Mitch stopped short and announced, "Oh, Gawd!" I thought he'd discovered his wallet was missing, but his eyes were fixed straight ahead on a commotion down the *prospekt.*

"Gypsies," Don said, and then I saw them, too. A group of about ten women and children swarmed through the pedestrians searching frantically for something. They didn't seem to see the Russians and went instead straight for the foreigners. Two men swatted and kicked them away like pesky dogs and then the group of Gypsies surrounded a third man. The Gypsy women hugged his arms while the children leapt at his sides. He yelled, broke free, and ran.

A woman in a trim yellow suit and high heels stepped from a cab and began walking down the sidewalk as she rummaged through her purse. She stopped to open a compact and check her face, and then continued on.

"Son of a bitch," Doug said. "They see her."

The woman only saw the Gypsies at the last second. The Gypsy women grabbed her arms and the children tore through her pockets and pulled at her purse. The woman pushed and shoved. She shouted in what sounded like German but they pulled her down like weak prey. And then the Gypsies let her go and moved on, and as they did I saw one of the children hand something to one of the women, which she quickly placed in the folds of her clothing.

I've encountered Gypsies many times before, but none so aggressive as these. I've also read a good deal about them, how they are thought to have come originally from India and are related distantly to Persian and Nepalese tribes. They had arrived in Europe around the fifteenth century and, because of their penchant for wandering and unwillingness to adopt Christianity, were persecuted and kept on the move. Gypsies were forced to survive by any means and became itinerant tinsmiths, storytellers, dancers, and fortunetellers. They also adopted an outlook that regarded other peoples' pockets like ripe berries alongside the road.

Many years ago I read the autobiography of Gipsy Petulengro, *A Romany Life,* and drank in his descriptions of a rich culture and lore, of feasts, trickery and cunning, and perpetual movement. But the book is largely a romantic recollection that makes even pick-pocketing seem merely mischievous and justified. It told little about what the modern world has done to the Gypsies, or what it is like to pass them in the street.

As we prepared to pass the Gypsies on Nevsky, I remembered a particular meeting with them while traveling in Bulgaria several years before. I was in a village near the Black Sea and outside it was a Gypsy camp. The camp itself was beyond a small train station and beside a garbage dump. A column of thick black smoke from burning tires marked the place, and someone told me they were training bears to dance there.

Some children approached me before I arrived at the camp. Their skin was soiled like a mechanic's, their black hair matted, and their clothes were old and worn. They stood in front of me with their small hands cupped for coins, chewing gum, or ciga-rettes. I offered coins and thought they would then lead me into their camp, but their excited chatter was like the noise bees make when they find nectar. In no time I was surrounded by still more children and several women, one of whom held a baby wrapped in rags. I tried to tell them I didn't have more coins but their dirty hands began to brush against my clothes and pull at my pockets. I tried to move through them but they only pressed closer to me. I stepped back the way I'd come but they moved as I moved. Then the woman with the baby did something completely unexpected. She tossed the baby high into the air above me.

I was supposed to catch it, and then once I had the baby in my arms the Gypsies would have been free to rifle through my pock-ets. But I didn't. Instead I watched it float in front of me, its tiny black eyes impassive as though it had been through this before. And then it fell into the maze of hands that pulled at my clothes. It teetered there, began to fall again, and was then snatched by a lit-tle girl. Collectively the hands fell away from me. I'd passed some test. I was left alone.

Our group waited until three businessmen passed us before continuing down the street in their wake. The Gypsies went for them briefly but then pulled back as one of the men raised and swung his briefcase. We hurried behind the men but were caught. Suzanne got behind Doug and me and we pushed through. "Get away! Get the hell away!" Charles yelled as they went for a small pack he had tied around his waist. A woman grabbed my arm and I felt the quick pat of little hands against my legs, pockets, and crotch. Doug and Suzanne pushed ahead. "Mah-ney," the woman pleaded with me. "Little mah-ney."

"No money," I said.

"Mah-ney!" the woman demanded and yanked on my arm. My arm, freed from her grip, rose, making the woman believe I was about to strike her.

"Ahhhhhhhhhh!" she screamed and whipped her arms at me. "Ahhhhhhhhhhhhh! Fahk-*u*! fahk-*u*!"

~~~

We walked for a long time, beside canals that wound through the city, beneath the walls of palaces and monasteries, through city parks gone half-wild. We walked across the long span of the Palace Bridge and over the slow, milky-green water of the Neva River. On the other side we watched a wedding procession pose for pictures with the World War I battleship *Aurora* as their backdrop. One of the ship's deck cannons had barked the order to begin the 1917 revolution that overthrew the last tsar, and she became a monument to that struggle. The ship looked almost cartoonish now with her rounded beam, blunt bow, and swept back smoke stacks. Suzanne insisted we all go aboard for a look.

Watching her lead us up the gangway I realized how at home she'd become with our group. I noticed it in her enthusiasm and curiosity, her quickness to initiate a turn down an alley or through a park, through her directives that we go here or there, or her desire to stop and look at things that caught her eye. She was beautiful in her strength, in her ready smile and laugh, the way she kidded with

the other guys. She seemed lighter. She moved with a confidence
I'd almost forgotten she had. I remembered how we had once been
like that together.

Farther along we came to a tall apartment block where sheets
and clothes hung from windows like ragged flags, and beneath the
shade of a tree two men methodically polished a rusting green car.
The tree grew in a small yard of overgrown grass and wildflowers
that was surrounded by an iron fence. In the middle of it was a
neglected brick-and-glass building that looked like a small arbore-
tum. A peeling sign outside the building explained its significance
in Russian, but we could only guess. The door was open and we
filed through it. Entombed inside the building was a log cabin.

"It's bloody auld," Alan proclaimed.

"Goooood Morn-ing!" a voice almost sang behind us. "You
want tour of Pay-ter's famous cabin?"

I turned and saw a thin man step from the shadows. He leaned
forward in his enthusiasm to greet us. His lips were parted in an
exaggerated smile that was sustained as he waited for our answer.

"How much?" I asked.

"For you?" he said, and included us all in the sweep of an open
hand. "Spez-ial price! Today, three hundred ruble for one man. You
like?" He smoothed a wedge of greasy hair over his brow, and as he
breathed he filled the space between us with the stench of stale
cigarettes and vodka.

We paid three hundred rubles each, about twenty-five cents,
and the man folded the bills and put them in his pocket.

"My name is Bar-is!" he said, and I noticed how his eyes
bulged when he spoke the last word of each sentence. "Like Bar-is
Yeltsin, yes? I am historical man, and I can see you are historical
mans, too!...and you, madam! That is why you come here!" He motioned dramatically for us all to turn and take in the little log
cabin. "Pay-ter. Pay-ter the Great! He had grand vision for most
significant city in all Europa, yes?"

We all nodded and Boris pushed between us to stand beside
the cabin. He put an elbow on the rough sill of a window and narrowed his gaze as he looked past us.

"See there, outside?" he said, and we all looked back through the open door toward the apartment block. "Outside is his dream! Nice dream, yes? And Pay-ter, he decide to build his dream here!" Boris said, and thrust a finger toward the ground. "In *this* place! Where *you* stand!

"Imagine when Pay-ter first come. Was only, some kind of water and mud...how you say?" and we watched Boris mime walking through something thick and unpleasant.

"Swamp?" Mitch offered.

"Ah-haaaaaaaa!" Boris exhaled, and we cleared a little place around him. "You is historical man?" he pointed to Mitch. "Good! *I* am historical man, *you* is historical man! Is wonderful!" he said, pressing the palms of his hands together as if he'd been blessed.

"Come close! Look!" Boris instructed us, and enthusiastically pointed through a window. We all took turns and looked into a single room that contained a wooden cot made into a snug bed, at a rug spread across the floor, some cabinets on the walls, and a wooden table with some writing instruments arranged on it.

"You know what this is?" Boris asked of the view we'd just taken in. As he waited for our answer he twitched.

"A bedroom," Doug said.

Boris looked disappointed. "*More* than bedroom!" he said. "In this window you see where Pay-ter dreamed the city! Where he write every part! Where he supervise everything! You understand?"

We nodded that we did, and Boris led us slowly around the circumference of the cabin. He told us of the long, frozen winters through which Peter toiled to create the city and how he struggled through spring floods that swept through and washed away months of work. He told us of the humid, muddy, mosquito-infested summers that Peter spent in his modest home. And as Boris told the story he continued to smile and pop his eyes in a crazed kind of way, as if he'd been there with Peter himself.

When he was done Boris thanked us for our time and waved as we filed out the door. I looked back and saw him return to his corner, where he nervously lit a cigarette and inhaled as if he was out of breath. Then he lifted a bottle to his lips and swallowed gratefully.

Around midday the sun emerged through a layer of clouds and burned brightly above the city. The air became warm and damp, and I grew languid from the heat and the comfort of the group. Our group moved of its own accord. We'd established a kind of collective mind that shifted direction without explanation or prodding. One of us only had to veer from the others for the rest of the group to veer too, and turn, and then we'd right ourselves and move easily along. I came to like our self-governance, the fact that after so many miles of concentrating on the bike, on the weather, on the roads, on other vehicles, I could just go along for the ride. And I liked, too, our ease with each other, the way we could break spontaneously into pairs and threesomes to talk, and then pull back together.

Our group took its time walking through the Peter and Paul Fortress, an island citadel ordered by Peter to defend the city. It later became a political prison and held many revolutionaries, including the writers Radishchev, Dostoyevsky, and Gorky. The entrance was crowded with t-shirt vendors, food stands, and women selling balloons. A little girl in a pink ballerina's tutu giggled as her father tied a string holding a balloon around her wrist. She let her arm rise with the balloon and her expression changed from a smile to one of profound concern. Then she grabbed her father's pant leg to keep herself from floating away.

On a patch of sand beside the river we watched a game of volleyball played by six men without a net. A hydrofoil skipped over the water, followed by a barge that seemed to barely move as it churned against the current. From a kiosk we bought open-faced cheese-and-cucumber sandwiches, sat on the riverbank, and ate.

On the way back to the hostel we walked past a casino where, for the length of the facade, the sidewalk was made of polished white marble. There were potted palms outside the door and the brass fixtures were polished to a high gloss. On the marble were parked several new Mercedes and BMWs, a gold Jaguar, and a fire engine-red Lincoln Continental. Another BMW pulled up and cut our group in half. Two men wearing dark glasses and snarls climbed out of the front and looked around before one of them rapped his knuckle on the passenger window. The door unlocked with an automatic click and the driver opened it. As he did so the front of his overcoat opened and revealed a machine pistol held close against his torso in a leather harness. A corpulent old man climbed from the back seat. He smoothed his suit and hair, then reached back inside the car and pulled out a girl, all of sixteen, as if she was on a leash. She was dressed in something so sheer that I could see her ribs beneath the fabric. The man kissed her roughly on the lips and gave her a little slap on the cheek. Then he took the girl's hand and moved impatiently toward the entrance. She stumbled on her high heels and long, almost shapeless legs, but the driver caught her by the arm and helped her through the door.

~~~

Each of our days in St. Petersburg was spent as a group. We began them along Nevsky, then radiated out from the center through concentric decades of the city until we brushed the edge of endlessly replicated apartment blocks. And then we'd be pulled back toward the neglected center, toward the palaces, cathedrals, mansions, canals, parks, and boulevards of old Petersburg. The Gypsies along Nevsky seemed to recognize us and left us alone. Mitch and Suzanne began handing the children coins, which they snatched gratefully. We spent a day around the fantastically ornamented facade of the Winter Palace. Its one thousand rooms now house the Hermitage Museum, where we wandered down seemingly endless corridors of sculptures, through ballrooms, halls, and chambers filled with paintings. And when we were full of sculptures and paintings, we studied the entries paved with elaborate mosaics, the inlaid floors, painted ceilings, and carved doorways of the palace itself.

When we were finished we moved across the vastness of Palace Square—Peter the Great's triumphal parade ground, and later the site of Bloody Sunday, a massacre of men, women, and children that precipitated the fall of the last tsar. We walked through the Field of

Mars, past randomly placed sculptures of sphinxes, rushing chari-
ots, lions, mermaids and mermen; we walked alongside the slow-
moving, pearly-green Neva. We walked until it was time to leave.

Alan and Charles announced they were going to Moscow,
while Doug, Mitch, and Don decided to take the train to Estonia.
Suzanne and I made plans to see them again in a few days in
Tallinn, Estonia's capital, before they boarded a ferry back to Scandinavia to begin the trip home.

We decided to have a celebration before departing and wandered through a street near the hostel that was congested with
small wooden kiosks for supplies. People sold cigarettes, tools,
pharmaceuticals and home remedies, blue jeans with names like
Cosmos and Boulevard, leather jackets with the American flag embroidered on the back, bottles of the finest liquors, green apples,
bread and caviar, boxes of Swiss chocolate, bottled water and bottles of herb beer, condoms and tampons, and songbirds.

In the hostel that night, in the room Doug, Don, and Mitch
shared, we unpacked our items and spread them on one of the
beds. There were chocolate bars, bottles of water and juice, bread,
and three jars of caviar. There was a nest of blush apples and two
bottles of vodka. Doug twisted the top from one and threw it away.
He put the bottle to his lips, drank it straight, and handed it to me.
Alan took it next and then passed it on to Charles. In a moment it
was back to me. Mitch poured juice for Suzanne, Don, and himself, and Charles opened the caviar and sniffed it. He poked it with
his finger, took a taste. "We've been ripped off," he said. "Tastes
like salted rubber."

I cut the apples into slices and Suzanne laid pieces of chocolate between them. The bottle of vodka came around again and I
drank. Don cut the bread and arranged the slices on a piece of
paper. They quickly disappeared.

We passed our address books around and made promises to
meet again. "In ten years," Suzanne said. "In ten years we should
meet here again."

"Or in South Africa," Charles said. "Alan an mae'd show ya
round."

Charles and Alan talked about their upcoming train trip to Moscow. In twenty-four hours they'd be in Red Square, and they'd say "Hi" to Lenin for all of us. Mitch said he was feeling that it was time to go home. He wanted to see about getting back together with a woman there.

"I want to land in New York and drive to California," Don said. The bottle went round and round, and I said how badly I wanted to be on the bike again.

The rest of the evening ebbed and flowed in front of me like a very fast series of tides. The room had a groove. Even for those not drinking, there was a collective wit that circulated and carried us along. Suzanne told jokes I hadn't heard before. She demonstrated the one card trick she knew, and nobody could figure it out. Doug showed us how he'd learned to kill people with his bare hands in the army. The South Africans sang drinking songs, and Mitch taught us all some Southern slang.

At one point someone banged on our door. Suzanne was closest and pulled it open. Outside in the darkened hallway was an older man. He was fat and completely naked. He just stood in the doorway and glared at us, a mass of flesh and body hair. In my drunkenness he seemed almost an apparition. Suzanne let go of the door and it closed slowly on its own.

"Who the hell was that?" someone asked.

"Naked Man!" Doug whispered, and the South Africans changed the words to one of their drinking songs, renamed it the Naked Man Boogie, and started a conga line, which faltered around the room like an old Russian train.

~~~

Suzanne and I waited alone outside the Europa Grand Hotel for the 6:00 A.M. bus to Helsinki. St. Petersburg was muted and still from the morning chill. Occasionally we saw a woman hurry along the sidewalk with a string bag of bread and vegetables, and occasionally a car puttered along like an arthritic animal. A flock of pigeons settled around us and waited for an early handout, but a moment later they left, and the clap of their wings was like the shuffling of cards.

The hotel was set on its own private lane just off Nevsky Prospekt and it looked oddly out of place. The sidewalk was new and smooth. Fresh paint covered the walls, and the exterior lacked the maze of pipes bolted to the sides of most buildings and the snarls of wire that dangled from other roofs. The window panes were so clean they looked as if they weren't there at all. A doorman dressed in a bright red livery coat embellished with swirls of gold braid, a matching tophat, and white gloves eyed us as we walked past the new luxury sedans parked along the curb.

Suzanne and I waited on a bench in a small park at the end of the lane. From there we had a partial view back toward Nevsky and of the buildings farther along. There was a beauty in the facades, in their decay and subsidence. It was the same worn look that makes so much of Greece, the Sphinx, Machu Picchu, and the Great Wall so appealing. There is a character and depth in that kind of decay, a mystery that invites us to regard our time here as something more than just time.

We watched an old woman in a dark blue worker's smock push a small cart into the park. She moved so slowly that watching her was like watching a far-off point and trying to decide if it was moving at all or if you're just imagining it is. She moved so slowly it took several minutes to realize she was there to empty the small, white metal cans set next to the benches. She'd position her cart just so beside each one and then methodically empty its contents onto a flat scrap of metal the size of a piece of writing paper. She wore a tattered pair of gloves, and almost painfully, she put her hand inside each bucket to extract scraps of paper, one at a time, pinched between her thumb and forefinger. Her movements were heavy and hydraulic, and reminded me of playing steam shovel with my arm and hand when I was a child.

The old woman stood up and lifted her piece of metal toward the lip of the cart with a studied caution, as though the contents were volatile. The pile, the entirety of which could have fit into my cupped hands, fell successfully into the cart. That done, she bent

down and hung her tool from a piece of twine. She then smoothed
her smock, aimed her cart at the next can, and leaned into the
handle.

The cart moved as if filled with heavy stones. Her thin body
was fully extended and she pushed with her toes against the gravel
walk. Her head hung between her arms like a counterweight. The
cart had only moved about five feet when the woman shifted her
weight in such a way that the cart stopped but her feet kept moving until she was upright again. Then she removed her tool from
its place, bent down, and prodded a pile of feces onto it with her
finger.

"How long do you think she's been doing that for?" Suzanne
asked.

"A lifetime," I guessed.

Three gleaming white buses with Finnish plates stopped in
front of the hotel, and we gathered our bags to leave. At the same
time the doorman stood aside from the hotel entrance, tipped his
red-and-gold hat, and began helping a long line of people aboard.
They were conspicuously Western, with jewelry, clean and coifed
hair, and good clothes. I guessed it was a tour heading home.
Each person wore a white name tag pressed onto his or her chest,
their American names written in precise, felt-tipped script. "Enid"
and "Bob Boyle" nodded as we waited patiently for a space in the
line. "Marianne Richards" looked concerned, as though our presence on the bus might jeopardize their chances of leaving Russia,
but "Helen Smith" held back so we could get on, too.

"Wait," Suzanne said, and she pointed to a white paper sign
taped to the side of the bus. "Jehovah's Witness Convention," it
said, and we stepped quickly away. Helen smiled and shrugged her
plump arms, as if to suggest we'd missed a golden opportunity.

Our bus arrived soon after. The driver collected our money,
asked our nationality, recorded our passport numbers on a roster,
and then welcomed us aboard. There were just thirteen people on
the bus. One was a pretty Spanish woman whom I overheard
telling her seatmate that she'd entered Russia just the day before.
She'd come through Poland and the Ukraine on a train and had

planned to spend several weeks in Russia. She wanted out, though, because in the middle of the night thieves had come aboard, sprayed a sleeping gas into all the compartments, and robbed the occupants. Several people were taken to the hospital. She said she'd had her passport and money in the space between her seat, but they had taken everything else. The bus to Finland, she said, was the quickest way out. There was a young man from the Netherlands who'd come from China on the Trans-Siberian Railway. It looked as if something had happened to him, too. Despite the warm air in the bus he wore a parka zippered to his chin, and for a while he had the hood pulled over his head. There was a young Cuban couple who looked scared. Six corpulent, middle-aged Chileans, who wore lots of gold and reeked of perfume and cologne, sat behind the driver. The bus was a luxury coach with reclining seats. I left mine in the upright position so I could watch the road.

The city gave way to a sprawl of Soviet-era high-rise apartment blocks interspersed with seas of mud and weed-covered fields bisected by trails leading, it seemed, nowhere. We passed small clapboard villages where adults were indifferent to our passing. Their children waved, except for one boy. He stood atop a hillock of rubble, with his eyes fixed on the bus, a smirk on his face, and his right hand raised as high as it would reach above his head. Each finger but one was furled, and that last was as erect and sharp as a cathedral spire.

We passed abandoned factories that materialized out of the forest and muddy farms that looked as though they needed to remain fallow for a very long time. The bus often leaned to the left to pass horse-drawn carts and smoking cars, which hugged the shoulder to let us by. I counted four petrol stations, one of which was pumping fuel to a long queue of cars and tractors. I saw no military installations we could have compromised, no gangs of thugs waiting in chase cars for prey, no burned vehicles riddled with bullet holes. There was only the road, the forest, the villages, and the people who lived in them. It would have been ideal.

The bus arrived at the border, and the formalities to clear everyone required a small bureaucracy. The Cubans were the only ones that aroused suspicion, but they passed and then acted as if they'd won the lottery. Then we all climbed back on the bus, took our seats, and continued.

"Settle down," Suzanne said to me, and laid her hand on my jiggling knee. "You'll be on it soon enough."

I imagined seven huge rubber bands, one for each of the seven slow hours of the bus ride. I imagined each hour as if one of the rubber bands was being drawn out, imagined the exertion required to bring each to its breaking point, imagined the satisfying snap that took us on to the next. A ferry was leaving for Tallinn that afternoon, and if everything worked out, we could be on it. I made a list in my mind of the things we needed to do: get the bike, pack, buy fuel and tickets. I couldn't find the ferry schedule I had clipped from a brochure. Did it leave at two or four?

Suzanne reclined her seat and slept. I looked around the bus and everyone but the driver and me was asleep. The Spanish woman was drawn across two seats, her knees tucked toward her stomach, and she'd folded her jacket for a pillow. The man with the parka had taken it off, and now it lay crumpled on the floor. The Cuban man slept with his head in his woman's lap, and she cradled it in her hands. I willed the bus forward and silently congratulated the driver when he passed a slow car or truck.

Then, after seven hours of watching, we arrived. As the bus rolled into Helsinki I thought how all the buildings looked like the Europa Grand Hotel with its windows as clear as water, its tidy facade and order. At a stoplight I watched as a small boy of about five or six pleaded with his mother for something. He was dressed in a nice leather jacket with a ruffed fur collar and a blue cap. His cheeks were round and smudged red from where his mother wiped his tears with a tissue. His face was contorted and his little hands struggled to reach toward a window display. On the other side of the glass were red and green plastic balls, a herd of plastic horses, a red race car, and a troupe of dolls. His mother was on her knees as she reasoned with him. The bus pulled away before I could witness the resolution, but I imagined how the woman made a deal with her son and the boy was allowed into the store where they emerged later, a balloon tied to his wrist and a white horse tucked beneath his arm.

twenty

The bike was just as we'd left it, tucked in a corner of the garage, the lock threaded through the frame and wheels. It was still carefully shrouded by our tarp like a piece of furniture in storage. I pulled the tarp back and remembered that the bike has a smell of its own—a sweet mixture of gas and oil, of plastic and worn rubber, and dust; the accumulated smell of all the miles. At that moment I was tempted to give the bike a name, to acknowledge the affinity and appreciation I had for it. We have this desire to name the machines we rely upon, to create the illusion they have a soul and feelings because we fear their indifference to us. It's an indication of our yearning for companionship when we can't find it in another, of our inclination to discover the human in something that doesn't really give a damn.

Suzanne and I packed our clothes and equipment. I fastened the tank bag and changed the map while she rearranged our stove and pots and tied our tent down across the top of our gear.

"That's everything," Suzanne said.

I pushed the starter. The engine caught on the first turn and settled into a reassuring idle. We were on our way again.

I let Suzanne off at the ferry terminal so she could book our passage to Tallinn, and I went in search of fuel.

The garage attendant shrugged when I asked him where I could find a gas station, so I began to ride through the city in search of one. I'd ridden what seemed like several miles when I stopped at a news kiosk and asked the old woman selling papers and magazines if she knew. She came out of her little stall to look at the bike. She took it all in, and then me. She wore a captain's hat that she pushed back onto the crown of her head, a thick wool vest, and boots. She seemed to find us worthy and playfully patted the empty space on the seat behind me and pointed back to herself.

"Benzin?" I asked, and pointed to the tank.

The woman pretended to look sad, and then smiled, as if to say she had to try. She straightened her hat and mimed directions with her hands by making little brushes left or right that indicated turns and quick chops that marked cross-streets. She gathered the tips of her fingers in a bud and burst them apart when she wanted me to see a street light. When she was finished she rubbed the empty place behind me, stepped back, and waved as I pulled away.

∽∽∽

I waited for Suzanne in the parking lot outside the shipping office. Through a window I could see the back of her head and jacket as she made her way to the front of the line, and for a moment I was struck by how much her hair had grown. She'd had it cut even with her collar shortly before we'd left, and now it was creeping slowly down her back again. Some scattered drops of rain from an errant cloud speckled the parking lot and the smell of finely crushed rock rose from the ground. A few drops smacked against the windscreen of the bike and hung there. Others fell on my head. They were surprisingly cool, and they felt like sadness.

Suzanne turned from her place in line and scanned the parking lot to see if I was back. She saw me, smiled, lifted her hand and waved. At that moment I loved her more than anything. I waved back and my imagination flared, as if called into motion to witness something. I imagined I had gotten into an accident while searching for fuel, and now watched the scene unravel before me. Suzanne would stand in that line not knowing. She would turn and look for me in the parking lot among the cars and trucks. I imagined how she'd think to herself I shouldn't take so long. She'd buy our tickets, and maybe ask about a buffet on board the ferry to surprise me. Then she would come outside and tuck the tickets into the inside pocket of her jacket, and she'd look for me again. Then she would sit down and wait. I wondered if she had her notebook or postcards to keep her busy while she waited. I climbed off the bike to check and found them tucked safely between her underwear and the dress she'd brought. I wondered how long she'd wait before realizing something must have happened, and then how much longer before she walked back to the garage, thinking there may have been a misunderstanding and that I'd returned there. Who would she call? I asked myself, and then realized we had very little to link the two of us together. Someone would eventually go through the luggage on the bike. They'd find her clothes and notes. They'd eventually find her name, but it would take time.

～～～

The sea was so calm we could see the sky reflected in it, and by looking down I could watch gulls cruise from side to side over the back of the ship as we sailed due south toward Tallinn. Clouds lay like stains on the water until the expanding wake of the ship broke them into froth. The vapor trail of a jet stitched its way west, intent on somewhere very far away. There was hardly a breeze except for the wind created by the ship as it moved, and for a while Suzanne and I didn't even need our jackets. In the distance we watched a freighter, riding high in the water, push past in the opposite direction. For a long time we were between lands. The far edge of the sea was our only horizon.

"If I squint my eyes and pretend," Suzanne said from her place in a cheap plastic deck chair, "we could be in the tropics. Porpoises could be racing the ship."

Her face was relaxed and content.

By degrees the sea darkened and began drawing the light from the sky. Stars came out, and later, to the south, the first lights of Tallinn appeared through the blackness. Europe. Passengers began to stir. A whistle blew. There was an announcement that in twenty minutes the ship would dock.

The ferry shuddered and rumbled as the engines reversed, and then it lightly nudged the pier and stopped. The droning of the engines subsided, and outside we could hear our first words of Estonian as men shouted back and forth while they secured the ship. Suzanne and I pulled our helmets and gloves on, climbed on the bike, and waited to join the press of vehicles as they rushed from the ferry. Metal clanged against metal, and then the whine of hydraulic rams signaled the opening of the sea door.

The driver of an old yellow diesel truck beside us started his engine, engulfing Suzanne and me in a cloud of thick, black smoke. Suzanne turned her face and coughed, and I tried not to breathe. There was some hollering toward the front of the ship, a crash, and the door became stuck half-opened.

I couldn't see what was going on. I couldn't move the bike because we were surrounded by other vehicles. The driver of the car in front of us rolled up his windows to stop the smoke from filling the interior. I leaned over and pounded on the side of the smoking truck to get the driver's attention. I waved and yelled, but the driver sat high up in the cab half a car length ahead of us, his gaze fixed on the stuck door. I honked our horn and the truck driver finally looked in his side mirror. I waved again. He rolled his window down and looked back at us to see what we wanted. The hot, gritty breath of his engine continued to pour over us. I twisted my helmeted head around and tried to find a bubble of air to sip from. I was getting light-headed, and it sounded as though Suzanne was about to retch. I signaled for the driver to turn his engine off. He twitched his nose as though he smelled something foul. Then he looked around to see where the smell came from, waved his hand in front of his face, and quickly rolled his window back up.

"Get off!" I said to Suzanne. "Walk between the cars and get to the front!"

"No! It's opening!" she said, and the first cars began to move slowly through the door.

The other vehicles around us started up, and I started the bike. The driver of the yellow diesel revved his engine to push the other vehicles along. The car in front of us moved. There was just enough space to slip in front of the yellow truck. We rode down the landing and pulled over to let our heads clear.

~~~~

A small section of the port was brightly lit by floodlights. They were aimed at the gaping mouth of the ferry, at an impromptu customs area most vehicles rolled through with a wave from a uniformed officer, and farther on they illuminated a sagging cyclone fence that had a gate cut into it. Beyond the fence was darkness.

I had expected lights that revealed the outline of the city, which our map showed lying just beyond the pier. I could almost conjure the city in my imagination through pictures I'd seen, the clusters of buildings that surrounded the port, the gray stone of the medieval wall, the round defensive towers with the red tile roofs, and the church spires on the hill.

Don had given us the address of a hostel on the edge of town, and he got it from Jim, the old man we'd met in Helsinki. Estonia had been his 101st country. According to Don, the hostel was just off the edge of our map, but now, in the dark, we weren't sure where to begin.

Two dented police cars were parked beside the gate, and a group of officers and civilians talked and watched vehicles pass through it. Suzanne and I walked over to them to ask directions.

"*Tere* (Hello)," I said. "Do you speak English?"

The officer nearest me looked as though I'd just asked him a riddle. He turned and pulled one of his partners by the elbow beside him.

"Do you speak English?" I asked again.

"Eng-lish?" the second one asked. "Eng-lish, ya?"

"Yes," I said, and he turned toward yet a third and brought him over, too.

The three of them could have been brothers. They were about the same age, maybe thirty-five. Each had the same color hair and identical mustaches. They wore matching white policeman's caps on their heads, and frayed, dark blue sweaters with badges sewn to the chest.

"You have problem?" the third one asked.

"We're looking for this address," I said.

He took the paper from my hands and held it up for the flood-lights to illuminate. He read the name of the hostel and street aloud, and knitted his brow.

"Tallinn?" he asked. "This address for Tallinn?"

"Yes. I think so."

The officer shared our piece of paper with his partners, and to-gether they discussed the address as if it were a place they had heard about in their youths but could only dimly recall. One of the officers reached into his car for a sheaf of papers and began flip-ping through them. He stopped twice and asked for the exact spelling. Another of them spoke into his radio and repeated the ad-dress several times. A voice called back and the officers consulted their papers again. They were excited now, on the trail of some-thing, and they followed it off one page and onto another.

"Ya, ya, ya, ya," the one who spoke English said. He tore a page from the bundle in his hands and anxiously began drawing as he explained where to go.

"From this ship place, drive, one, two, three roads," he said, and drew a straight line with three others that crossed it. "Then left...and, one, two roads...then big billing," he said, and described a building with both hands that was so big we had to move aside.

"Three roads. Left. Big building," Suzanne recorded.

"Ya," he confirmed. Then one of his associates spoke up and pointed from the paper to the map.

"Ei!" our guide said. "Not two roads. Three roads," and he added another to our map.

"Do we turn left before or after the building?" I asked.

"Building?"

"Billing. The big billing," I said, and described it with my hands.

"Ya. Big billing. Here," he said, and pointed it out with his pen. "One, two, three, four roads. Go right."

"Four roads?" Suzanne asked. "Four?"

"*Ei!*" the first officer we'd met said. He pointed at his associate's work critically, at the lines and building, and responded with a string of syllables, long vowels slung like rocks between them.

"Maybe there's a cheap hotel nearby," Suzanne whispered.

The officer who spoke English defended his work while the first seemed intent on pointing out its flaws. Finally, our cartographer shoved the paper at his associate and said something that sounded like, "Well, you do it then!" At that point the third officer shouted for them to stop and then said, "Follow us."

The city was almost completely blacked out. There were hardly any cars, and those we saw drove with their lights off, as if to conserve energy. Even the left taillight of the police car was dead. There were no street lights, and only a few curtained windows were dimly illuminated.

The police car sped through the city, through narrow cobbled streets, and around turns that I had to slow way down for. There were bumps and potholes the driver of the police car drove right over but which were big enough to bend a rim, pop a tire, or cause us to crash if we hit one on the bike. I narrowly missed the gaping mouth of a coverless manhole.

We followed them through the city, past still factory complexes, past the darkened hulks of apartment blocks. The odometer clicked three, four, then five miles. The police car turned often and abruptly, making dangerous and illegal turns. The police car finally stopped. An arm appeared through the driver's window and waved us alongside.

"Here. This billing," the English-speaking officer said, and pointed to one of them.

"Are you sure?" I asked. "I don't see anyone. There aren't many lights. It looks deserted."

"Ya, sure. This billing," and they drove off before I could say anything more. The car came to a quick stop, though, reversed, and came beside us again. "Not leave motorbike in outside," he said.

"Why?"

"Thieves!" he said, and the car sped away.

~~~

"We're not staying here," Suzanne said as we watched the car disappear. "I'll spend a hundred dollars for a hotel before I stay here for the night."

"Let's at least check it out," I said. "Doug, Mitch, and Don might be inside."

"You can, but I'm staying here. Those places look creepy."

The metal door into the building was broken, and it scraped loudly on the concrete landing when I pulled it open. The air inside was stale and reeked of urine and mold. I'd left the flashlight with Suzanne and had only matches. I lit one and tried the light switch. Nothing happened. There was no elevator, and the handrail was missing on the first flight of stairs. I followed them up and kept one hand against the dirty wall. The match burned out and I lit another on the first floor. I held it up so I could read the numbers above the doors, and I could tell that the one I was looking for was near the top.

I felt my way along the wall and up several flights to save matches. The blackness was almost total and I felt carefully with my feet and hands as I climbed from one landing to the next.

I found the right number near the top floor. There was a name card inserted in a metal slot on the door, and it matched the name of the hostel Jim had talked about. It was almost midnight, and I debated whether to knock, but did because I didn't know what else to do.

My knocking sounded so loud I was sure Suzanne could hear it outside the building. There was no answer. I knocked again. Someone called and I wanted it to be Doug.

"Hello!" I called back.

There was some noise. A thin band of light from under the

door lit the tips of my boots. A man's voice called from behind the door, and I said I was looking for the hostel.

Locks were turned, the door opened a crack, and a single eye appraised me.

"*Tere.* Sorry to disturb you. I'm looking for this hostel," I said, and passed the slip of paper through the crack. The man sighed and the door opened. I had woken him up.

"No hostel!" he said.

"But we got your name and address from an old American guy...Jim."

The man shook his head in exasperation, as if this had happened before. "Yim!" he said, and ran his hands over his tired face. "This Yim give you wrong address. This not hostel. This my home!"

Then I remembered how Jim liked to collect the names of people he'd met, just as he collected the names of countries. He'd collected Don's and the South African's. This man, I realized, probably worked at the hostel, had done something nice for Jim, and had added his name, too.

"But where is the hostel?" I asked.

"Tallinn! Hostel is in Tallinn! Go there. It open night and day," he said, and began to push the door shut.

"Where? Can you please write the address?" I asked, and he did only reluctantly before closing the door.

~~~

We became so disoriented trying to find our way back into Tallinn that I finally just stopped the bike on the edge of the biggest road we could find and waited for a car or truck to come by so we could follow it. The cool stillness of the night surrounded us. Fields stretched away from either side of the road, and though I couldn't see how far they extended, they felt endless after the closeness inside the apartment building. My eyes slowly adjusted to the darkness. I made out the shapes of what looked like bushes and trees a short distance off. I saw stars in the sky and the drifting bulk of clouds that rolled over them.

"I'm so tired," Suzanne said as we waited. "How could Jim have made such a mistake?"

"Don't be too hard on the guy," I said. "He was trying to be helpful. It's just an unfortunate time of night to have discovered his mistake."

"There you go again," she said. "Always minimizing everything. We could have gotten robbed out there." She sighed behind me and began to hum a song as if to drive the night away.

"We can't change the fact that we had the wrong address," I said. "We can't turn this night into day."

"Just let me be a little miserable," she said. "I need some sleep."

"We could ride into that field and spread our bags on the ground," I said.

"It's too spooky out here," she said, and I felt her turn on her seat to look behind her. "We have no idea where we are."

A light appeared in the mirror of the bike. I turned around and watched a miniature sunrise on the horizon. We watched it move slowly across the flat landscape toward us, watched the single light become two, watched it disappear behind some trees or dip through a swale. The lights appeared again, and grew, and were accompanied by the laboring sound of an engine.

"Get ready," Suzanne said.

It was a transport truck that pulled a trailer bearing a shipping container, bound for what we hoped was the port. We were able to ride slower behind it than behind the police car and take in the strangeness of the dead city. Besides the dark there was also an absence of street signs, which we later learned was because the old Russian signs were being replaced by Estonian ones. We stuck behind the truck until, in the distance, I saw the lights of a hotel. I decided to peel away from the truck and go toward it, and in that instant I understood something about the attraction insects have to light.

The doorman of the Palace Hotel watched as I parked the bike beside a neat row of new cars. He wore a burgundy suit and smoked. He combed his slicked back hair as Suzanne took off her gloves and helmet.

"Tere," I said, and watched as the color of the doorman's suit changed to a burnt orange as he walked beneath a neon sign that said, "Disco!"

"Two hundred dollars," the doorman said when Suzanne asked him the price of their cheapest room. "With breakfast," he added, as if to sweeten the deal. "And, I guarantee no Russian steals your motorbike."

I told him it was too much, and he just shrugged his shoulders. "I cannot make new price," he said. "Not my hotel." He said the cheaper hotels in Tallinn were all full, that an international symposium was being held, one of the first, he said proudly, since Estonia had declared independence from Russia.

"What about the lobby?" Suzanne asked. "Can we sleep in the chairs? It's two in the morning."

"Impossible," he said. "We have reputation."

I showed him the paper with the old and new address of the hostel written on it, told him that we'd been duped, and he said we were lucky to have made it back. "That is Russian area. Many, many Russian mafia man lives there. Estonians are okay. But these Russians, they kill you for a match!"

The doorman said that the hostel was probably also full since the rooms were so cheap, and that I should at least call before we left. He said I could use the phone in the lobby and he helped me to find the number. Despite the late hour a woman answered. She spoke English and said there were plenty of rooms, and that we should come on over. She confirmed the address and even spelled it out slowly so I could make sure I had it right. The doorman helped us with directions. He walked out into the street and pointed into the black. "Not far. Maybe three kilometers," he said, and gave a casual wave of his hand as if it was just down the block.

The directions seemed simple enough, until we were on our way. The doorman had said the building we were looking for would be quite obvious, and the sign above the door distinctly illuminated. But in the dark, on those winding, narrow streets crisscrossed by alleys and passages, without street signs, we became disoriented. We rode back, almost as far as the Palace Hotel, and began again. We scoured each side of the street for any hint of a hostel, of an illuminated sign, lit windows. Two kilometers, three, four. We rode another just to be sure we'd gone far enough. We rode until the city gave way to apartment blocks, empty lots, and factories, before turning around for another try. I saw someone walking along the sidewalk and rode toward them to ask for help, but they scurried into the shadows of a building.

We were slowly narrowing down our options when a car, on an otherwise empty street, pulled behind us and matched our speed. I moved over to let it pass but it moved over, too. I sped up and the car remained behind us. The driver flashed his lights twice, and a block ahead of us, another car flashed its lights back. The second car began moving, in our lane and directly toward us. Suzanne gripped me with her knees and hands, and I thought how tragic it would be if those people who had warned us of all the dangers of this trip would be proved right.

The car behind us flashed its lights again and the other car sped toward us. I leaned the bike to the left and turned the throttle. We lunged forward in a turn so tight the end of my footpeg scraped the asphalt. Suzanne pulled me into her and I thought for sure we would go down. I found my mind racing to remember where my knife was, while at the same time I shoved my leg out and down to push the bike upright again. Then we were upright and rushing toward the center of town. The lights of the vehicles receded quickly behind us, and then they were gone.

～～～

We eventually found the hostel at the end of an alley that was cluttered with rusted iron and empty shipping crates. Above the door was an unlit sign. I was so tired I wouldn't have minded falling asleep on the steps, and Suzanne wavered after she peeled herself from the back of the bike.

The entrance had a glass door, and I looked through it into a small lobby. A young couple sat on stools beside a bar. They looked bored as they smoked and regarded the fat bottles of beer before them. An older woman in a blue smock sat at a desk writing something. She looked up once, and I smiled and waved to let her know we'd made it.

The door was locked when I tried to pull it open. I knocked, and the couple turned slowly toward us. The woman looked over the top of her glasses and squinted to see who was there. I waved, and she walked over, opened the door, and asked what we wanted.

"A room," I said. "We called a while ago from the Palace Hotel. Sorry we're late, but this place was a little harder to find than we'd imagined."

"No rooms," the woman said, and blocked our way in.

"Excuse me?" I said. "We called a little while ago, and you, or someone, said to come on over."

"What did she say, Allen?" Suzanne asked from behind me, where she was unpacking our bags from the bike.

"Was not me," the woman said, and turned and walked back to her desk. I followed her, and she snapped open a ledger on her desk. She ran a finger over just a few names. "Is no rooms," she said, and was about to close it. The last three names were for Doug, Don, and Mitch.

"We're traveling with them," I lied, and held the ledger open. Suzanne came up beside me with her bag in her hand and our tent in the other. "We'll stay in their room," I told the woman, and Suzanne and I walked up the stairs.

"Who is it?" Don called from inside their room.

"Naked Man," I whispered.

~~~

I dreamed that Suzanne and I crashed. I dreamed that while turning the bike to evade the cars that I wasn't able to push it upright again, and that instead of rushing down the street toward the center of town, the bike went off balance and we started to fall.

In our falling Suzanne hugged me and I wanted to disappear into her. I wanted us to dissolve together and to have never begun this trip. The bike went down and a sharp pain rolled up my leg as the weight of everything—of the motorcycle and our gear; as the weight of Suzanne and of my own ambition—ground it into the road.

My ears rang. The cars were almost on top of us and their lights burned my eyes. I tried to call Suzanne, tried to turn and look at her, but my helmet became like a towel wrapped around my head. I felt her struggle behind me, heard her call, *"Allen? Allen? Are you okay, Allen?"* And I heard the incomprehensible voices of men coming from the cars, heard the quick scrape of their shoes against the asphalt. Suzanne screamed, and then she cried a slow, wailing lament.

The bike's engine still ran and I revved it so the noise would scare the cars away. The exhaust pipe was like a torch, and I turned the throttle as far as it would go so the flame burned the men before they could reach us. Someone kicked the back of my helmet and the nape of my neck went numb. The engine sputtered and died. I felt the concussive echo of blows as they fell onto Suzanne's body, and then on my own. Someone grabbed me by my jacket and pulled me away. I twisted my body and reached for Suzanne. For a moment, I held her arm and our eyes met through the dirty visors of our helmets. A boot came down on my hand and I let go. I had to let her go.

~~~

Doug's alarm went off at seven. I reached beside me and found the soft warmth of Suzanne's arm. I felt the thrumming of her pulse with my fingers and she stirred. Her body tightened and shivered as she stretched. She inhaled deeply, and then let her breath escape in a sigh through her body's tautness.

"Reveille, boys and girls!" Doug called.

"Gawd!" Mitch groaned. "I wish you'd quit sayin' that."

Doug, Don, and Mitch were leaving on the morning ferry to Helsinki at ten, and then, later that same night, they'd get on another to Stockholm. Both cities seemed like far-off places now.

There was a bathroom down the hall, and Suzanne and I went there to clean up. The doors to the rest of the rooms stood open and each was empty. The hall was strewn with old papers and debris. "There's no one else in here," I said.

"Of course not," Suzanne said. "This place is a dump."

"We shouldn't have a problem getting a room tonight," I said.

"Agh!" she said, as we entered the bathroom. "It smells awful in here!"

"At least we can get clean," I said, and turned on the spigot in the bath. "I'm filthy after yesterday."

A stream of rust-colored water ran from the faucet, and I moved so Suzanne couldn't see until it cleared.

"What would you like for breakfast?" I asked.

"Sleep," she yawned.

I put my hand under the faucet and the water was as cold as if it had been drawn from the bottom of the sea. I arranged our soap on the side of the tub, and we began to undress.

"I had a bad dream," I said.

"I don't have any clean clothes," Suzanne said, as she held her shirt up for inspection.

"We can wash some now," I said. "Do you want to hear about my dream?"

"I'd rather not right now. Everything still feels a bit nightmarish."

I put my hand under the water again and wanted it to be warm. Suzanne put her hand in, too, pulled it away, and shivered. We waited a minute more and tried again.

"There is none," Suzanne said dejectedly. "Is there?"

"We can at least freshen up," I said, and I climbed into the tub and squatted at one end to make room for her, too. I held my breath as I splashed some water onto my crotch and under my arms, as if by doing so she'd see that it was fine and would follow me. "It's not bad," I managed.

I splashed water over my face and rubbed as the skin hardened in resistance. I turned to see if Suzanne was coming in, but instead she had begun to dress.

~~~

Our group walked outside. The bike was beside the front door where I'd parked it. The piece of plywood from one of the shipping containers I'd leaned against its side for camouflage was there, and I checked to see that the lock was still threaded through the rims and around a sewer pipe bolted against the building.

We walked down the alley to the street Suzanne and I had ridden up and down just a few hours before. It was wider than I'd remembered. The dark shadowy buildings looked only neglected and dirty in the morning light. A horse-drawn cart passed us heading into town, and the man driving it returned my wave. A bus full of faces went the other way, toward Russia. An old woman waddled past hauling a heavy canvas bag that caused her body to list to the right with each step. Two boys with book bags flapping against their backs hurried past, as though late for school.

The guys took Suzanne and me to an outdoor market held in a dusty lot. Old wooden tables were set in rows, and on a few of them people sold mounds of small muddy potatoes, bundles of fat carrots with long green tails, piles of yellow onions with peeling skins, a pyramid of carefully arranged eggs, leeks as big around as broom handles, and little bundles of herbs. We bought baskets of wild berries, a loaf of bread, two bottles of milk, and then sat on a curb and ate.

"So," Mitch said. "Jimbo burned ya'all, too?" He said they'd taken a cab to the same address after arriving on the train the previous morning, but that they hadn't even bothered to go in the building.

"We got out there," Doug said, "and I told the cab driver, 'Screw this! Get us back to town.'" He tore off a corner of bread for himself and passed the loaf on. "It looked like a war zone."

"Can't imagine what it was like at night, riding around like that," Don said, and passed the berries to Suzanne.

"I was really scared," Suzanne said as she carefully pressed some berries into her bread like jam. "It was so dark. I swear there were people wandering around in the shadows watching us. And then Allen disappeared inside that building. I felt trapped...afraid to go in after him, and afraid to stay where I was. It seemed like he was gone forever."

"I didn't know what else to do," I said. "That address was all we had to go on."

"You should have followed the police back into town," Suzanne said frowning. "It was stupid to be out there."

"You saw how fast they drove away," I retorted. "I did the best I could."

For a moment nobody said a word, and I wished the sounds of the market were loud enough to hide behind. Then Don cleared his throat. "Anyway, Tallinn's a one-day town," he said. "You can actually see it in a few hours."

"Yeah," Mitch concurred. "Takes no time 'tall."

As Suzanne asked about the town, and the guys obliged with descriptions of the main square and the narrow streets, I felt the sting of her judgment. I hated that she was talking to me through others again. It was as if she'd spoken out of desperation and left some kind of note the guys would remember should anything happen to us, a kind of note before we rode into the abyss.

I shook the thoughts off. They were ridiculous. It was just a road south through a couple more countries. I could think of doom and gloom or I could stay focused on all the good things that would unfold before us. We had to be in accord, especially for the rest of the trip. Traveling had everything to do with faith. I felt I'd been called to go to the places I went, and I hardly questioned that calling. There was faith in the listening, in the patience of planning, in the saving and the sacrifices to save more, in the packing-up and leaving. There was a faith in knowing there couldn't be a wrong turn or a bad trip because if you listened, you'd always be right where you needed to be. And with that faith came the rewards of travel: the experiences and insights, the connections and friends, the limitless peace of mind that I rarely felt at any other time.

Mitch stood up, wiped the crumbs from his lap, and looked around. He said he wanted to do some shopping; he'd seen a sweater in a window he wanted to look at for his girlfriend. We walked down the street, past the Palace Hotel, which looked overexposed in the daylight, and then through the medieval wall of Tallinn's old town.

There would be no dishonor in changing plans, I told myself. I'd be a hero in Suzanne's eyes if I were to suggest that we get on the ten o'clock ferry, too. It was strange to think that after so many miles and weeks that we could be in Stockholm in less than twenty-four hours. We could return to Harö or travel to Norway with the guys, and then head south, somewhere warm and sunny on our own. I put on the idea like a coat and followed our group.

Tallinn was an ideal medieval town. The cobbled streets were narrow and bent. The buildings were weathered so the stone showed beneath the peeling layers of paint. The mortar between the stones was charged with sea shells that looked like layers of fossils suspended in geologic time. Someone played a piano and the music rushed along the stream bed of streets and washed over us.

Along one narrow street we walked around a mound of coal that had been dumped there. A woman and her two small children scooped it with their blackened hands onto squares of fabric they'd laid on the street. When each square was full they tied the corners in a knot and cradled the bundle in a leather sling they carried on their backs up the narrow steps of their building. I wanted to stop and help, to take the bundles from the children so they could play in the street, but I had already fallen behind our group.

Mitch found his shop and we went inside. The sweaters were knitted from hand-dyed wool by local craftswomen, and Suzanne helped him look through them. She looked happy as she instructed Mitch. She giggled as she held a sweater up for him to comment on. She laid several against her chest so he could see how they'd fit.

It bothered me that my peace of mind could be so affected by her unhappiness, that everything could be as black as she saw it now. I wanted it to be the other way around. I wanted my faith and pleasure to inspire her as it once had. It felt as though at any moment now what it was that still held us together could vanish and she'd just as easily wander off with the three guys as with me.

We continued through the old town, through squares and passages, iron-studded oak gates and portals, and then up the steep steps to Castle Hill where we looked over the red-tiled roofs below. The sun reflected off the stones there. From our place on the hill we had an impressive view of St. Olaf's cathedral with its tall spire and I imagined that from the top I could look west toward Latvia and get an idea of what lay ahead. Beyond the spire was the sea, and on it was the approaching ferry that could take us to Helsinki. The choice was there and I knew where I had to be.

~~~

Suzanne and I said good-bye to Don, Doug, and Mitch outside the hostel, and then we watched as they disappeared around the corner to find their ship.

"You could have gone with them," I said cautiously as we packed the bike. "I'd understand."

She didn't say anything for a moment, and then she looked at me. "That's not the answer," she said. "Not yet anyway."

"Thank you," I said.

I removed the lock, and together we backed the bike into the lane.

"Ready?" I asked.

"As I'll ever be."

twenty-one

While researching the trip I had discovered a reference to Saaremaa, a large island that lies off the coast of Estonia. Before the Second World War it was known for its unspoiled nature, folk traditions, and a small spa resort in the town of Kuressaare on the southwest edge of the island. Since the war, the island was closed by the Soviets to all but a few islanders and the military. Most Estonians had never set foot on its shore. After some research I found that the Estonian government was issuing travel permits on a limited basis. I'd made inquiries and was issued one.

Because of its isolation and remoteness, the island had reverted to what the literature accompanying our permit defined as a "pre-natural place." I had figured that after negotiating Russia, Suzanne and I would be ready for a little "pre-natural." That was all we knew about Saaremaa as we left Tallinn.

The old town passed quickly to apartment blocks which in turn gave way to pastures and woodlots, fields of ripe grain, and meadows of purple, blue, and yellow wildflowers.

Then it began to rain.

It was only a little at first, a few fat drops from some loitering clouds. I felt Suzanne stiffen behind me and I wondered if she didn't regret her decision about the ferry after all. We turned onto a smaller road near the village of Klooga and I thought about trying to outrun the storm. Then the clouds rushed in to greet us. With the rain came a gusting wind. I leaned the bike just so and it seemed as if the tone of our journey had been re-established. It was as though during the past week of relative sun and calm, something had been amiss, and when that storm hit I heard a sad voice say, "Oh, yes. This is just as it should be."

We turned onto an even poorer road at the village of Risti, just a pocked ribbon of asphalt and gravel laid over the landscape. I slowed and began to weave around monotonous miles of potholes that induced a rhythmic back and forth. Gray curtains of rain and rising mist hid all but a very small portion of the world. I became lost in the leaning, lost in the infinite gray mist that encircled us, lost in Suzanne's sadness as it seeped through my jacket and soaked my soul.

The road came to an end at Virtsu, a village no bigger than the dock and the few boats that were tied against it. A small open-decked ferry was among them and we drove on. We parked the bike between the tall tires of a tractor and the rear wheel of a truck.

The ferry had a small, bare room behind the wheelhouse, where we stood pressed against a window overlooking the back of the ferry and the receding land. The other passengers were there, too, and they talked in a collective drone that suggested they all knew each other. They gave us furtive glances, and I could tell that they were trying to piece our story together. I heard cousins of the word "motorcycle" and "American," and I smiled whenever eyes lingered on us, but no one reacted. It's been written that Estonians are some of the most stubbornly distant people in Europe, a defensive reaction adapted after hundreds of years of brutal foreign occupation. I wanted to make a connection nevertheless, with the old man in the tattered sheepskin coat and leather knee boots, with the young couple and their baby, and to have entered into a

long conversation that continued over dinner and an evening at
their farm.

The rain fell harder on the open sea, and the wind, without obstacles, whipped up clouds of mist that filled the air. The ferry
rolled over waves and I looked out the window and watched the
horizon to keep from feeling sick.

~~~

The ferry stopped at the small island of Muhumaa and everyone drove off. It was set like a stepping stone between the mainland and Saaremaa, and our map showed a road that crossed it and
led to a bridge that linked the two islands. A heavy man in a dark
wool uniform covered by a gleaming green poncho checked our papers as we rode off the ferry. He took them in his big hands and
shuffled each page as though they were out of order. When they
were to his liking, he studied each as if it were a test. He had fat
blue lips that trembled as he read. Beads of rain fell from his
hooded head onto the pages until the ink began to run. Our papers became translucent and relaxed like tired skin over the frame
his fingers made. Then he waved us on.

We rode quickly across Muhumaa and came to the bridge. Our
map showed a vague sketch that had invited me to imagine an old,
steel span built sometime in the twenties with ornamental stan-
chions and illuminated globes hanging from each to light a trav-
eler's way on a dark night. Instead, the bridge was just a single lane
constructed of granite boulders laid across the sea floor, and then
covered with gravel and dirt. The bridge stretched over a mile
across the churning sea, and at the end we could see the dull, gray-
green outline of Saaremaa. Waves beat against the rocks and ex-
plosions of spume and water cascaded over the road. Flurries of
mist and rain concealed the other side, making it seem as though
the road led to oblivion.

It felt as though we were in the very center of all the storms that
had hit us on this trip, and I was overcome with a desire to stop and
look into their very center. Midway across the bridge I did stop and

turned off the engine. Suzanne asked what on earth I thought I was doing and I said that for just a moment I was going to look. The sea boiled on either side of us, and when I looked past the strip of ground at our feet, the storm was all that existed. It was infinite, and I thought of those storms on Jupiter that rage for ten thousand years.

Then we were across the bridge and into the protective cover of a forest of ancient oaks and pines and beech, where the wind was reduced to a breeze and the rain a shower. The road wound across the middle of the island, along the edge of meadows and small farms. Occasionally the name of a village was posted on a sign beside the road, but most of the time they were only marked by an old church, a fork in the road leading somewhere else.

Like all the islands in the Baltic Sea, Saaremaa is still rising about three millimeters a year after having been submerged beneath the weight of the last ice age. It is quite flat and has only a thin layer of soil over a solid stone base. From east to west it is roughly fifty miles long, and from north to south some thirty miles wide, but it lacks all classical island proportions. It is not round or crescent shaped or oblong. Rather, it is shaped like an ink blot, with distorted ganglia and protrusions that make it difficult to describe.

Our destination was the town of Kuressaare on the far south coast, and when we arrived there we rode up and down several of the quiet little streets, past old homes and new inns that had recently been renovated in anticipation of a wave of tourism. Suzanne tapped me on the shoulder, pointed at one, and we stopped.

A young man who insisted we call him Ivar quoted us seven dollars for a room, with breakfast. He was tall, with neatly combed blond hair and a nervous smile. He announced the figure with trepidation, as if he was prepared to go lower if we objected. Before we could say yes or no, Ivar promised there was a nice view, that we'd share a bathroom with only one other room and, that at least in this hotel, there was plenty of hot water. As proof he handed us the key and encouraged us to take a look.

There was a double bed pushed against a gleaming white stucco wall and, above it, an oil painting of what looked like one of the farms we had passed. There was a small wooden desk, a chair, and a large window that looked onto the backyard of the adjacent house and the tile roofs of some buildings beyond. Suzanne sat on the bed and tested the springs. She let the bag she had in her hands fall to the floor. Then she lay back and sighed. "This is it," she announced. "We'll stay here until we leave. We're not camping on Saaremaa."

"Perfect!" Ivar said when we agreed to take the room. Then he handed me some papers to fill out. He said he'd arrange space in the garage for the bike, free of charge, that it was necessary because of the Russians still living on the island. Ivar said the hotel was a training facility for the developing tourism industry on Saaremaa, and that downstairs there was an excellent restaurant. "Should have some stars," he said, in reference to its quality. "Three. Maybe four."

He said he'd been in training for two months and had done everything from cleaning, bed making, window washing, cooking, check-in, and "customer happiness."

"The customer happiness is most serious," he said as he gave me a receipt. "You call for Ivar if you need something."

The shower was running when I returned to the room with our bags, and Suzanne's clothes lay in a pile outside the bathroom door. She was in there for a long time, testing what Ivar had said about the hot water. I was hanging up our rain suits to dry, and separating our clothes for washing, when I heard the hiss of the shower stop. Suzanne emerged a moment later with a towel turbaned around her head and another draped around her shoulders. She pulled back the cover of the bed and lay down. I dried the warm, damp skin of her back and legs, and asked what she wanted to do with the rest of our day. She didn't answer. I pulled the cover over her shoulders and listened as the ebb of her breathing lulled her into a deep sleep.

～～～

Later that afternoon the storm broke, and in the distance beams of sunlight burned through the clouds. I opened our window and sat on the sill. The light changed and the geraniums growing in the window boxes of the adjacent house became inflamed. The leaves of the apple tree that filled the yard began to glow, and the drops of rain resting on them shone like beads of mercury. The back door opened and a woman stepped out, her hands on her aproned hips. She reached up and took her long, auburn hair in her hands and tied it into a twist at the back of her head. I waved, but she didn't see me as she surveyed the sky and then went back inside.

Her house was two stories and built of brick. The windowpanes were clear and polished, and I could see into the two upper rooms. One looked like a study, with a dark wood bookcase partially visible. The spines of old volumes crowded together on the shelves, and on the top were some blue and green bottles and a bunch of dried flowers arranged on a piece of fabric. I could see the back of a chair and a lamp. The other room was darker, and a white lace shade covered a portion of the window. A tropical houseplant grew from a shiny brass planter and snaked along the sill.

The woman stepped back into the yard. She carried a yellow plastic bowl and a plate. She set them on a weathered wooden table against the fence and arranged them in a row. The yellow bowl contained a bunch of silver herring, each about six inches long, and she filled the bowl with water from a white pitcher. From a pocket in her apron she produced a pair of scissors and began to open each of the fish along its belly with a quick snip. A gray cat pressed at the screen door at the back of the house and the woman called to it softly. The cat meowed, rubbed its face against the screen, and the woman walked over and let it out. The cat curled around her legs as she scooped the fish entrails out with her fingers, and then leapt as she dropped them onto the grass. The woman hummed the melody of a song and I hummed along softly, too. It sounded happy, and so was I.

When the fish were gutted, the woman rinsed them in the yellow bowl and arranged the clean ones on the plate. When she was done she scattered the pink water on the vegetables growing along the back fence. Then she rinsed her hands in a basin near the back steps, dried them on a white cotton cloth hanging beside the door, and went inside.

∼∽∽

There was nothing so very remarkable about Saaremaa. There were no volcanoes or towering mountains with immense views of the surrounding sea. There were no hot springs or gorges or navigable rivers that led through jungle to waterfalls, no crescent-shaped white sand beaches that extended to the ends of the horizon. The water was cold, the shore rocky, and the bent junipers along the coast showed that the wind blew hard and often from the cold north.

The beauty was subtle. We found it in the way we were drawn aimlessly along chalky gravel tracks and lanes just to see where they'd take us. We found it as we lingered at yet another view of the sea and watched the clouds gain mass before heading over the continent. The rhythmic kneading of the waves along the shore pulled our attention down to notice how a wildflower thrived in a thimbleful of dust collected between two stones, and we found beauty as we combed a beach for swan feathers and clam shells, polished rocks and fossils. We found it in the way all roads led back to where we'd begun, like a riddle, and in an odd idea I had one day that the island was all there was of the world, and that it was somehow knowable.

We rode hundreds of miles on Saaremaa. I made a point to search for the end of each road and lane and peninsula, of stopping as often as possible. On one ride north we passed a meadow with some of the largest oaks I'd ever seen, trees that rose like huge fountains from the earth, their long branches tapering to fingers of spray. On the other side of the road was a field of grain an old couple was harvesting by hand with scythes. Their heads were bent in observance of their task, or from so many years of such work, and they didn't notice our presence. We could see where they'd begun together that morning in the same corner of the field and how they'd worked away from each other toward opposite ends. I could see that midway in the woman's progress she'd discarded a rose-colored shawl and draped it like a blanket over the fallen grain, and how farther along on the man's side he'd hung his black coat on a fence post. Suzanne and I stood there for some time and watched as the steady sweep of their scythes fell row upon row of grain-heavy stalks, their polished blades reflecting the sun at the beginning of each stroke, and we watched the precise steps they took as they stepped farther into their work.

The roads narrowed the farther we went. They divided often, or ended abruptly in the woods, at the sea, beside a seeping stream, and once at a lonely stone church kept tidy in a clearing. We stopped there and found a trail leading into the forest. The sun filtered through the canopy onto the ground in shifting plate-sized dapples, and the earth was so soft from the accumulation of decades of shed vegetation that our footfalls were like whispers of our passing through. Suzanne took my hand as we walked toward an opening so bright I had to squint my eyes. Quite suddenly we were on the edge of a low cliff about ten feet above the sea. We slid down the face and loosened a clatter of shale shingles that settled behind us. Suzanne noticed something and picked a piece up off the ground. It contained the fossil of a shell. We bent down and discovered that nearly every bit of shale contained a fossil, or a portion of one, like scraps of torn pictures.

As we walked along, the cliff rose higher above us and the beach narrowed. The shore was littered with jagged slivers of rusted metal amid the stones. We rounded the point of a peninsula and climbed back up the side. There was an abandoned trench there, and I realized we'd stumbled across one of the island's many World War II battlegrounds. I climbed down into it but Suzanne stood well away and looked at me like I'd climbed into a grave. The trench was about six feet deep and lined with stones. I pushed down nettles with my boots and cleared spider webs with my hands. There was a small wooden shelf built into the rocks where the island's defenders had probably stored ammunition, food, books, and pictures of those who waited for them at home. There were depressions in the wall that were at the right level to have been improvised seats. Just past a destroyed gun emplacement the trench was filled with garbage from more recent times. Among the rusted cans, broken bottles, and faded plastic containers were a burned baby carriage and an old umbrella that had been inverted by a gust of wind from a long-forgotten storm.

~~~

Suzanne and I remained all but invisible to the local people while on Saaremaa, but the bike received plenty of attention. On one occasion Suzanne and I were walking back to the bike after a lunch beside the sea when two boys rode past on an old moped. The engine buzzed like an insect and left a blue trail of smoke that expanded like a stain in the air. They saw our bike parked on the edge of the road and sputtered to a stop. Suzanne and I remained hidden in the brush beside the trail and watched. The boy on the back held two fishing poles and a metal pail for their catch, and as he dismounted he worked his way free from a tangle of line. The two boys walked carefully toward our bike. They pointed at the engine and tires and fairing while circling, but didn't get too close, afraid the bike might spring at them. They were edgy, especially the driver, and once he stepped backward so one of the fishing poles brushed his neck. He squealed and jumped. Suzanne and I laughed, and the boys ran for their machine. They pushed it to a start and were off. The boy on the rear kept looking back to make sure they weren't being followed.

Another time we parked in the Kuressaare town square so we could buy some food before heading out for the day. Our bike glowed beside the Estonians' ancient Russian vehicles and created a commotion. Cars slowed and stopped so people could take a long look at the bike. People stopped on the sidewalk and leaned over the handlebars to inspect the instrument cluster, study the tires, mirrors, paint, and seat. I was standing right there but I may as well have been a road sign. I said, *"Terre.* Hi! Can I help you?" but no one moved or looked at me. A man got down on his hands and knees to inspect something under the bike, and while he was looking up I waved my hand in his line of sight. *"Terre,"* I said as I waved. "I'll take you for a ride if you say something." A woman carrying an armful of bread loaves stared into the headlight as if it were a television screen. I cleared my throat and for just a moment our eyes met, but then she went back to staring. I had a desire to poke the man on the ground or take one of the woman's loaves, just to cause a reaction.

"Yes," Ivar nervously confided one night in the hotel. "Estonian people are very inside-looking. With each other is the same. We say very little."

"We'd just like to meet a few people," I said. "They like the bike, but they don't seem to notice Suzanne and me."

"You must not cry over this," he said. "Machine is easy. Not so difficult to know. People are a problem. For so long the Russian people only want Estonians to say nothing. Many people was sent away, or killed, because they talk. You understand? Some person like you comes. You want to talk, ask questions. Has been a long time since that happens here. You must come back another year. Maybe many years. Can be different then."

～～～

In the afternoons Suzanne and I returned to Kuressaare and walked the streets. The town began along the edge of a bay where a thirteenth-century castle still dominates. It was constructed quite simply in the shape of a block with sheer stone walls and surrounded by a moat that was partially filled with silt, the deadfall of trees, and litter. Kuressaare radiates inland from there along a neat grid pattern. The center of Kuressaare was built around an oblong square with a broken fountain. The buildings are a mix of single- and two-story baroque structures painted a dusty gold or white with red tile roofs. They accommodate a mix of food shops, a barber, a bank, some government offices, and a church. The store we bought our food from was on that square and I liked going in. It was big and airy and smelled of meat, bread, dust, and the sour odor of two monumental women who sat near the door and added

our purchases up. There were shelves of canned goods with tattered paper labels. Blurred pictures of the contents were described
with Cyrillic text. Next was a shelf filled with gallon jars of preserved fruits and vegetables in milky solutions. There were eggs
carefully laid on straw, as if the hens had laid them there, and
loaves of bread in dented metal bins. Along one wall were crates of
bottled beer, vodka, and juice, their labels askew and peeling.
There were jugs of milk with paper caps, a stringer of smoked herring tied to a nail in the ceiling, slabs of meat hanging from metal
hooks above a bloody counter, and wilting vegetables laid out on
newsprint on a table in the middle of the shop.

Suzanne and I walked up and down most of the streets and
commented on flower and vegetable gardens and windows and
doors and paint schemes that appealed to us. We imagined ourselves sitting quietly on the porch of a house we liked as we
watched another day end. We leaned into yards to smell roses, to
pet a cat that arched its back for us while it balanced on the top
rail of a fence. We guessed how much it would cost to buy a small
stone house with a red tile roof and overgrown yard, and we allowed ourselves to wonder where we could order stone and grout
to fix a sagging wall and buy plants to fill the garden with.

"Do you think you could write here?" Suzanne asked one warm
and still afternoon as we stood outside a house we both liked.

"Fall begins in another month," I said. "The winters here go on
and on."

"That doesn't seem possible right now, does it," she said, and
squinted her eyes as she looked into the empty sky. "It seems like we
could put some of this weather in a jar and have it for the winter."

There was a park with a band shell and gazebo, a snack kiosk
that was locked-up for the year, a memorial to victims of Nazi
atrocities, and a bench where a young couple sat pressed against
each other as they silently watched their toddler crawl across the
grass. Suzanne and I sat on another bench and she laid her head
against my shoulder.

"Where do you think we'll be in a year?" she asked.

"I don't know," I said, and pulled her closer. "At home, I suppose. Working, and saving our money for another trip. What made you ask?"

She thought a moment as we watched the baby delight in the feel of the grass beneath its naked hands and arms and legs.

"What is it?" I asked again.

The baby pressed its face into the grass and sneezed. It giggled and then looked at its parents with a big smile.

"I was just wondering," she said. "Wondering where we'll be."

It was while on Saaremaa that Suzanne began sleeping more than usual. It was as though she had never caught up on her sleep from the long night of riding through Tallinn. I thought she might be coming down with something, but she insisted she was just tired. She'd take a long nap each afternoon before dinner, and she'd sleep late while I went down for breakfast alone. In the afternoons I'd lay beside her until she fell asleep, and then I'd move to the windowsill to write and wait for the woman to appear in her backyard.

One afternoon the yard was filled with drying clothes hung on lines strung from the back of the house to the branches of an apple tree. Crisp, white sheets, yellow-and-blue hand towels, and underclothes quaked in the breeze. It reminded me that we had clothes that needed to be washed before we left, so I gathered them up and took them into the bathroom. I filled the tub with warm water and shampoo, and swirled my hands around until a layer of suds grew like clouds on the water. I dropped in Suzanne's two shirts, her underwear and socks, and mixed them all together with mine.

I slid my hands inside Suzanne's socks and rubbed one against the other. She'd bought them new before we'd left home, but I noticed the places along her heel and toes where the fabric was so thin I could see through to my fingers. I traced where the ball of her heel lay, traced the rise and fall of her arch, traced each of the five points where her toes rested, and I thought of the great whorl of miles that had worn them so. I rubbed my hands together until the watermarks of her sweat disappeared and the soil from the cuff of her boot had loosened and washed away. I picked up her shirt next and noticed how the collar was beginning to fray. There was a black oil stain on her sleeve that rubbing only dulled, and a button was loose that I promised myself to fix for her. Her underwear remained and it moved lazily in the water, like a leaf in the tide. I swirled my hand around and watched them roll and crumple. I thought how little, and how much, she was asking of me to make things better.

I hung our clothes on coat hangers around the room and then moved back to the window. The woman was in her yard and I watched as she moved in small sidesteps down each line. She stopped just long enough in front of each article to pull it from the line, snap the wrinkles out, and fold it with a choreography that involved her hands and chin and the smooth slope of her breast. She did it with an efficiency and grace that I studied. It was an efficiency and grace that Suzanne and I had somehow lost.

I looked at Suzanne asleep on the bed. Her body was curled beneath the covers and her pretty face rested on a pillow. I wondered where, exactly, we'd lost our grace. On which trip? In which city? Or did it happen at home? Did we lose it all in one piece, a piece we could recover? Or did it happen slowly over many miles, a dispersion of particles that could never be found?

~~~

Breakfast—a buffet of coffee, bread and butter, tomato and cucumber slices, herring filets, sausage, and hard-boiled eggs— was served from six to eight-thirty in the restaurant. Because I went down alone now I chose the same small table against the wall from which I could watch the few other guests. For two mornings there was a Dutch couple with a small child who said they'd come to see the island where the man's father had been born. Tonu said his father was still alive, but that he'd refused to return with them. "Bad memories," he explained. "First Germans, then Russians. All his family was killed."

They'd been out to see his father's farm, but a new family lived there now, and they hadn't allowed Tonu and his wife to look around. "They think we come back and push them out," he said. "That happens now. People who left because the Germans or Russians, they want their homes and farms back. It's a big problem."

I asked them how they liked the island, and Ingrid, his wife, smiled and said she preferred the south of France. "But it is so open here," she said. "So quiet. Sometimes Tonu's father talks about his life here, how wonderful it was. I see that now. But the people, they are like stones in the field."

The next day Tonu and Ingrid were replaced by a Russian man and his young girlfriend. The man was about fifty. He was heavy and balding, and each morning he had the same sour expression on his face. He wore tight-fitting clothes with the shirt opened at the top, revealing a mat of black hair and a heavy gold chain. His girlfriend was no more than eighteen. She was tall and thin and had long, brown hair that followed the natural curve of her back, suggesting the meandering bends of a river. She should have been wearing shorts, a t-shirt and hiking boots. Her face and arms should have had a red glow from the sun. Each morning she wore the same tight black dress that covered no more of her body than a slip, and high heels she walked stiff-legged on. She wore black nylons, and each morning the run behind her right knee reached a little higher. The man smoked as he ate sausage and bread, and he mumbled gruffly, as if reminding her of all the ways she'd disappointed him. She ate painfully, as if each mouthful was poison. I tried to talk to her in the buffet line once, but she just looked at me sadly and turned away. I recognized them twice on the island's roads in an old, rusted Mercedes. He drove madly, an angry expression on his face, as though chasing someone down.

Another morning I met an excitable German bicyclist named Rudy. He was riding to St. Petersburg alone, but he admitted he'd taken a ferry and trains most of the way. "Stupid idea," he said when I asked him about his trip. "Bad place if you are German. In Poland, they throw stones at me and try to steal my bike. I went back to Germany and took a ship to Lithuania. Forget Poland. They take everything. Made me so mad," he continued maniacally as he chewed his food. "Okay...maybe my father shot some Polish people long time ago, but I do nothing. I just want to go on my bike."

"I've been to Poland," I said. "I liked it very much."

"When? Hundred years ago? Pwah! Animals!" he declared, and filled his mouth again. "St. Petersburg should be okay. I have a friend there, and then I can take a ship home."

I asked Rudy about Latvia and Lithuania, and he said they were okay. "Wind. Rain. Last year I was in Spain. Perfect!" he said, and kissed the tips of his fingers. "You go to Latvia now?"

"Yes," I said. "My girlfriend and I are riding our motorcycle to Germany."

"Crazy. Latvia and Lithuania are okay. A ship take you from Memel, in Lithuania, to Germany. Take it. You can go overnight to Kiel. Much better. Besides, you never make it to Poland," he said decisively.

"Why?" I asked.

"The border. Five days crossing," he said, and held up a hand with five erect fingers for me to see. "In five days they kill you. Take everything. This is for sure!"

Rudy was talking about the only border crossing into Poland through which tens of thousands of people from all over Russia and the Baltic States had to pass. I'd read about it at home, about the line of people and vehicles up to five miles long all headed west in search of jobs, or to sell contraband, antiques, rugs, caviar, knives, vodka, their bodies, and whatever else they could carry with them.

When I had read about the line at the border I'd imagined the wait would be interesting. I'd thought of the people we could meet, craftspeople and artists, magicians, and village folk following a dream. There would be nights around bonfires on the side of the road, days of swapping stories, a camaraderie we would never forget.

But now I wasn't so sure.

"How do you know it takes so long?" I asked him.

"I know!" he said, as if I was a fool to doubt him. "In Memel you find this ship. I show you on the map."

～～～

It rained our last afternoon on Saaremaa. It was an easy shower of big silver drops that came and went, and left in its wake a fresh calm and quiet.

"Just washing the dust off the roads for us," I said to Suzanne.

And then the sun came out, and Suzanne lay in its rays as they soaked our bed. I heard a door open and went to our window. The woman next door stepped into her yard and walked barefoot beneath the canopy of the apple tree. The leaves and branches shook as she pulled at the fruit, and a cascade of drops fell to the ground. She laughed, and her voice sounded like warm light. I wanted to hear it again and she obliged me by laughing full and long as the cool drops fell upon her skin. A moment later she walked back across the yard. She'd made her apron into a basket that held the apples, and she wiped her brow with her free hand. Drops rested on her bare arms like gems. She sat on her porch, pulled her dress above her knees, and set the apples down in a nest between her legs. Then she picked up the first one, turned it slowly, and peeled the skin off in a long, single strip with a small knife hidden in her hand.

"What do you see?" Suzanne asked sleepily behind me.

"Some woman," I said. "Just some woman."

twenty-two

From a distance the Hotel Pärnu looked like a discarded box. We had only traveled a hundred miles from Saaremaa to the town of Pärnu on the continent, but the wind and rain, the lightning and thunder, had dogged us all the way. The hotel was shelter, and we rode toward it.

"Every time we start it's the same," Suzanne had said that morning as she looked through the window of our room into another storm. She was close to tears as she contemplated another day in it. I wanted the wind and rain to be something I could go out and fix for her, but all I could do was hold her in my arms.

I had lain awake most of the previous night listening to the storm. It rolled over as if we were the roadbed for its passage. I listened for signs of its passing in the pauses between each rush of wind. I filled the intervals between squalls with hope for its passing. But the storm persisted and grew, and I expected to feel its weight roll over us like a stone.

"*Tere,*" I said to the heavy woman behind the desk of the Hotel Pärnu. "Do you speak English?"

"Yes," she said, and stared at our dripping bodies. Her hair was thin and rolled into loose curls I could see her scalp through. Big, thick glasses magnified her eyes and cheeks. Her lips were small and tight, like the mouth of a bag drawn closed with string.

"We'd like a room," I said, and a flash of lightning illuminated the lobby. "For two people."

"Two," she said, and strained to push the words through her lips. She moved some papers around her desk as she searched for something and seemed oblivious of the weather that raged outside.

"Quite a storm," I said.

The woman stopped her searching and looked at me. "You say?" she asked, and her lips opened just enough to let the words escape.

"I said it's a big storm," and I pointed outside.

She looked through the front door and squinted her eyes to see what I was talking about. Another bolt of lightning flashed and shadows raced across her desk. A clap of thunder followed, and she resumed her search.

"Seven floor is okay?" she asked.

"Yes. Fine," I said.

The woman inserted a worn piece of carbon paper between the pages of a booklet and began to write.

"Pass?" she asked, and Suzanne handed her our passports.

"You has motorbike?" she asked without looking up.

"Yes," I said.

"Not good to park outside hotel. Is thieves. At petrol station," she said, and absently pointed over her shoulder as though it was just behind her. "My friends. Is good place."

We paid the equivalent of five dollars and she handed us a key.

Suzanne and I carried our bags to our room on the seventh floor, and then I said I would move the bike.

"Right away?" she asked sharply.

"It's not safe out front. You heard what she said."

"Fine!" she said, and turned away from me as she climbed out of her rain suit.

"Is that okay?"

"You'll go out of your way to find a nice place for it, but you drag me here!" she said, and swept her arm in a wide swath that could have included our entire path around the Baltic Sea.

"What do you see?" she asked. "I want to know what you see here."

I looked around the room and knew that whatever I saw it would be the wrong thing.

"*What do you see?*" she repeated vehemently, and a clap of thunder shook the room.

"I see a dry room. A bed. A nice view. We even have our own bathroom," I said, and opened the door to show her. I was greeted with the stench of an outhouse, and I quickly closed it.

"Know what I see? I see these water stains here on the wall, and these stains on the curtains. The paint's peeling from the ceiling," she said, and pointed it all out to me. "I see this sagging bed, this filthy floor. And that's after spending the day on the back of the bike. I feel like I've been sitting in a cold shower all day, Allen. I'm beat-up by the wind. And now I'm in this dirty little room in this God-forsaken town for a few hours before we have to do it again!"

"This is Estonia, Suzy, not France. Fifty years of Russian rule would make France...."

"*Don't* lecture me! I know that!" she said, and threw her suit on the bed.

"I didn't make the weather," I said. "I didn't intend for you to be unhappy here. This was supposed to be a good thing for us."

"But you're not helping!"

"Not helping? I feel like I'm the only one who *is* helping. Just once I'd like to complain, but I don't. And you know why? Because you're not there to help me hold things together. Every time there's a cloud in the sky, I think, 'Oh, no. I hope it doesn't rain and upset Suzy again.'"

"You love this, at my expense."

"Yes. I love this. I love that we're not at home stuck in a dead-end job, that we're doing something interesting with our lives, that we're taking a chance and following our dream. Don't you feel that anymore? For a few months we've been free, Suzy. In a while our money will be gone. We'll be back home, working to make some-one else's dream come true. This is like flying! Get beyond the rain and wind and think about what we've accomplished! *This is* our dream!"

She stared at me and crossed her arms over her chest. *"Your* dream," she said.

I hated her for saying the truth. I clenched my hand around the motorcycle keys and knew it would take me less than five min-utes to gather my things, walk downstairs to the street, and ride away. She'd never find me. I could finish the trip alone. I could take my time and linger no matter how hard the rain fell or the wind blew. I could even ride back in the opposite direction if I wanted, or head off to any point on earth.

"It was our dream," I said. "You're the one who's letting it go."

"But my dream changed. Doesn't that count?"

"And mine is still alive."

"You're crazy, Allen. You're really crazy!"

"Look," I said. "I know all too well how you feel. You've made that clear miles ago. I can't do this with you much longer. I'm get-ting tired."

"Maybe you shouldn't try so hard, then," she said, her voice trembling. "Maybe you should just admit this is terrible and we could get out of here."

"It's not like that for me at all. Yes, it's been difficult. It's been challenging. And it's the most important trip I've ever been on."

"Why do you need to finish this? Do you want to get rid of me?"

"No, I don't want to get rid of you, Suzy. I can't imagine being anywhere else. This is exactly where I'm supposed to be, on the bike, going around the Baltic Sea. I know that."

"Why? It's not like it's so beautiful here, or that the people are so great."

"Do you really want to know? Because it feels to me like you got off the bike miles and miles ago, and the trip is all that I've got left." I stood motionless before her, drained of the truth I'd been carrying.

She dropped her arms and stared at me. "You better go move the bike," she almost whispered. "You heard what the woman said."

Once outside I searched all the windows on the seventh floor for Suzanne. I wanted to see her standing there looking for me, watching as I moved the bike to make sure I came safely back. I climbed on, started the engine, and looked again. Then I waited for her to walk through the front door after me. The rain fell harder. Lightning flashed and thunder rolled over me like a wave. The sky became as dark as soot. The cloud ceiling dropped and consumed the church spire across the way. It seemed as if the storm would soon smother the entire town. I pushed the bike back into the street, looked for her once more, and rode to the gas station.

~~~

She was in bed when I returned. Her body was curled protectively in a ball, and the bedcover was clenched in her fist. There was a chair in the corner of the room and I set it in front of our window overlooking the city. Lights illuminated the windows across the way, making each room look cozier than the last. The lightning and thunder continued as the storm settled in like a siege. After a while I undressed and lay down beside her. I gently put my hand on her hip, felt her stir, and she laid her hand over mine.

twenty-three

The road from Pärnu to Riga ran beside the edge of the sea for more than a hundred miles. The sea was a frothy, dark jade; the sky a mottled, weeping gray. The trees beside the road rocked back and forth as they brushed the bottoms of the clouds, and the meadows were so bright it seemed that all the shades of green were distilled from them.

The ride to Riga should have taken days. There were countless gold-sand beaches we had planned to camp on. They were long and straight and abandoned. I thought, had the weather been clear and warm, Suzanne and I could have picked any one and it would have been ours alone. I could have rigged together a drop-line, caught herring, and cooked them on an open fire. From the local villages we could have bought sweet new potatoes no larger than a bird's egg, dandelion leaves for salad, wild mushrooms, and berries. We could have swum and sprawled on the sand.

But the wind and rain herded us along and we passed them all by.

We did stop once. There was a lull in the storm and I remembered how Suzanne had read that the soil of this coast was filled with amber. The article had also said that the best time to find it was along a beach after a storm because the churning water forced the sand to give it up. I remembered how Suzanne had once been so happy in the Outback of Australia while fossicking for opal discarded with mine tailings. It had been so hot that our sweat evaporated as it came through our pores. We were covered in dust, and flies gathered around our eyes, noses, and mouths like animals around watering holes. We'd found a few worthless but brilliantly colorful shards, and Suzanne had packed them with her the rest of the way around the world. She would take them out to show people and delight in licking the glass-smooth edge where the stone had been shattered, and then hold it up to the light to show them the fire inside. Sometimes she'd bring the pieces out when we were alone and remember how we'd found each one.

I rejected several more beaches until I saw the perfect one. It was long with a curve like a cupped hand, perfect for collecting bits of amber. I slowed down, pulled off the road, and stopped the bike.

Suzanne climbed off from behind me. "What is it?" she asked through her helmet.

"A little surprise," I said, and took her hand in mine. "We can look for amber here. I think this beach is perfect."

She flipped her visor up and looked toward the beach, then back at me.

"Over there. See?" I said, and pointed to the curve where the amber lay. "Remember that article you read?"

She looked down the beach. "But it's raining, Allen," she said, as if to say there was quicksand on the beach, and if we went down we'd become stuck in it. She just looked at me then, and as her eyes rested on mine I saw the rain streaming down her helmet, the wet sheen of her suit. I heard the wind rush through the pines. I turned back to where the amber lay and watched the surf compress, spring onto the beach, and push clear to the edge of the forest, where it licked at the exposed roots of trees destined to be pulled into the surf.

"You don't want to go," I said.

Without saying a word she closed her visor, climbed behind me and adjusted herself. I started the bike and we rode to the Latvian border.

~~~

The traffic leading into Riga was frenetic. Cars and trucks wove impatiently around us and honked angrily at nothing. The streets were dangerously slick with a psychedelic mixture of rainwater and oil that had leaked from old cars and trucks. There were enormous potholes that appeared as suddenly as hazards in a video game. I saw a car, and then a bus, go down in one with a lurching movement that reminded me of the time I saw a running horse step in a hole and break its leg. Both times the vehicles were running smoothly along the street. Then a wheel dropped, and the heads of the occupants floated and then began to fall as the wheel fell. The tire bottomed out with a whack and just as quickly snapped back like a dribbled ball. The body of the vehicle was still dropping, the wheel was rising, and the two met. The occupants' heads compressed into their necks and then fell toward their laps. Both vehicles groaned as if kicked in the belly, and then heaved violently forward.

Traffic became congested and slowed as we approached the center of Riga, and Suzanne and I were able to slow too and look beyond the road and vehicles around us. At the same time, the dense gray veil of the storm began to part, revealing harmless white polyps in the sky. Suzanne pointed out a row of baroque buildings down a side street, and from one of them came a troupe of girls dressed in dark blue uniforms that matched the sky. They began to run and skipped across a park.

We stopped at the address of a room rental service. It was on a street lined with neglected buildings. Stains bled down their facades. Three old women sunning themselves against a warm stucco wall watched as we pulled up. Suzanne said she wanted to take off her rain suit and warm herself, too, and I went in alone.

The building was a three-story baroque apartment house. There was a central entrance for carts and automobiles that led to a muddy courtyard. A door leading into the basement was open and I walked down a flight of rounded stone steps. A small wooden table was set at the bottom of the stairs. A lamp stood on it and the light illuminated a painting of a pastoral scene. The bottom third of the canvas was taken up with a swatch of brilliant green and the rest was filled with a royal blue. A wagon, full of brightly dressed people, was being drawn by a gray horse along a country lane. A small dog ran alongside. I was looking at the painting as I walked down the steps, comparing it to the countryside we'd ridden through that day. I didn't notice the basement was flooded until my feet were submerged to my ankles.

I sloshed down a domed hall to the door of the rental agency. It was also open, and inside the room was a wooden desk cluttered with papers and folders and a green ledger with scraps of paper sticking out from between the pages. The desk chair was pushed back as if someone had just left.

"*Labdien* (Hello)?" I called. "*Labdien?*"

I stepped back into the hall and called again. I heard the sound of water being poured from a cup, and then it stopped.

At the end of the hall was an identical table and lamp, and above it a painting that looked like the first. I walked toward it and saw that the hall continued to the right.

The sound of water came again, this time like water being wrung from a sponge, and then it tapered off. I continued into the darkness of the hall. I called again, but there was still no answer. Fragments of light reflected off the agitated water and flashed against the domed ceiling. The corridor turned sharply again and in the middle of the next section was an old woman. She stood on a small island of brick that rose above the water. A dark shawl covered her head and stooped shoulders. She leaned on a mop, and a metal bucket was on the floor beside her feet. A gas lamp hung from a hook on the wall and lit the space around her.

Her eyes regarded me for a moment, and then she dipped the mop into the water and slowly stirred it. Her body bowed as she lifted the saturated mass above the bucket. She strained as she positioned the handle across her thigh, then took the long hairs of the mop in one hand and slowly turned the handle with the other, until the hairs twisted and released their load of water.

"*Labdien*," I said, but the old woman ignored me. Instead she put her mop back into the water and stirred.

I stepped closer. Her eyes met mine as she lifted her mop above the bucket, and I suddenly realized what she was doing. She was soaking up all the water into her mop and was taking it, bucket by bucket, from the basement like an ancient sorcerer's apprentice.

I felt as if I'd stumbled upon something forbidden. I wanted to leave but the woman was clearly waiting for me now. I stepped closer still and handed her the piece of paper with the address of the room rental service. She kept her eyes on mine until the paper was in her hand and then looked slowly down at it. She squinted, lifted it closer to her eyes and studied it. When she was finished she looked back at me. Her look was expressionless, as if I wasn't even in the right world.

~~~

Suzanne was sitting in the sun against the wall of the building. She had our map of the entire Baltic spread before her. She was smiling.

"I was just looking at how far we've come," she said when she saw me.

I stood beside her and looked at the familiar map. Each evening I had marked every mile of our progress with my pen.

"It's so far," she said, as if seeing it for the first time. "We've come such a long way."

Her words made me bitterly sad. I wanted to remind her the trip was almost over, that her sudden wonder at the miles and distance were no help now. I felt possessive of the map and wanted to take it from her hands.

"Look," she said, and I followed her finger up the length of Sweden, across Finland, through Russia and Estonia.

If her finger had been a stick, I would have broken it over my knee. I wanted to yell at her, say it was too late, say the miles and months were gone forever.

"We don't have a room," was all I said. "We'll have to keep looking."

"What happened?" she asked as she folded the map and stood up.

"The building's flooded. There's no one there."

"Flooded? What's flooded?"

"The basement. And there's a woman down there trying to get the water out with a mop and a bucket."

Suzanne took a step back and looked at me. "What are you *talking* about?"

I couldn't explain. I reached for my helmet and slipped into its obscurity. Suzanne finished folding the map and put it away. She pulled on her helmet and we rode back to the main road leading into town.

~~~

We found a room in a vacant music academy on the other side of the city. The building appeared to be abandoned. The concrete facade had so many cracks that it looked shattered. Tall weeds grew from between the uneven cobbles that lined the courtyard, and the windows were covered with grime. The front door was open and we went inside. A very old woman sat near the door in a closet that had been made into an office. Inside it was a tiny cot, some clothes hung from the ceiling, a television the size of a toaster, books, a loaf of bread, and a tea kettle.

She seemed surprised to see us there, as if the rooms weren't really for rent after all. We tried to communicate with the few words of Latvian and Russian I'd copied from phrase books. She kept trying to ask us something that had nothing to do with the room, but eventually she grew tired and waved her question away with her thick hand. She assigned us to a small room at the end of a long hall. We put our bags there and went into Riga.

The center of Riga reminded me that we were approaching the

West again. The neoclassical and art nouveau architecture would reside comfortably in parts of Berlin or Paris. The oldest part of town, a small area beside the banks of the Daugava River, had a few archaeological reminders of the city's early beginnings in the 1300s. Founded by the Teutonic Knights, Riga became an important commercial center, and the seed pod of Christianity for the entire region.

We walked through a park where the remnants of the Riga Castle are preserved, across what is left of the moat, and into the small old town. Its makeover had just begun. Scaffolding covered the facades of many buildings, and white plastic tables shaded by bright café umbrellas had sprung up outside others. A few BMWs and Mercedes, signs of an emerging business or criminal class, roamed the otherwise quiet streets. A brand-new tour bus was parked beside the thirteenth-century Dom Church, and a group of elderly German tourists looked approvingly at the surrounding square.

Beyond the facades of the old town was the major portion of Riga, the portion of flooded basements, potholes, and shattered facades. We walked for hours through it, until the light began to fade, a cold wind blew up the river from the sea, and our feet gave way. Suzanne suggested we stop to rest along the edge of the Daugava. The shell of an old barge was moored along the edge of the river. Long ago someone had added a roof and a row of wooden benches. The roof was filled with holes. The benches were mostly gone, or broken, but there was one whole one that overlooked the river.

We sat on the bench and I zipped my jacket against the wind.

"I'm sorry about last night," I said.

Suzanne shifted beside me and moved a little closer.

"Me, too."

"I'm sorry about where this has gone," I added.

Suzanne was quiet as we looked over the water. Farther down the river two boys threw stones toward the center. A thin line of white agitation broke the dark surface, and then a small black bird rose into the air and flew out of their range.

"Hey," I said gently.

"I heard you," she said, and I watched as she worried the toe of her boot against a bottle cap laying on the steel deck of the barge. It made a rough, scraping sound, and I had to resist the temptation to move my foot beside hers and help.

"I can't see beyond this," she said. "I've tried. I really have. You say this is going to be over soon, that we'll be home and wish we were here again. But I just want it to be over. I can't imagine going anywhere like this again, or ever getting back on the bike."

She flipped the cap over and it rolled across the deck until it bumped into a piece of broken board. Someone had used it to cut fishing bait on. It gleamed with dried blood and the pearly luster of fish scales. Flies buzzed over it and nervously settled to feed. The head of a small anchovy was tilted upwards. Its mouth gaped open, revealing tiny, almost translucent teeth.

"How did we get to this point?" I asked. "After all our years together, after all we've been through, how did we get so far apart?"

I looked down the river to where the boys had been. They were gone, and the river was turning a bruised purple in the evening light.

"Short of leaving, what can we do?" I asked.

"Let's just get through the Baltics. Maybe things will be better in Poland."

~~~

Getting through the Baltics meant that we wouldn't continue along the coast. It meant that when we left Riga we wouldn't ride along a jutting elbow of land that projected so far into the sea that it came within sight of Saaremaa. It meant we wouldn't ride through the remote coastal towns of Roja, Kolka, and Mazirbe. We wouldn't ride around the elbow and over the wide mouth of the Venta River, through the towns of Uzava, Jürkalne, Pävilosta, and Saka. We'd ride instead across the flat inland plain of Latvia, straight through Lithuania, to Poland.

"It's probably just like the part we've already seen," Suzanne reasoned as we consulted the map the night before leaving.

The deviation looked all wrong to me. I wanted the irregular coastline, the beaches, the sand spits, forests, swamps, and villages that our map promised. Maybe things would be better there, too.

"Let me have this," she said.

~~~

We found our way out of Riga early the next morning and entered a vast agricultural plain. It was the middle of the sugar beet harvest and tracts of earth had been churned to mud. Teams of mismatched horses plodded through the muck pulling wagons, their great heads bowed toward the earth as workers lobbed beets the size of pineapples into the carts. A flock of white gulls rioted in the sky and dove toward the newly turned earth.

Fifty miles south of Riga we came to a small wooden shack set in the middle of the road. I slowed the bike and a young man in military fatigues with a machine gun stepped in front of us. Beyond him was Lithuania. He looked at the bike, at us, then at the bike again, and his eyes remained there—a young man dreaming of going quickly away.

Suzanne and I gathered our papers and stepped inside the guardhouse. It was small and windowless, and smelled like an old campfire. A gray-haired officer and a young recruit sat on a dirty brown sofa against the back wall. They were both smoking. Their hands rested lazily on the rim of a hubcap filled with cigarette butts. I spread our papers on a folding card table. The officer nudged the recruit. The recruit stood up, stretched, and flipped through our passports until he found a blank page. He stamped them, then yawned and fell back onto the sofa as though he'd been up for days.

The road narrowed to a single lane of asphalt, the edges of which disintegrated into a swath of washboard gravel. The landscape was bare and desertlike, and for as far as we could see there were only anemic fields of weeds. At times the land looked barren, as if we were riding through an area cleared by a Chernobyl-like accident. The rounded slope of the horizon fell away and the sky buried us beneath its dome. The long, straight road before us fell away somewhere over the horizon. The end of the earth seemed just a little farther ahead of us, and soon enough we'd ride over a sheer continental shelf into an eternal landscape of clouds.

~~~

We stopped for gas outside Marijampole, a town of uniform apartment blocks just thirty miles from the Polish border. It was the last town of any size, and earlier in the day we'd decided to stay for the night before trying to cross. The station was a collection of oil drums and a wooden kiosk set alongside the road. A thin man with greased-back hair, a pencil-thin mustache, and the sleeves of his shirt rolled to his shoulders worked the pump as I filled the tank. Suzanne sat on the raised edge of a discarded palette beside the barrels, and I watched as she ran her fingers through her helmet-matted hair and rubbed her eyes. She unzipped her jacket, shed it like a skin, and folded it on her lap. She rested her chin on her fist and watched a horse-drawn cart pass. The animal's unshod hooves quietly clapped against the pavement.

When the tank was full, the man added the total on an abacus in the kiosk and wrote the amount on a slip of paper. There was an assortment of candy bars and soft drinks arranged in the window. Their labels were faded from the sun. I bought a thick Cadbury bar for Suzanne and two lemon sodas.

I joined her on the palette and she smiled when I showed her the bar. She tore the wrapper off and breathed in the rich smell of the chocolate. It had melted and solidified many times since being placed in the window. The Cadbury logo on the top of each square was an indecipherable doodle.

"Hmmm," she said, as if it was perfect.

I pried the caps from our sodas with the motorcycle key and took a sip. I could smell the sweet perfume of the chocolate as Suzanne ate. Cars and trucks drove past. Another horse went by, this one pulling a cart full of pigs, their legs stiff and set wide against the irregular movement.

"You hear that?" Suzanne asked. "Something behind us."

I turned and saw nothing but tall weeds.

"There. It's a little boy," she whispered, as if it could have been a deer. "A Gypsy."

There was movement in the weeds, a rustling, then a flash of blue. A boy wearing ragged shorts and a torn shirt came into view, and then stopped and stared at us.

"He's scared," she said. "I think he's hungry."

Suzanne broke her bar in half and extended her hand toward the boy. His face brightened a little and he began to move shyly toward her. A truck with an exhaust leak approached. It sounded like a machine gun and the boy crouched on the ground. The truck passed and he stepped tentatively forward. Suzanne stood and moved closer to him.

"It's okay," she said gently.

The boy's eyes shifted from me, to the chocolate, to her face. He turned sideways so he could cut and run if either of us tried anything. He leaned toward her, his body and arm stretching. Suzanne leaned toward him, too. She took a small step and leaned farther still. Their eyes locked and then the boy leapt forward and snatched the chocolate away so quickly it surprised Suzanne. She let out a little shriek that chased the boy back into the weeds. He stopped partway in and we watched as he sniffed the chocolate, then tasted it by shaving off a corner with his teeth.

There was a bang behind us. Yelling. The door of the kiosk opened and the station attendant ran toward the boy. He yelled and screamed and threw a stone that crashed through the weeds. The boy was already running, and then he was gone. The attendant stopped at the edge of the field. He threw another stone in the direction the boy had gone and waited for a response. He stooped to pick up more stones, and I guessed he was going to stand there a while and pepper the weeds like a ship dropping depth charges on an enemy submarine. But then he turned, pocketed his remaining stones, and returned to his kiosk.

A policeman pointed out the Hotel Marijampole, an exact replica of the one in Pärnu. We were still a mile off, but it was plainly visible, a dark-gray edifice in the middle of town. We parked in the loading zone near the service entrance because there was no other parking, and a plump woman with a pleasant face came rushing out and greeted us with joy. She didn't speak English, but we were able to converse in German. *"Wunderbar! Wunderbar!"* she kept saying when we'd made it clear that we did, in fact, want a room. She nervously ushered us into a big, empty lobby and kept looking back at us as though she was afraid we'd leave. Her manner made me think travelers were rare in Marijampole, and that she looked at Suzanne and me as omens of a bright future.

She seemed relieved after we'd filled out the necessary paperwork and paid the equivalent of four dollars for our room. Then she quickly called her brother, who worked nearby, and insisted he show me where I could safely park the bike. He and I rode to a fenced compound where a man saluted me with his machine pistol as his assurance that the bike would be just fine under his watch.

The woman was waiting for me at the door of the hotel. In my absence she had helped Suzanne with our bags to our room. I asked if she had a map of the town. She didn't, but offered to draw one for me on the back of an old receipt. While doing so she asked if everything was okay, and why I wanted to leave the hotel.

"To look around," I said.

Her eyes roamed the huge lobby as if everything we could possibly want was contained within it. When she was finished with the map I asked about the border crossing into Poland. She looked grave and spoke haltingly, but we didn't have the words in common. She called her brother again. He came and translated with a mixture of English and German. They said the border took three to five days to cross, that the line of waiting cars and trucks extend several kilometers. The wait was so long, they explained, because most of the people crossing were heading west to sell carloads of goods that had to be inspected. It was an imposition on people like us, they assured me, and there were some things we should be aware of. They told me about the horrible latrines improvised in the fields along the road, the mud, the need for plenty of food and water unless we wanted to pay the extortionate prices food sellers demanded. They warned me we shouldn't trust anyone, especially the Gypsies, and that we shouldn't both sleep at the same time or we'd lose everything. The man said we did have an option—we could employ a professional line sitter, someone who would wait for us while we stayed in the comfort of the hotel. Then the woman had another idea, which her brother quickly translated. Because the bike was small, she reasoned, and because we had nothing to declare, we could jump to the front of the line. They both gave me but-of-course looks. I asked if this was ethical, whether someone wouldn't run us down for cutting to the front. The woman thought, then shook her head back and forth. Her brother held his hands to his side and shrugged, as if to ask, what do you have to lose?

With our business concluded, the woman ushered me to the elevator that would take me up to my room. When I was safely inside she reached through the open door and pushed the right button for me. We smiled at each other until the doors began to close. Then she cocked her head to one side and waved good-bye.

Suzanne was lying across the bed when I entered the room. I asked her about a walk through town, but she said she was tired and would rather sleep. I lay down beside her and put my arm across her chest. She yawned and turned until she found a more comfortable position. Then she was quiet, and within a minute she was asleep. I listened as her breathing slowed and fell into a pattern of untroubled regularity.

I heard the clipped sound of thin, hard-soled shoes crossing the concrete plaza outside the hotel. I went to the window and saw a woman in light summer clothes walk quickly past. The sound of her passing was immediately followed by others. A trickle of people, then a flow, all moved in the same direction as though they'd been let out of a factory.

I went outside and watched them pass. It was as though the entire town of Marijampole was migrating from one side to the other. There were people of all ages, some alone and others in tight chattering groups. A man carried a small pig, his arms wrapped tightly around its body and head. Another carried a bundle of wood tied with a cord slung over his shoulder.

I joined them. A young man wearing a frayed blue Mao cap stopped short so I could enter the stream, and from there I moved toward the center. I brushed against a woman holding two live chickens by their feet. Startled, they began cackling and beating their wings, and lifted the woman's arm as if they'd fly away with her. Two girls sang a song and clapped their hands in time against their thighs and chests as they walked. An old woman looked angry, her chapped lower lip hanging loosely from her chin, her eyes sharp and wild.

We walked over the same road Suzanne and I had come in on. Our progress slowed as we funneled into an alley. Everyone short-ened their steps and used the time to fill the air with greetings to a neighbor, to adjust a load, to begin a new song. The path beneath our feet turned to rough dirt, then gravel, then pavement again. We filed over several boards and sheets of metal siding that cov-ered an open sewer. A dog barked. The chickens stirred. The girls stopped singing and laughed.

The alley opened onto a wide street. On each side were rows of weathered apartment blocks the crowd streamed past and then dissolved into. I kept walking until the crowd was gone and I was left at the edge of the city, at the end of the road, at the lip of a bare field, as though I'd been washed up onto a beach.

~~~

I scoured Marijampole for food. I wanted to buy a loaf of bread, some cheese, tomatoes, meat, and a few bottles of some-thing to drink. Because the weather was decent I thought Suzanne and I could have a picnic. In one store I found beer, vodka, some stale bread, and a pan of tripe and offal that hadn't been cleaned very well. I bought nothing. In another I found two glazed and shrunken herring, all of three inches long, on a plate behind a big display window. The herring were surrounded by two plastic fish and a lobster, faded and cracked from years in the sun.

I tried some kiosks across from the bus terminal but only one of six was open. It had a compelling arrangement of objects in the window. There were four zippers: two brown, one blue, one white. Beside them was a single ping-pong ball, a valve stem to fill a ball with air, four withered cucumbers, and a bunch of sandy carrots the size of my thumb bound together with string. Two heads of cabbage lay on a shelf. The outer leaves were yellow and dry like old skin and covered with black fungus. There was a set of colored pencils in a paper box, a small pat of creamy green eyeliner in a black plastic case, a set of sewing pins stuck like arrows into a wad of fabric. Behind them was a ball of string, a bottle of shampoo, a pink plastic racquet with two yellow foam balls, and a faded blue box containing a plastic model of a World War II Russian fighter plane.

～～～

"Experience our boo-fay," the brother suggested when I asked at the hotel about finding food.

"Buffet? Here?" I asked.

"No restaurants in Marijampole," he said as if the thought put a bad taste in his mouth. "Best food in boo-fay. Number three floor. You see."

I imagined a large room with tables along one wall loaded with country food: baskets of bread, a bowl of steaming boiled potatoes, rice, a tureen of borscht. I imagined there might be a plate of sliced tomatoes, cucumbers, and juicy red onions. And there would be platters of roast pork, beef, or lamb, and a bowl of thick brown sauce made from the juices of the meat. Perhaps there would even be fish.

"Oh, God," Suzanne strained through her teeth when she saw the "buffet." She balked at the door, but just then a woman stood-up from the chair she was sitting in and greeted us with the sweeping gesture of a game-show hostess. She looked like a retired Las

Vegas show girl—tall and lean, a pile of frosted hair atop her head, and a movie star's smile punctuated by a polished gold incisor.

"Vel-cum," she said seductively, and beckoned us into the room.

It was a converted bedroom, and the buffet was arranged on two folding card tables draped with a stained red tablecloth. The woman stood at attention behind the buffet, beaming with pleasure that we'd come, and waited expectantly for us to make our selections. She presented us with a bowl of shredded cabbage in what looked like buttermilk, a platter with a few wrinkled tomato wedges, a plate with four chicken legs, another with pieces of boiled fish, and yet another with what I realized were fried eggs that a pair of flies played tag over. Then, as if it was something of a great value, she showed us half a cake cut into thin wedges. Everything was cold.

"Are you sure there's nothing else in this whole town?" Suzanne whispered.

"I looked everywhere," I assured her.

Suzanne pointed to a chicken leg, the cabbage, and a slice of cake. I chose the cabbage, chicken, fish, and tomatoes. The woman nodded her head in approval. She carefully weighed each selection on a small scale, wrote the price on a piece of paper, and then arranged the food on two plates. She smiled the entire time and made small noises of pleasure, as if we were in for something especially good.

She watched us as we ate and Suzanne reminded me to look pleased. "It's not bad," Suzanne said of the cabbage.

"The chicken's fine, too."

"Is that really fish?" she asked of the flaking mass on my plate.

I tasted it, decided it was, and Suzanne ate half.

We ate everything, except for the cake, which Suzanne said clung to the roof of her mouth and tasted like grease and sugar. When we got up to leave the woman frowned and pointed to it. Suzanne quickly rubbed her stomach and feigned fullness. The woman smiled, waved her manicured hand, and we began to leave. Then the woman hurried behind us and laid her hands on our shoulders. We turned, and after a long pantomime understood she was inviting us back for breakfast in the morning. Suzanne promised we'd come, and the woman smiled as though an important date had been set.

~~~

For a moment it seemed as if the night hadn't passed, that Suzanne and I hadn't entered the elevator and returned to our room and slept through the night. Instead, it was as though we'd turned back so Suzanne could finish her cake. When we walked into the room for breakfast the woman rose from her chair just as she had before. She wore the same clothes. She pulled us in with the same flourish of her hand and smiled so her gold tooth caught the morning light. When her hand had paused, and moved again to introduce the food on the table, we saw that it was the same food, in the same bowls, and on the same plates, placed exactly as it had been the night before. There was the cabbage, the two remaining chicken legs, the fish, and the fried eggs. Suzanne began to laugh, and the woman laughed, too, as if we only now realized how wonderful it all was.

~~~

Our map showed we would cross into Poland just past the town of Kalvarija, but a few miles before that point a pile of fallen trees blocked our path. Members of a road crew, fleshy men tattooed with flecks of hot tar, lounged on a band of grass on the side of the road. I stopped the bike, and while Suzanne and I consulted our map, one of the men pushed himself from the ground and approached us.

He made a cross with his hairy forearms, nudged his chin down the blocked road, and shook his head back and forth. Suzanne showed him the map and drew a line across the border into Poland. The man studied it until he recognized something to take his bearings from. He looked over the landscape, then down at the map. He marked his place with his finger and looked out over the land again. Suzanne pointed out Marijampole on the map and traced a line to where she thought we were at the moment. The man seemed to agree and turned another ninety degrees until he faced back the way we'd come. He lifted his right hand and drew a line across the empty fields behind us. Then he described a road with his hand that went up and down valleys, shimmied through turns, and came to several stops. There were more turns, and then a long cautionary pause I understood to be the border. We thanked him and left.

They were the smallest of roads, the kind that had begun as animal tracks and had been widened and paved. Nothing was marked. The land began to rise and fall like bubbles in a softly boiling pot. Villages materialized where there were none on the map. A river appeared on our right, the wrong side of the road. The roads began and ended randomly, and once we found ourselves at the end of one where the gravel dissolved into the empty field beyond.

We stopped and asked directions from some kids outside a barn, but they didn't know what we were asking for. A few miles farther we stopped again, this time just beyond a man walking along the road in the same direction we were headed. We got off the bike, removed our helmets, and waited for him to catch up. He wore a tattered tweed jacket and a cap pulled across his brow so his eyes were hidden. Patches of coarse gray hair hung over his ears and brow. As he approached I waved and smiled and held up our map. He turned to look over his shoulder and crossed to the other side of the road. I pointed to our map again and moved to meet him. He stopped, then turned as if to head back the other way.

"Be careful!" Suzanne called behind me.

The man carried a chapped, brown leather suitcase. The leather latches were rotted off, and when he set it on the pavement at his feet the suitcase bulged open as if it needed to breathe. I saw the curved green skin of a cucumber inside, the fabric of some clothes, and the neck of a bottle with a wad of paper for a cork. Perhaps he was headed west, too.

I pointed to where I thought we were on the map and then pointed to Poland. I shrugged my shoulders questioningly and ran my open palm over the landscape hoping he'd point the way. He took the map from me and held it open in front of him. I watched his eyes pore over the lands it described, watched them run from Tallinn to Minsk to Kaliningrad as if he were searching for something himself. He held the map closer to his face, then at arm's length. He began to mutter and point as if he'd found the answer to something. Then he looked at me and handed the map back. But he didn't wait for my hands to reach it. As the map was falling, so was his hand, which took the sweat-stained handle of the suitcase and pulled it from the road. I picked up our map. The man was already several paces beyond me.

~~~

We came to a road that was wide enough to lead somewhere else. It ran west, and was paved and worn in a way that suggested we follow it. The land became green and fertile as if the soil in neighboring Poland leached something beneficial. We passed a transport truck, its load covered with tarps and ropes. We, in turn, were passed by two low-riding cars filled with people. Large parcels wrapped in plastic were held to the trunks and roofs with a web of rope. Four arms reached through the windows of one car, two on each side. They were balancing a wooden bureau, supplementing the bit of cord that held it in place.

We shimmied through the turns the man in the road crew had described. There were several stops as we rode through the town of Lazdijal. Then came the multiple rise and fall through the softly rolling landscape, and then brake lights flared ahead. The car in front of us slowed, pulled over, and stopped.

"This is it!" Suzanne yelled.

I hesitated for a second, wondering if we should first stop at the end of the line before riding on. But I didn't, and the first, second, third, fourth, and fifth cars fell behind us. Nobody yelled or threw anything, and we kept going.

We passed new arrivals to the line who had just climbed from their cars and were looking around and stretching. Some stood in groups as they decided what to do next. Others checked the ropes that held impossible loads to their cars—big bundles wrapped in plastic, old wooden furniture, tubs and sinks, chairs, lumber and metal, boxes and trunks, machine parts, and the parts of other vehicles. A man and a woman walked from behind a bush adjusting their clothes. Some boys were lighting a cooking fire.

Farther along there were tarps attached to the sides of vehicles for shelter. There were tents and plastic shelters. Groups of children played ball and tag and chased each other between the cars. There was a soccer game in progress in a field. Men worked on their cars. Fires burned. Clothes hung drying on bushes. It went for almost four miles. A crawling town.

The line became dense and chaotic at the border, as if the momentum of the cars and people, and the weight of their possessions, shoved from behind. We slowed to a walking pace, and then a crawl, as we wound our way through a sprawl of people and vehicles. People moved their vehicles over, stepped to the side, took their children's hands and moved them out of our way. A man guided us between two cars that couldn't move any farther. We pushed clear to the front, all the way to the covered Lithuanian inspection building where trucks, buses, and cars were being unpacked and disassembled as uniformed officials barked instructions and pointed with thick metal batons.

One of them came and demanded our papers. The guard disappeared into the building and another pointed to our panniers, the tank bag, and we opened them. He probed the insides with the end of his baton and our clothes and notebooks spilled out. He motioned for me to remove our tent, and I began to unroll it on the ground until he was satisfied. Then he moved to the vehicle behind us, a yellow Russian Lada with a family of four. He motioned to the roof where a canvas tarp lay swollen and bound with ropes. The ropes came off and the canvas was peeled back, revealing cardboard boxes and plastic bags. The guard pointed again and the family began to lift each item to the ground, where the baton was thrust into them. The guard motioned to a box and the father carefully extracted large glass jars wrapped in paper. The guard shouted something and the man unscrewed the tops from each. Unsatisfied, he summoned a muzzled German shepherd that sniffed its way through all their possessions.

Suzanne and I were allowed to continue a quarter mile farther to the Polish border, where we went through the same process. A guard took our papers while another pointed to our bags. He rapped the tent with his baton. All around us the occupants of cars and trucks and buses unloaded their possessions and cargo for a second time. A guard watched as a man removed a spare tire from beneath his car. The owner was dirty and tired. The seats had already been removed and the carpet pulled up. The man's wife sat slumped on one of the seats and slowly unpacked a suitcase. The contents of another were spread at her feet. Someone handed our papers back and then, mercifully, we were through.

~~~

At the first opportunity Suzanne and I turned off the main road and found ourselves riding beneath the cool canopy of a pine forest. The trees were tall and the foliage was multilayered so that light was almost excluded. The smooth, easy whine of the bike's engine surrounded us. The air was damp and cool. It smelled of earth, mushrooms, and sap. Suddenly, like a camera's shutter, the forest opened onto a brilliant green meadow, and then we were enveloped by the twilight of the forest again. Then another meadow. The land began to gently roll. We passed a sapphire blue lake cupped in a vale, its surface busy with rafts of yellow and white lilies. It was the first of the thousand or so that comprise the Mazurian Lakes.

Suzanne and I rode for another hour and then stopped in the town of Mikolajki. It was a small town of white stucco buildings set on the edge of a long, sprawling lake. The weather was clear, and we rode down a rough cobbled lane to the shore. I maneuvered the bike between tents and around bicycles, canoes, and inflatable boats. A group of children waved at us.

Suzanne chose a place beside the water with a view down the

lake and of the town. Behind us a boy played his guitar as if to greet us. He was an enthusiastic, though limited, player. He kept beating out the same three chords as the girl beside him howled and rocked back and forth with her eyes closed. For a while Suzanne and I leaned against each other and watched small sailboats skate slowly across the water. A group of kayakers loaded with gear and provisions paddled away from town and headed across the lake, toward what looked like wilderness.

"Maybe we can rent a kayak tomorrow," Suzanne suggested.

I said I thought it was a great idea.

"We can pack lunches and head that way," she said, and pointed down the lake after the other kayakers.

She was smiling and her eyes seemed brighter then they'd been in a long time.

"How far would you like to go?" I asked, wanting to hear the happiness in her voice again.

"As far as we want," she said.

As we set up the tent Suzanne danced a little to the guitar music. I joined her and we moved back and forth with the tent stretched between us, its blue skin flashing in the sun. I wrapped it around her and pulled her against me. We finished putting the tent together, and I handed our things through the door to her. Then she took my hand, pulled me inside, and zipped the door shut.

~~~

We bought grilled sausages for dinner, fat ones that a man shoved into sliced rolls and topped with a big spoonful of sautéed wild mushrooms. We had two each and ate them on a bench on the shore of the lake. More swans found us and we fed them pieces of bread that they plucked from the water. Then we followed the edge, holding hands and talking about how we'd spend the following day. Fish broke the smooth surface of the water as they jumped for insects, and I said we could catch some. We came across rowboats for rent and decided one of them would be fine if we didn't find a kayak. We talked about staying a few days, perhaps a week if we could find a little cabin to rent.

Several miles down the shoreline the wind picked up. Night was coming on and we'd lost ourselves in the changing colors of the sky. Suzanne zipped her jacket up and pressed against me. The smooth surface of the lake was broken and wavelets were driven against the sand. I thought I smelled rain, but the sky was clear. Suzanne smelled it, too, and she began to scan the sky. "Look," she said suddenly.

"Where? I don't see anything. Just forest and sky."

"It looks like fire," she said sadly, knowing that it had to be rain.

Then I saw it, too, a boiling mass that seemed to rise like smoke above the trees. The sky rumbled and split. We headed quickly back.

We were soaked before getting halfway to the camp. Suzanne stopped running and began to walk as if she didn't care anymore. She looked as though she was going to cry.

"Why can't it stop?" she asked. "God! Why can't it stop?"

She went right inside our tent. She lay down on her sleeping bag with her wet clothes on. I took off her jacket and boots. I dried her hair and kissed her. I said the storm could be gone in the morning, that we could wake to a perfect day and still row down the lake. I reminded her what an incredible day we'd had: waking up in Marijampole and going down to breakfast, the people along the border, the easy crossing. The warm, clear weather. The beauty of the lake district. She didn't respond, and I realized that I didn't have the energy to try and lift her hopes again. I went outside.

～～～

"Four. Five days!" a young man shouted above the sound of the storm when I asked how long he thought it would last. I had joined him and his two friends beneath a leaking metal roof that covered some picnic tables.

"Has been rain, rain, rain," said the young man as he lit a cigarette. "Most wet summer in history."

He introduced himself as Premek, and his friends as Jozef and Fryderyk. There was a candle set between them that illuminated their slim, open faces. Premek explained that they'd ridden their old, single-speed bicycles from Warsaw for a holiday before school began again. "But we go home on bus," he said, and Jozef and Fryderyk nodded in agreement.

They passed an almost empty bottle of vodka between them, and I wished at one point that they'd divert it toward me and offer me a smoke. I tried to ask them questions about their ride and what they planned to do before heading home, but they were already drunk and could only giggle. When they discovered I was from California they wanted to know if I'd been to Hollywood. They asked about several heavy-metal bands I'd never heard of. They asked if I lived in Malibu. Then they grew bored with me and went back to their drinking. I sat there a while longer listening to the incessant rain. Then I turned toward the darkness and began to cry.

twenty-four

I should have insisted that we stay. I should have just walked into town and found a room where Suzanne and I could have slept for as long as we wanted. A place where we could take hot baths until our skin wrinkled and our bones warmed, and the memory of the previous night's wind and rain, of the water that seeped through the zipper and into our bags and kept us awake and shivering through the night, was only a dim memory we could wash down the drain of a warm bath. Instead, Suzanne was in a gray mood. I made her breakfast beneath the metal roof and put away her wet sleeping bag and clothes. I wrestled with the tent in the rain as cold, muddy water ran down my arms and neck. She sat and watched me as if I deserved it all. I suggested we stay and she said, "Stay? For what? To watch the rain?"

"You want to go?" I asked. "We'll go."

I washed our bowls and cups and put them away. Suzanne and I climbed onto the bike, and we headed west toward Gdansk.

Our mood seeped across the landscape. It made the cold. It made the fog and the wind that carried the fog across the land like smoke. It made the rain that washed down on us like water from a hose. The roads were narrow, winding, and slick. I rode cautiously, which meant we weren't fast enough for the cars that came speeding behind us. Most were older Audis and Opals, more powerful than the under-powered Russian cars we'd become used to. One after another passed us dangerously. One came from behind and slowed just short of hitting us. The sound of the over-revved engine, of the tires tearing over the wet asphalt, made it seem as though the vehicle was on top of us. And then, while in the middle of a sharp turn, the car swerved into the outside lane and began to pass. It was beside us when another vehicle appeared coming fast in the opposite direction. I applied the brakes, a dangerous maneuver on a motorcycle while in a turn, and I felt the rear tire begin to slip from beneath us. The driver of the car swerved back in front of us, just missing our front tire. As he pulled away I noticed a crucifix swinging from the rearview mirror.

I began to wonder what it is about drivers like these. Perhaps they just lack imagination and don't think about what could happen when they pass on a turn. Perhaps they don't think about all the crosses on the side of the road that mark where lives have been lost. Like tribal warriors who believe the enemy's bullets will pass through them, the Poles seem to have a similar faith that God will slow down oncoming vehicles as they pass without enough room, that He will clear the way around sharp turns as they pass there, too, and that He will see everyone safely home.

It happened again. We were slowing down to turn onto another road. I had the signal on, my left hand out and up. From behind I heard the scream of tires, followed by the rage of a racing engine. Suzanne's arms and legs constricted around me. Her hands bit into my waist. I quickly turned my head to the left to see what was happening, hating my helmet because I couldn't see enough to make a decision to turn or dump the bike or twist the throttle and speed ahead. All I could do was hold on, follow through with the turn as my body surged with adrenaline. The car screamed past, so close to our side I thought it would sideswipe the bike and cause us to crash; so close that I was able, in a suspended moment, to notice a spider web pattern in the cheap white finish on the right front fender. I hugged the edge of the road and was able to move a few more inches away. I hit the horn. The car pulled away in a cloud of smoke and mist.

I found myself hating the drivers. I wished we would round a corner and see the guy in the white Opal, the guy in the black truck, the woman in the rusted blue Mercedes, buried in a heap of twisted, smoldering metal. I found myself hating the narrowness of the roads, the bumps and potholes. The landscape itself was transformed from a place of beauty to one of concealed hazards. I became paranoid. I clung to the edge of the road when vehicles rushed from behind. I focused too much attention on them and not enough on the road ahead. While rounding turns I began to flinch and overreact when other vehicles approached. My mind raced as I determined whether we were being passed, how much the wind pushed against us, and how much we needed to lean; in the space of a second I had to determine our speed, the width of the road, where our escape routes lay, and whether there were potholes or puddles ahead.

Then the road widened. The surface became smooth. We crossed the Vistula River and approached Gdansk. Traffic slowed, and so did the rain. Even the wind relented and the eddies of swirling mist that blew over us became tiny things, gusts like potshots to remind us not to let our guard down. The city came into view—the low, angular darkness of factories, apartments, and churches, then the slender towering cranes of the shipyards along the coast.

~~~

I had been in Gdansk before, in 1984. It was the first stop on my first Eastern European trip. I went there at the height of the Solidarity crackdown. It was a time of intrigue and suspicion, and I'd fallen in love with the place. I remembered it as a city of passions and subterfuge set in an atmosphere of medieval architecture, blackened brick buildings, and heavy industry. It was a city beside a shining sea, one with a thousand-year history of sieges, wars, and long periods of independence. So much had happened to me in 1984 in Gdansk: I learned about black markets and how to play the cat-and-mouse game of eluding authority that allowed me to travel alone through the rest of Eastern Europe. My love of industrial landscapes was refined there. I learned about the particular kindness that comes from people who have very little. I met an amazing woman. I was arrested.

I had always wanted to go back. Now I looked for reminders of my previous trip as we rode into town. I recognized the peaked roof of the town hall, the cranes of the Lenin Shipyard, and the spire of St. Catherine's Church. But much had changed. There were many more cars than in Communist times. Buildings looked cleaner and citizens now walked with determination along the busy streets. Shop windows were clean and brightly decorated, and every vacant lot was filled with busy, open-air markets. We came to the main train station, where a bright plastic banner announced "Tourist Information" in English, and we stopped.

I waited in line while Suzanne went to the bathroom. We'd agreed to find a hotel, preferably something in or near the medieval old town so we could easily walk to the many places I wanted her to see. My turn at the tourist information booth came before she returned, and I stepped up to the counter. The woman there looked overworked and ready to leave. I smiled, said hello, and asked her to recommend a hotel that met our needs.

"Fool!" she exclaimed.

"Excuse me?" I asked.

"Fool!" she repeated, and then I realized she meant "full."

"What about something in the suburbs?" I asked.

"No!" she said, as if she'd already answered the same questions an unreasonable number of times. "Is a medical conferenze. No more room. No hostels. No private home. Nothing."

"God," I said, "there has to be something."

"Is not for God to make place for you," she scolded me.

"There isn't *anything?*" I asked.

"Brzezno," she said after a moment of thought.

"Brzezno. Is that a hotel?" I asked.

She impatiently took a map from a stack of brochures and circled a spot outside town with a blue pen. *"Brzezno,"* she said, and tapped the point of the pen on the spot. "Camping place. Cabins. Near to the sea."

"We're in luck!" I said to Suzanne when she came out of the bathroom. She'd washed her hands and face. She'd brushed her hair and pulled it back. She was doing her best to smile.

"Don't tell me...you booked a room at the Inter-Continental?"

"Not exactly...."

"A nice room in a bed and breakfast?"

"No. There's a medical conference in town and the doctors got all the best places. But the woman behind the desk said there's a place down by the sea. It's called Brzezno, and..."

"Don't tell me we're camping again," she said, and her face began to crumple.

"These are cabins. They're in a campground, but she said they're very nice. Sounds good, doesn't it?" I said, and knew it didn't sound good at all.

I busied myself folding the map so it would fit into the tank bag and I could read it while riding. While doing so I felt Suzanne's eyes upon me, searching, as if I'd let her down, as if I hadn't tried hard enough to find a nice place. I avoided her gaze and tried to think of something reassuring to say. I felt the weight of her disappointment settle on me.

"Maybe they're great old homes that look out onto the water," I said, and knew it was a bad gamble to say such a thing.

~~~

Brzezno was by the sea, though we couldn't see or hear the waves. There were cabins, and we rented one for three days. It was a single room and had a tiny porch, which we shared with the connecting unit. It was just right, I thought, for a young newlywed couple from the flat, interior plains. The room was furnished with a bed, a table and two chairs, and a small shelf I placed the keys and my wallet on. There was a sink and a hot plate for cooking. Above the sink was a picture from a magazine in a chipped, white frame that showed a woman and a child walking along a beach. The woman held the child's hand and her arm was stretched as far as it would go because the child was leaning against it, like a dog on a leash straining to get away.

I turned from the picture and said I thought it was a nice place, that we would have a good time there. Suzanne said nothing. She was sitting on the edge of the bed with the wide eyes of a cat set down in a strange place. She peeled back the covers and looked at the sheets. She brushed something to the floor and then inspected her hand.

"We could walk down to the sea if you like," I said. "Or, we could go into Gdansk on the streetcar."

"It's raining," she reminded me flatly.

I went outside and unpacked the last of our things from the bike. I was removing the buckles that hold the tank bag when a Gypsy woman with five shouting kids orbiting about her hurried past and then walked onto our porch. I watched as the woman ushered the children inside the cabin adjoining ours. Their clamor lost all inhibition once their door was closed. *This can't be. This is not good,* I thought to myself, and thought next of Suzanne who I imagined, on top of everything, was looking up from the bed at the wall separating the two cabins and wondering what in hell I'd gotten us into now.

"Hear that? Do you hear?" Suzanne asked, her hope unraveling before my eyes when I went back inside. Her hand pointed at the wall separating the two units as though she'd discovered a great, damning truth. *"Hear?"*

I could hear. At least two of the children were crying in long, wailing spirals of sound. The woman was screaming at them to stop. Another child began shouting, and then what sounded like hammer blows fell against the floor.

"I'll go see if they'll give us another cabin," I said.

"No! It's more than that."

The shrieking continued. The children screamed louder. The hammering stopped.

"What is it?" I asked, and sat beside her on the bed.

Suzanne's head dropped to the middle of her chest. Her hair fell forward, exposing her neck. She began to convulse with grief.

I put my hand there and asked her again what the matter was. She took a deep breath that seemed to lift something heavy from deep within her soul.

"Everything!" she said, and it sounded like a summation of our seven years together.

"What do you mean, 'everything'?"

The woman behind the wall began screaming an ultimatum. The wailing of her children grew and sharpened as she began hitting them.

"I...feel...broken," Suzanne said between sobs.

"It's almost over. Just a few more days," I said, realizing the emptiness of anything I could say to her.

"I can't get through this. Today was it. This isn't a trip, Allen. This is a fucking mess. You hear me? A fucking mess!"

"Come on, Suzy. We're in Poland. Gdansk. We're almost done."

The crying and shouting in the other room subsided. The adjoining door opened with a slam, and the children ran through it as if escaping. I watched as the colors of their clothes flashed in front of our window, swatches of dark green, light blue, and pink. The rain had stopped and the sun was breaking through.

"What's our plan?" Suzanne asked suddenly.

"For tonight?"

"No. Our *plan*. What are we going to do when this is over?"

"You know what I think we should do."

"Just one trip after another? That's not good enough anymore. I can't do this again."

"What do you want, then?"

"I want to be home. I want a week in bed. I want to ride in a nice car, with the windows up. I want to finish college and get a normal job. I want a plan, Allen."

My ears began to ring. My throat went dry and a sharp pain ran from my stomach through my bowels. One of the kids screamed outside our window, but it was a scream of delight. They were playing.

From where I sat on the bed I could see the bike through the window. I studied its parts: the bronze fairing, the windscreen and instrument cluster, the handlebars, fuel tank, tires, engine, and seat. I had never seen a picture of Suzanne and me on it and I wondered how we looked. I tried to imagine how my hands held the grips, the position of my helmet relative to the windscreen, the curve of my back down to my hips, the way my legs point forward to the knee and then run down to the footpegs. I positioned Suzanne behind me. I put her helmet behind mine and to one side like she was looking past my shoulder at the road ahead. Her gloved hands rested on my hips, and the curve of her back matched mine.

"Does that mean you want to leave?" I asked.

"I think I should."

"From here?" I asked.

"I'm sorry."

~~~

I went outside and leaned against the bike. My legs and hands shook so violently I thought I would fall to the ground. Suzanne's words echoed through my mind and I ran through them again and again to see if they wouldn't play differently. I wanted to hear her say that she had to finish the trip with me, that we'd go home together and fix everything. I went to the window and cupped my hands around my face to look in. She was lying on the bed, her face to the wall. I turned around and three of the kids from next door were standing on the grass staring at me, not saying a word.

"Hi!" I said sharply, and the youngest of them, a small girl in a stained pink shirt, flinched, and then ran off with the others. I wondered who they thought I was. I imagined, over dinner, they'd refer to me as the man with the motorcycle. "The man with the motorcycle," I repeated aloud, and in that moment I felt myself slipping. I felt they could be right and that Suzanne could be dead-on. Perhaps after all, that's all I was, and everything else—this journey, my dream of more journeys and of writing, my entire life thus far—*everything,* led to this pathetic cabin beside the Baltic Sea.

I had to do something, so I decided to wash the bike. I would wash it gently, as if it was wounded. I would go about it the way some people pray. I filled our collapsible bucket with water from a spigot, hung it from the passenger's left foot peg, and noticed for the first time how Suzanne's boot had worn a depression in the rubber. I got out the sponge I kept for cleaning the bike and began by squeezing water over the windscreen and fairing to loosen the crushed bugs and grime that covered it. I scrubbed the mud and dirt from the tires, rims, and spokes, from the forks, and around the exhaust pipes. I wiped between each heat fin on the engine. I cleaned the valve cover and scraped bits of tar from the bottom of the transmission. I washed the drive line, under the rear fender, and around the license plate. I filled the bucket again, and then used a scrap of rag to rinse anything I had missed. I polished everything I could. And when I was finished I rinsed and dried the bucket, wrung out the sponge and rag, and put everything away.

Suzanne woke as the sky was growing dark. I heard the bed creak as she turned and lifted herself from it. I was sitting on the grass on our tarp beside the bike, watching as a German couple in a fancy van effortlessly made camp on the grass opposite us. It took them just a few minutes from the time they'd parked. The woman left her place in the passenger's seat and moved into the body of the van. She crouched and turned a crank that lifted the roof so she could comfortably stand. The man got out, stretched, and rubbed his hand over his extended girth. He walked to the side of the van, where he pulled an awning from the roof, connected two poles, and had himself a covered area the size of our cabin. He opened a door that exposed the inside of the van and pulled out two chairs and a folding table, and set them up. His wife came out with two beers. They sat down and took in the view. I waved, but they either didn't see me or didn't respond. To hell with them anyway, I thought. They'd just invite us over and we'd have to see the fancy implements and tools, the well-stocked refrigerator, the cleverly designed bed, and hear all about their tour.

My view of them was blocked anyway by a rusting yellow Mercedes sedan that pulled in front of our cabin. The car knocked and coughed after the engine was shut off, and the driver seemed used to stopping it by popping the clutch. A big man stepped out. I knew by his look, his olive skin, black hair and mustache, the gold rope necklace, that he was the father of the family next door. I smiled as our eyes met. He looked at the bike, then back at me. He puffed himself up, nodded cautiously, and went inside his half of the cabin.

There was a tapping on the glass behind me. It was Suzanne. Her face was drawn but I saw the trace of a smile. I waved. She waved back. A moment later the door of our room opened and she came and lay on the grass beside me. After a time I moved closer to Suzanne, until our bodies touched, and she laid her head upon my shoulder as we looked into the sky. I told her that I loved her, and she said that she loved me. We were quiet for a time, and then I said, "If only we were still chasing the same thing."

A flock of pelicans winged across the patch of sky above us, and then disappeared over the roof of our cabin as they headed toward the sea.

"For some reason I need to finish this trip with you," Suzanne said when they were gone. "But when it's over, you have to promise me that we try to find that same thing again."

"I promise," I said.

The adjoining door of the cabin opened and banged against the wall. The father pushed through it leading the little girl dressed in pink by the hand. They headed to the car and I thought they would drive away. While watching them I suggested we stay a few days, that in the morning we take the streetcar into Gdansk and spend the afternoon there like tourists. Suzanne suggested we find a nice restaurant and treat ourselves. She said she wanted to buy an amber pin or necklace, maybe both. The father opened the door of his car and slid a cassette into the radio. He turned the volume up so there was a loud hissing, followed by a rush of distorted sound. It was Michael Jackson singing "Billie Jean." The man, moved by the song, placed his daughter on the hood of the car. He stepped away from her and began gyrating his heavy body as if it wasn't heavy, moving it as Michael does in a series of staccato leaps and thrusts that were extraordinary in their spontaneity. "Billie Jean!" the man sang in a high falsetto, and with each "Billie Jean!" his daughter jumped and moved like a broken spring, her face alternately bright and twisted, the hood of the car deforming and reforming beneath her feet. The song ended and Suzanne said a few days in Gdansk was a great idea. And while she was saying this the man rewound the tape to the beginning of the song and let it roll again.

Suzanne and I went inside and closed the door. She drew the thin curtain, through which I could still see the man and his daughter jerking and twisting to the song. I pulled Suzanne toward me and she began to sing, too. "Billie Jean," she whispered in my ear. "She's so fine."

~~~~

Each morning we woke with our neighbors. The father's alarm buzzed promptly at five and we listened to his deep voice as he groaned and then muttered a few words to his wife. The bed springs complained as he pushed himself up, and I pictured him bending over to pull on his pants and shoes. He coughed and dredged his throat with a complex workout of snorts and heaves. Then he farted, admonished his children, and went outside and started his car. We learned he was a rug seller, and as the car warmed up he went to the back of the cabin, where he kept a trailer filled with colorful, woven rag rugs. He carried armloads of them around until the trunk and back seat were full. Before leaving he popped his Michael Jackson cassette into the player and then drove off into the darkness. The cabin became quiet again as our neighbor's wife and children settled back into sleep, and we followed them.

Then, later, Suzanne and I got up and took the streetcar into Gdansk, where we walked through the stunningly restored alleys, squares, cobbled streets, and marketplaces of the central city. We visited the many cathedrals and churches, the monuments to countless leaders and to victims of atrocities committed through the centuries. The weather was warm and most of the time we walked with our jackets slung over our arms. We walked along the Radunia canal, the boat-lined Motlawa River, and along the Royal Way, a wide, cobbled boulevard defined by the facades of fine Renaissance homes. Suzanne made a point of walking through each of the many carved defensive gates that once limited access to the city in medieval times. We were both caught off-guard by the atmospheric beauty of St. Mary's Street, a short and narrow lane lined with Renaissance and baroque homes decorated with intricate friezes, terraces, columns, statues, and gilded ornamental iron. Farther along we discovered fountains, towers, astronomical clocks and sundials, and ruins, reminders of the destruction caused by World War II. We ate well: fresh Baltic herring and eel, strawberries, cherries, and fat loaves of bread that smelled of roasted nuts. Suzanne bought her amber and a new blouse. We each bought a pair of cheap sunglasses.

On the morning of the third day we got up with the father. I pushed myself from the mattress as he did, and then I went to the window and checked the sky. I saw the glitter of a thousand stars, and in the east the first glow of morning.

"How does it look?" Suzanne asked sleepily from the bed.

"Perfect," I said.

We rode out of Gdansk along the edge of the sea, through the old resort town of Sopot, and the gritty, gray continuum of the port of Gdynia. After the town of Reda the landscape opened itself to us with a vibration of light and clarity I had almost forgotten. I had forgotten how heat vapors cause a field of grain to melt before the eyes, forgotten the smells the heated earth exudes—of resin, loam, honey, the tindery smell of dried straw. I had forgotten how a bloom of wildflowers can erupt like fire beneath the sun, forgotten how a forest can stink of pitch. Suzanne felt supple behind me, at ease with the swaying of the bike, the undulations of the road, and with me.

Past Koszalin we stopped along the side of the road where a farmer had set up a stand. We bought grilled sausages and bread and had a picnic on the grass. After we had eaten we lay in the sun with our faces full into it until we were sweating. The sky was cloudless and of a color I named infinity blue because of the way I fell spinning into it. I became dizzy from looking, disoriented without the reference of a cloud. I began to spin wildly and put one hand on Suzanne to make it stop. A pair of storks flew overhead. I turned to ask Suzanne if she'd seen them, too, and the shadow of one crossed her face.

"I'm blessed now," she said. "Blessed with fortune and luck."

"How is that?" I asked.

"If they fly over you, they'll bring good luck."

The storks were black and white with long, bright red legs, serpentine necks, and sharp, red bills that looked inflamed. We heard the husking sound of their wings as they circled above us. As if on cue they stopped flapping their wings and began to fall. Their long legs reached for the ground. Their great wings billowed with air and just before touchdown they gently flapped them and slowed. Once on the ground they greeted each other by noisily clapping their bills together. Then they folded their wings, quickly preened, and began to sift through the stubble with their bills, searching for insects, mice, and snakes.

As Suzanne and I continued riding across the northern edge of Poland, I, too, felt blessed. The sky remained cloudless and the temperature rose through the afternoon. I felt the knots of difference between Suzanne and me dissipate like tight muscles under the touch of a masseuse. I felt our fortune turning as if I were turning to a more comfortable position in bed. I grew indifferent to our recent squabbles. I allowed myself to dream that soon

Suzanne and I would both look on the trip as a great one and that together we had accomplished something extraordinary.

We passed dozens of mushroom pickers, one after another, selling their wild harvest along the road. Men, women, even children, they waited patiently to turn their full baskets toward the few cars that passed them. They looked sentimentally peasantlike with colorful scarves over their heads, long dresses, and embroidered blouses. The men wore leather knee boots, thick jackets, and worn hats.

We were ambushed by a pack of boys and girls on single-speed bicycles as we entered the village of Trzebiatów. They followed us over rough cobbled streets through the center, a noisome pack of squeals, shouts, clanging bells, and pumping legs. Their intent seemed to be to surround and capture us, to keep us as their own. We rode once around the town square to show them they had no chance with us and brought smiles to the faces of the old men and women sitting on the benches there. Then we rode out of town and left them all behind.

We stopped for the night at Rewal, more a place-name than a village. We stopped there because the German border was less than an hour away and to continue would have been too large a step that day. Rewal was a place of golden fields and large, green trees. There was a campground set on the edge of a cliff that looked over the Baltic.

It took some time to locate a place to set the tent that was free of mud. As the German guy who was camped next to us with his girlfriend said, "It rains like shit here." His girlfriend, he said with excellent English, wouldn't come out of their camping van anymore because of the rain. Suzanne scanned the clear, blue sky and promised the man his girlfriend was safe for a while. He said it didn't matter, and pointed over his shoulder to the van, where I could see someone's back pressed against a window. "As a matter of fact," he continued, looking around and speaking in a low voice, "my girlfriend...she is bothered by many things here in Poland. And, well, to be honest, so am I."

I thought he would tell us a story of how they'd been mistreated or how someone had ripped them off.

"Have you been here long?" he asked, wringing his pudgy hands. "Have you not noticed anything, well, strange?"

I started to tell him about our ride from Gdansk, of the light and air, of our picnic, infinity blue, the storks, mushroom pickers, and the children on their bicycles, but he cut me off.

"The, how do I say this...*hygiene,*" he said. "Does it not bother you? Your girlfriend?" he asked, as if Suzanne was no longer there. "As a matter of fact," he said, getting closer to the point, "Helga and I find it...lacking. You see," he said, and leaned closer to us, "she will not even *go* anymore. You understand? She hasn't had a movement in a week."

~~~

Suzanne and I spent the afternoon walking on a long, golden sand beach. We'd left our jackets in the tent and our feet were bare. The air was still and the sea looked lacquered.

"It should have been like this," Suzanne said, holding my hand, her face turned to collect the sun. "The whole time. From beginning to end."

"Yes," I said.

"Do you really think so? I'm not criticizing, but I'm not sure you do."

"Despite everything," I said. "I think it's been a great trip. Maybe the most important for us yet."

We walked to a drainage pipe that stretched from the middle of the beach into the sea, where it gradually disappeared beneath the surface. A boy was walking on the submerged portion as if he were walking on the water itself. He stopped and pushed the front of his suit down and began to pee. The sun caught his stream and transformed it into a golden thread.

"You have to say that," Suzanne said. "You have to say that because you gambled everything on this one."

"I didn't know I was gambling," I said. "I thought we were just taking another trip."

The boy adjusted his swimsuit and dove into the water. His

round wake grew outwards, toward all the places we'd been on our journey. As it grew I began to recite place names in my mind, the wonderful names: Sonderburg, Roskilde, Copenhagen, Åseda, Gotland, Stockholm, Luleå. . . .

"So you think it was all worth it?" Suzanne asked.

"Yes," I said.

twenty-five

Our plan was to cross the German border at the coastal city of Swinoujscie. From there we would ride to Rügen, our last Baltic island, for a celebration before heading back to Bremen. I'd seen pictures of the high, white cliffs that overlook the sea there, and I had once imagined Suzanne and me camped on the edge, dancing around a bonfire in an orgy of self-congratulation. But as we were leaving that morning Helga's boyfriend informed us the border at Swinoujscie was closed. "You must go south, to Szczecin," he said. He was packing up and said we could follow him if we didn't know the way. His girlfriend was already perched in the passenger seat ready to go. I said thanks, but no, and we headed off on our own.

We left Rewal in the glare of another perfect day and rode south through a low-lying region of meadows, slow streams, and forests. We merged onto a wide, four-lane road and in no time at all we came to the border. We crossed so easily it could have been a tollbooth. We were in Germany again.

I pulled over beside an apple orchard that had been left to go wild and adjusted our map. We had come to a fold, a portion of the map I'd bent and pushed beneath another so it would fit in the clear plastic pouch of the tank bag. When I removed and reset the fold I saw Bremen, the end of this journey.

A flock of starlings lifted themselves on blurred wings into the sky from the gnarled limbs of one of the apple trees. They leaned as one toward the east and streaked back the way we'd come.

At the first opportunity we turned onto a small road heading north. The map showed we could ride northeast, back toward Poland to the village of Linken, then west toward Pasewalk, and north again for a direct route to Rügen. The road turned to a narrow path of up-thrust cobbles and depressions the bike juttered over. Our bones shook. My cheeks vibrated and rubbed against the inside of my helmet. Suzanne began to hum behind me, her voice a staccato that broke into a ragged laugh. The front shocks of the bike wheezed as they compressed and released between our weight and the rough surface of the road. I held my jaw open to prevent my teeth from clapping. My hands grew numb and twice slipped from the handlebars. Suzanne shook behind me and I could feel the complication of her weight coming down on the tail of the bike.

"C-a-a-a-n-n-t y-o-o-u-u d-o-o s-o-m-m-t-h-i-i-n-g?" she called through the back of my helmet.

I tried different speeds, as pilots try different altitudes to escape turbulence. At faster speeds the shaking quickened. It became harmonic and penetrated my bones, penetrated to the core of the bike so the engine sounded different. I tried slowing and the bike began a sharp bucking that felt like the tires were square. A truck appeared behind us. It pulled close and impatiently rode just a few feet behind us. I put my hand out for the driver to hold back and he interpreted it as a signal to come around. The lane was too narrow but he came anyway. The left mirror of the bike filled with part of a headlight and a portion of the grill. I moved as far as I could to the side and let off the throttle. We rode through a pothole, some mud. The front tire slipped and I felt Suzanne wobble behind me as she caught herself. The truck continued to move past and I saw it was a flatbed loaded with hay. It smelled green and fresh. The truck was its own universe of sounds: clattering valves, worn springs and metal seams abrading like the fiddling of cricket's legs. It finally pulled ahead of us and I moved the bike onto the road again as tufts of hay swirled over the cobbles.

We stopped twice to feel the solidity of the earth and to restore feeling into our arms and legs. While stopped near Locknitz Suzanne asked me if I smelled it, if I smelled the rain.

We looked and saw an assembly of clouds in the west. I hoped that by heading to Rügen we would pass clear of the storm, and from a spot farther north we could turn and look back as it passed harmlessly out of reach. The road improved and we sped toward Pasewalk trying to beat it.

"Did you see that?" Suzanne yelled. "Lightning."

I followed the trajectory of her gloved finger past my head. I saw a wall of roiling black clouds.

We rode into an open plain that revealed the size of the storm. It made me think of pictures of sandstorms in the Sahara, the way they curl and bloom, explode, and then envelop everything in their path. Thin veins of lightning projected like feelers from the front of the storm, as if they were feeling for us. We crested another rise and the road began a gentle, well-engineered turn to the left. Off in the distance I saw where our path would soon disappear beneath the clouds.

Of course, I said to myself. *This is the way it has to end.*

I searched for a building or barn but there was nothing. We rounded another turn and rode through a saddle I considered stopping in. Then from nowhere we were struck head-on by a gust of wind that felt as though someone had jammed our brakes on. The force pushed me forward. My arms compressed and my head struck the windscreen. An instant later the front of Suzanne's helmet struck the back of mine. Her chest collided heavily against my back, and for a moment I could only see a portion of the instrument cluster from the corner of my left eye. The bike wobbled and I thought to myself, almost with a sense of relief: This is it. We're finally going down. I pushed backward from the handlebars and we swerved into the opposite lane. There was a strip of broken pavement, some gravel, and then an open field I was thankful for. Then the bike corrected itself. I eased it back into our lane and we rode on.

The storm rolled right over us. The air was charged from the lightning. I felt the rumbling of the thunder in my chest. Light was drained from the sky. The first sad drops of rain whacked against the windscreen and my helmet. Suzanne hunkered down behind me and her arms circled my waist. I looked again for a place to stop but there were only churning meadows of grass and the narrow band of road ahead. We passed a wreck, a car upside down and a battered truck on its side. Flashes of lightning exploded around us like strobes.

We stopped beneath the roof of a gas station on the edge of Pasewalk. Suzanne bought us coffee in thick paper cups, some sandwiches, and we leaned against the side of a pump and watched the storm. I thought if we ate slowly enough the storm would pass and we could continue to Rügen. The car from the wreck was hauled past on the back of a truck. We bought more coffee and continued to wait.

"Allen," Suzanne said. "I haven't asked for very much on this trip, have I?"

"No. No, you haven't."

"Well..."

"I know what you're going to say," I said. I realized immediately our journey was over.

"I think," she began, "I think Rügen is an unreasonable goal in this storm."

I was watching a man fill his car with gas. He wore a yellow raincoat with a plastic hood that kept filling with wind and flipping off the back of his head. His wife sat comfortably in the passenger's seat looking straight ahead. The man kept pulling the hood back over his brow, but each time it filled with air like a parachute and blew backward.

"Allen. Is that okay?"

The man's wife flipped the rearview mirror over and checked her appearance. She turned her face from side to side, licked a finger, and wiped the lower lids of her eyes. She bared her teeth and picked at one. The wind took the man's hood again and he reached angrily back and jerked it over his forehead. He used his knee to hold the gas nozzle in place and began to tie the hood around his neck. A gust of wind shoved him as he was doing so and the nozzle fell to the ground. He began swearing and flipped the hood off his head. His wife turned to see what happened. She opened the window just enough to say something though it. The man yelled at her. She closed the window, shook her head, and went back to her teeth.

"Yes," I said to Suzanne. "You're right. There's no need to go to Rügen."

twenty-six

Suzanne and I were checked out of the hotel at six the next morning. As we stood beside the bike and pulled on our helmets and gloves, she made me promise we would stay in the same hotel where we began this journey. I promised we would. She climbed behind me, gripped my shoulders, and shook them lightly. The sky was still spotted with clouds but they were frail and spent. The storm had passed.

We rode from Warren to Parchim on a small road, and then merged onto the autobahn to Hamburg. I accelerated across a wide expanse of concrete to the middle lane and settled in at seventy-five miles an hour. Traffic was light and I remembered it was Sunday.

We passed the exit for Schwerin, another for Lübeck, cities that were arranged like the last minutes on the clock of this trip. The next exit was for Kiel, and I realized that if we were to do this trip over, we would exit there and head north to the Danish border. It was such a perfect day for riding, and I couldn't help but imagine what it would be like if we started the trip again. If we did, perhaps the weather would hold long enough for us find our perfect beach on the edge of the sea.

More than three months had passed since that first morning when we rode out of Bremen. I looked down at the odometer and calculated we'd ridden almost six thousand miles. As we moved along I began to think of all we'd experienced during that time, the endless variety of winds and rains, the limitless forests and plains, the borders, the mountains, rivers, and clouds. The sea. I thought of Eddie at the shipping office and wondered if we'd see him again when we dropped the bike off to send it home. I thought of Jesse King, the blues musician. I thought of Hanne from our first ferry ride, of Kary and his "wife," of David from The Hooters and how carefully he handed us the pictures of his wife and son. I wondered if Jan and Cory had found their orchids, wondered if my Uncle Chester remembered that he loved me. I remembered the feel of the rope in the church on Gotland. Midsummer. I thought of Tord and wondered if he stopped to tell every motorcyclist about his accident. I hoped that Malin remembered how our fingers moved among her spare parts. Where on earth was David Barr?

Traffic slowed as we negotiated the knot of exits and on-ramps around Hamburg, and in the distance we saw the outline of the taller buildings in the city center. A truck driver waved at us. An old man driving a red Mercedes honked and gave us a thumbs-up. Traffic thinned as we merged onto the road to Bremen, the road we began on.

I thought of our first miles, our first nights, our first storms. To our left I saw the first gas station we had stopped at. I saw the pump we used, the area to the side where I'd added air to the tires and convinced Suzanne that those first winds were nothing to worry about. Headlights flashed impatiently behind us. Suzanne pinched me with her knees and I pulled into a slower lane. The first Bremen exit appeared. I slowed to sixty and thought how endings are, for most of us, very quiet things.

We left the autobahn at the exit for the center of Bremen and rode through almost empty streets. We rode past the train station, through the central square, and came to a stop in front of the hotel. An elderly woman in a dark blue suit looked down at us from the window of the hotel's restaurant where Suzanne and I had shared breakfast that first morning. The woman took a sip of coffee, wiped her mouth with a napkin, and turned back to the man sitting across from her.

Suzanne climbed off, removed her helmet, and stood beside me. I thought some kind of ceremony was in order but I was at a loss for what to do. The engine idled smoothly beneath me, ready to continue if that's what I asked of it.

"I'll go see about a room," Suzanne said, and she turned and walked toward the door.

When she was gone I took our bags from the bike and set them on the ground. I folded our last map and put it with all the others inside the tank bag. Then I carefully threaded the lock through the wheels and frame and put the cover over the bike.

Suzanne didn't see me when I walked into the lobby of the hotel. She was laughing and joking with the woman behind the front desk. I watched her from behind as she signed her name to something. One leg was bent at the knee as she leaned against the counter, and her head was bowed forward, revealing the soft skin along the back of her neck. I knew every inch of that skin. I could recall its scent. I knew where the mole lay just below her collar, the easy angle of her torso as it blended with her waist. She felt a world away from me then.

When she was done she walked to the front door and looked out for me. Then she turned and saw me standing at the back of the lobby. She smiled and jiggled the room key as she held it up for me to see. "The manager upgraded our room," she said. "For free."

Once in our room Suzanne began peeling off her clothes like dead skin as she walked into the bathroom and turned on the water to fill the tub. I opened our bags on the bed and laid out the new blouse Suzanne had bought in Gdansk, clean underwear, socks, our razor, comb, and toothbrush. I found Suzanne's dress and shoes, which had been put away in a plastic bag since Stockholm, and unwrapped them for her. Underneath them I found a polished green stone from a beach on Gotland, Suzanne's collection of spare change from each country we'd ridden through, some sand, and two leftover packets of soap for washing clothes by hand.

"Come on!" Suzanne called from the bathroom. "Get your clothes off and come in with me."

I picked up the stone and began rolling it in my palm the way I imagined the surf had.

"I think I'll take a walk," I said, and slid it into the pocket of my jacket. "I'm not quite ready."

"It feels great," she said excitedly. "You don't know what you're missing."

The bathroom was like a steam bath. A mountain of suds covered all of Suzanne but her face. "I'll be back in a little while," I said, and kissed her forehead.

As I left the hotel I stopped and looked up at all the empty windows facing the square. Behind one of them was Suzanne, immersed in the simple pleasure of a bath. I knew I should be there with her, but I could only feel the unbearable sadness of the distance that lay between us.

I walked across the square to the train station. As I walked I instinctively checked the sky for signs of weather but there was only blue. Once inside the station I bought a can of beer and a pack of cigarettes from the man at the newsstand. The station was almost empty and he seemed to want to start a conversation, but I wanted to be alone. I checked the board announcing departures and arrivals and looked for the destination farthest away. A train for Budapest was due in half an hour on track five. I walked through the station and found an empty bench alongside the track. I sat down and waited.

ABOUT THE AUTHOR

Allen Noren is a veteran of seven extended journeys and many shorter ones. He's traveled by foot, single-engine airplane, bicycle, train, car, and kayak, through more than forty countries. His poems, short stories, and articles have appeared in several small print publications and on the Web. *Storm* is his first book. While writing *Storm,* Allen has worked for O'Reilly & Associates, a print and online publishing company, as the managing editor of their Web sites. He lives in Northern California with his wife and daughter where, at night, they plan their next journey. Allen has just completed the manuscript for his second book.